Living with Capitalism

Living with Capitalism
Class Relations and the Modern Factory

Theo Nichols
and
Huw Beynon

ROUTLEDGE & KEGAN PAUL
London, Henley and Boston

First published in 1977
by Routledge & Kegan Paul Ltd
39 Store Street,
London WC1E 7DD,
Broadway House,
Newtown Road,
Henley-on-Thames,
Oxon RG9 1EN and
9 Park Street,
Boston, Mass. 02108, USA
Set in 10 on 12 pt Ehrhardt
and printed in Great Britain by
Western Printing Services Ltd, Bristol

© Theo Nichols and Huw Beynon 1977

British Library Cataloguing in Publication Data

Nichols, Theo
Living with capitalism.
1. Chemical industries—Great Britain
2. Industrial sociology—Great Britain
I. Title   II. Beynon, Huw
301.5'5   HD6957.G7
ISBN 0-7100-8594-X
ISBN 0-7100-8595-8 Pbk

Reproduced with permission
Reprinted by Athabasca University, 1987, 1990, 1998.

Contents

Preface

OPEN THIS BOOK at any page and it is likely that you will read the words of men who spend their lives working for 'ChemCo'[1]—a giant, British-owned multinational chemical producer. We talked to these men—workers, foremen and managers—many times and at some length between 1970 and 1973. We were concerned to find out, above all else, what it meant to them to be working for ChemCo; how they understood the work they were expected to do, the Company they did it for and the society within which they lived.

Thirty years ago Bob Edwards of the Chemical Workers Union wrote a good book about the chemical monopolies. His Preface carried the clear statement that 'the author looks at the industry through socialist eyes, and is biased in favour of public ownership'.[2] A lot has happened since 1945; to capitalism, to the working class, and to 'socialism'. Not least, the practice of successive Labour Governments, and the experience of 'public ownership' as the accommodation of nationalisation to a new 'statist' capitalism, has done much to erode a view of an alternative (and better) society.

Now by its very nature the book that we have written cannot hope to offer a view of an alternative socialist society. But what it does seek to do is to look at things as they are: thereby indicating the tendencies that are becoming clear in large corporations, and the way they are affecting the people who work in them. What becomes clear from this—and what we came up against time and again during the time we were at ChemCo—is the immense waste of human potential that is locked up within capitalist factory production. This experience strengthened our central political conviction that the need for a fundamental restructuring of British society is both a desirable and urgent one. And we hope that this book carries the conviction that the struggle for that new socialist view is now a matter of great importance.

In attempting to document the waste involved in capitalist society we have also sought to offer some explanation of why it occurs—to point to the mechanics of capitalist production. We have not found this an easy task because so much of what passes for 'theory' (even Marxist theory) fails to connect with the lives that people lead, whereas most descriptive social surveys too often fail to grasp the structure of social relations and the sense which people make of them. It is almost as if another way of writing has to be developed; something which 'tells it like it is' even though in any simple sense this is not possible; something which is theoretically informed yet free from theoretical pretentiousness, and which destroys the gap between the abstract and the concrete. We don't think for a moment that we've succeeded in doing this. What we have arrived at is a succession of pieces which, we hope, has a cumulative effect in building up the picture of ChemCo.

We have worked together on this book—a book which is in every sense a joint project—on and off for the past six years. Over that length of time we have built up many debts which we can only touch on here. We are grateful to Peter Armstrong and Martyn Nightingale for the help they gave us between 1970 and 1973 when we were working together on a research project financed by the Social Science Research Council.[3] Also, amongst those who had great patience with the innumerable redrafts and corrections that we asked them to type for us, we have to acknowledge a special debt to Mrs Doris Macey and to Margaret Rowe. Undoubtedly though, we owe our greatest thanks to the people we met at ChemCo; to those who talked to us, drank with us, and invited us into their homes. We learned a great deal from them. To one in particular. In writing any book you can have doubts, about how to write it and about why. It was at one such moment that we happened to spend an evening with a man who operated one of ChemCo's control rooms. He told us he thought that a book like this could be important. That it could indicate to him, and the many thousands like him, that he was not alone in his feelings that things as they are, are just not right. ('Trouble-making feelings', he called them, because to act on them was to be branded a 'trouble-maker'.) We hope we haven't let him down; and there's more than one sense in which this book is for him.

Notes

1 'ChemCo' is, of course, a pseudonym. We regard this as less than ideal but some people we talked to asked us not to reveal their identity, and the site manager made the anonymity of the Company a condition of our being allowed on the site. To this

end no individual is referred to by his proper name and certain minor details about the factory, etc., have been changed. There were some other problems of this type. The book, for example, contains no detailed examination of the situation of the craftsman and this is something that we regret a deal more deeply. Again this was a condition laid down by management and to have gone against this—in spite of the interest that the craft workers had in what we were doing—would have seen ChemCo's gates closed to the research. We can only hope that in spite of these inadequacies what we have written makes the research as it stood, worth while.

2 *Chemicals: Servant or Master? Life or Death?*, National Labour Press, 1945.

3 One book has already been published which was based on this project (Theo Nichols and Peter Armstrong, *Workers Divided*, Fontana, 1976). This focused upon the ways in which workers who work in the same factory can become divided against themselves. In this book we have taken a wider view; we look at the situation of managers and foremen as well, and attempt to locate these groups within the broader context of capitalist society.

Introduction

DRIVING OUT OF Teesside toward Redcar at night you pass a thousand shining lights—a giant chemical complex, the Wilton site of Imperial Chemical Industries. While the lights shine, men work. Chemical production in sophisticated process plants makes no allowance for the night or Bank Holidays or anything else for that matter. Except the market, that is.

Wilton, of course, isn't the only chemical complex in Britain. In fact chemicals is a major growth point in the international capitalist economy. In Britain the three firms which top the table of corporate size—as measured by capital resources in 1973—come from the petro-chemical sector: Shell (£2,700,000,000); BP (£2,661,000,000); ICI (£1,972,000,000). And to these have to be added the foreign owned multinationals like Exxon, now the world's largest corporation, the other American giants and the Germans Hoechst, Bayer and BASF. The petro-chemical sector marks an immense centre of capital. The motor vehicle industry, for example, had in 1971 an average of £3,000 worth of capital assets to each worker who added something like £2,800 worth of value to the raw materials that made up the finished product. By contrast each worker in the petro-chemical sector added £120,000 worth of value and worked on £400,000 worth of capital. Once located in relatively small plants in the north of England and Scotland, chemical production now takes place on a massive scale throughout the British Isles, often and increasingly in places remote from large centres of population. Chemicals is huge business.

Chemical production has a long and none too savoury history. It was singled out by Karl Marx in his discussion of 'victims of industry', and in 1899 after intervening in a strike of Glasgow chemical workers Keir Hardie wrote:[1]

I wish I could adequately describe a day's work so that my readers could fully understand its horrors. The men on the day shift go in to begin work at six in the morning. The vapours and fumes of the chemicals are about them all the time, eating away the cartilage of the nose and poisoning the blood, so that the stomach in time will only contain certain kinds of foods and an intense desire for stimulants is generated. A dry dust floats in the atmosphere, which gets into the throat and produces an acid, burning feeling. The surroundings . . . are all of the gloomy depressing kind.

It is ironic therefore that an industry with such a history—a history of an injured and poisoned workforce—should now be singled out by managerial theorists as the one around which the whole future of capitalist society rests. To these people the new process technology of the new chemical industry—a system whereby production takes place continuously within enclosed vessels being monitored and controlled by the manipulation of levers, etc.—marks a unique symbiosis between production and consumption. It produces in great quantity all the elements of the new plastic age, without, apparently, any of the inhuman costs of the past. In this view the chemical industry serves the needs of both consumer and worker, and makes big profits to boot. In 1972, D. T. N. Williamson, an engineer employed by a large British capital equipment firm, addressed the British Royal Society on the theme of the 'Anachronistic Factory'. He began by claiming that:

The present trends of professional management in industry and commerce [are] misconceived and have been steadily veering into opposition with the values, aspirations, and expectations of the people who will have to keep the industrial system working.

Williamson shares the belief of many other 'progressive' managers and politicians that the working classes of Western Europe and America are no longer prepared to endure quietly the pressures and monotony of capitalist factory production. Process production—and with it the possibility of establishing 'enriched' work—is seen as a solution to this. Harshly critical of assembly line techniques—particularly as they are found in the motor industry—he offers in its stead what can only be described as a eulogy for the modern factory:

The current technology in the process industries represents the summit of man's achievement in manufacturing. In a modern oil refinery, chemical works or power station a few men control and maintain plant which generates physical wealth at an unprecedented rate. Productivity, in terms of output value per man, is at least an order of magnitude higher than other engineering industries. High skill is demanded, but working conditions are good, and as a result the relatively few jobs available represent the elite of manufacturing industry, and are highly prized and rewarded.

Much recent writing about process technology by sociologists follows a not dissimilar line. Thus, in Britain, Stephen Cotgrove:[2]

Marx's description of wage workers as 'physically exhausted and mentally debased' can hardly be applied to process workers, however appropriate it may be to those on the assembly line.

And one of the most influential studies of the 'new working class':[3]

The second industrial revolution was sweeping aside the satanic mills of the first and creating new types of factory. Managements were becoming increasingly concerned with 'human relations', while automated or process production systems gave rise to conditions of work which, from both a physical and social point of view, differed markedly from those characteristic of an earlier age of industry.

In America Robert Blauner has described this new work:[4]

Very little of the work of chemical operators is physical or manual, despite the blue collar status of these factory employees. Practically all physical production and materials-handling is done by automated processes regulated by automatic controls. The work of the chemical operator is to monitor these automatic processes: his tasks include observing dials and gauges; taking readings of temperatures, pressures and rates of flow; and writing down these readings in log data sheets. Such work is clearly of a non-manual nature.

It would be very interesting to know just how many chemical workers recognise themselves from these descriptions. But there is more to it than this. Blauner, for example, moves from this description of work within the new process technology to argue that such work is accompanied by a 'secular decline of the workers' class consciousness and militancy'. Basically, this argument asserts that capitalism has witnessed a new industrial revolution since the last war, and that the basis of this revolution—the new technology, the 'white heat' of which formed an important

plank in Harold Wilson's 1964 election platform—facilitated the placation
and integration of the working class into the structure of the corporation
and, by extension, into the very fabric of capitalist society itself.

Undoubtedly technology has great importance but the nature of this
importance can only be appreciated if 'technology' is understood in
relation to 'capital'. 'Process technology' has not been introduced to ease
manual work, nor simply because of the usefulness—or otherwise—of
the products it can make in such gigantic quantities. Process technology
comes about as a result of investment decisions based on profit, and any
'integration' of the workforce that has taken place has not been 'automatic' but has again been part of this same logic. Productivity deals, for
example, cannot be understood as simply a by-product of technological
advance. They have to be located within the ideological framework of
advanced capitalist production. The capital intensive nature of chemical
production makes it vital that as much 'co-operation' as possible is gleaned
from the people who tend the biggest of big machines; for this is what
process technologies are. It is no coincidence that the most widely praised
productivity deal took place at the Esso oil refinery at Fawley,[5] or that
ICI have, for the past ten years, been involved in attempts to 'humanise'
work, thereby to 'involve' their workers in the better performance of it.[6]

The chemical industry plays a fundamental role in modern capitalist
society. It is a leading growth point in a growing international economy.
Its products have been central to the 'cultural transformation' that has
affected these societies since the war. The industry's management has
been well aware of the industry's importance. They have been most
likely to take up 'progressive' management ideas and they have been in
the van when these ideas are discussed and propagandised at conferences,
in management journals and in the media. What happens in chemicals
matters; both for the economic and ideological structure of capitalism.

These considerations led us to visit several different 'process technology'
sites between 1970 and 1973. Each of these sites produced a range of
different chemical products and used—as we shall see—a variety of
technologies. What we have written draws upon what we saw in these
places, and the conversations that we had with the people who worked in
them. The core of the book however draws upon just one chemical site: a
chemical fertiliser complex in the south of England which we visited
regularly throughout the three years of our research. In it we try to do
several interrelated things.

To begin with, in Part I, *Labour for Capital*, we are concerned to describe what we have seen; to offer a description of what work is like in the chemical industry and to recount the ways in which the people who do that work feel about it. And by this we don't only mean manual work. The talk about the 'new worker'—talk which we will want to criticise quite severely—has by and large paid little attention to the ways in which middle management and lower level supervision have been affected by the massive accumulation of capital in the petro-chemical sector. Our chief concern is to demonstrate that while often living quite different lives— and belonging to different social classes—*both* managers and workers can increasingly be seen as *labour*, whose future is structured by the needs of *capital*.

Class in process, though, needs to be understood at one level as the experience of individual men and women. And, as statements about class relations involve a consideration of history, so concern with an individual's class experience relates to biography. Part II, *Individuals in a Class Society*, is therefore based upon just this: five of the people who work for ChemCo talking about their lives.

Part III, *The Politics of the Factory*, switches from the *individual* to the *collective*. This is where we look at company-union relations, give due recognition to the fact that the managers, though labour themselves, are agents of capital, and to the fact that the relationship between 'management' and 'men' is a class relationship. Our concern here is to look at what this means in the context of a 'progressive' management in an 'advanced' industrial sector; and at the sorts of organisation that workers develop, their strengths and weaknesses and the nature of the challenge that they pose to capital.

Part IV, *Living with Capitalism*, broadens the discussion beyond the factory. It raises questions about 'affluence', politics and political change, points to what it means to live in a society where 'success' and 'failure' are reproduced in the way they are in this one and, in the absence of major political change, to the waste—the human waste—that gives a unity to production and consumption.

Notes

1 Quoted in Bob Edwards, *Chemicals: Servant or Master? Life or Death?*, National Labour Press, 1945, p. 22.
2 S. Cotgrove, 'Alienation and Automation', *British Journal of Sociology*, December 1972, p. 447.
3 J. H. Goldthorpe *et al.*, *The Affluent Worker in the Class Structure*, Cambridge University Press, 1969, p. 6.

xvi *Introduction*

4 R. Blauner, *Alienation and Freedom: The Factory Worker and His Industry*, University of Chicago Press, 1964, pp. 132-3.

5 See A. Flanders, *The Fawley Productivity Agreement*, Faber, 1965.

6 This being something which has been 'celebrated' (the author's term) in a recent book: see Joe Roeber, *Social Change at Work: The ICI Weekly Staff Agreement*, Duckworth, 1975.

Part I

Labour for Capital

I
ChemCo

PLUMES OF SMOKE—white, grey and green—thin spirals of orange fumes. Ten miles away on a clear day, this is your first glimpse of the Riverside site. As you get closer it takes on the form of a giant, science fiction stage set; all pipes and tubes and spheres and cylinders, painted in different colours. An eerie, unreal, ominous presence; planted amongst green fields.

Fifteen miles to the south is Provincial—a large urban centre. Employment in the area is centred on the factories of several large, and often paternalistic, employers. The wage rates in the area generally have never been high, but employment has always held a degree of security, and you would have to go back to the beginning of the century to find any evidence of extensive unemployment or of militant union activity. It is, in the words of a national union officer, 'a dozy part of the world', but part of the world that is changing nevertheless. Every year of the 1950s and 1960s saw a large increase in the population of the county. People moved there from London, from the north and, particularly in the early 1960s from the West Indies. Provincial was the centre of an 'expansion area'.

ChemCo bought the thousand acres of fields and marshland that make up the Riverside site in 1960. Some £30,000,000 were spent on plant and equipment, covering over 300 acres with roads, pipes, chimneys, huge sheds, canteens and offices. In the words of the site manager Riverside is 'a multipurpose site', one of many which make up this gigantic, multinational company. The main product is chemical fertiliser, but tankers filled with nitric acid, sulphuric acid, ammonia and carbon dioxide leave the site every day, as do lorryloads of cement from a subsidiary cement plant and drugs from the site's large pharmaceutical plant.

Two types of fertiliser are made at Riverside: a straight nitrate which we have called Zap and a compound, Zap X. On the Zap plant a nitrate solution is dropped from the top of a shot tower, filling a hopper at the base with Zap 'pearls', ready for packing. The Zap X plant is dominated by 'the Grinder'; a huge rotating steel cylinder which mixes and spews out huge loads of Zap X—hundreds of tons at a time. These two plants are served by smaller acid and ammonia plants which process the raw materials. Stored there in mountain loads in the corrugated storehouse that dominates the site, potash and phosphate rock from Senegal has to be moved around by hand, shovel and dumper truck.

When ChemCo arrived at Riverside it came with its own managers and foremen, and a few experienced workers (encouraged by the promise of a 'staff job', in the future, as the site expanded). The majority of the 'pay roll', the manual workforce, was to consist of local people from Provincial and its environs, who had never before worked in a chemical factory. Riverside was to be a 'green labour' site, located in green fields, far away from the traditional chemical wastelands of the north. Chemical towns like Billingham and Runcorn are part of another world.

By 1970 ChemCo was firmly established in the area. It is still farther away from Provincial than any of the other factories and this helps to keep it in the back part of people's minds. They only ever see it from a distance when they're making a journey north. But they know it's there. As one dockworker put it, 'a bit of a myth has built up about ChemCo over the years. It's a bit of a special place to work. A good firm with real high wages. I don't expect it's like that really but that's how a lot of blokes see it.'

ChemCo faces the world with its administrative block, its staff car park, its security guardroom and its flags—the Queen's Award for Industry having a special prominence. The administrative block houses the plant managers whose offices look over the river. Their secretaries and assistants are there with them, but their offices are across the corridor—overlooking the site. The plant managers have bikes, painted in different colours and initialled. Every morning they ride them over to their plants to check on things—and then ride them back again, in time for their meetings, or for work on costings, or possible technical improvement on the plant. There are other managers in the administrative block. The site manager has a large room on the top floor, with his senior managers alongside him, each responsible for part of the site. Then there is the personnel manager and his assistants. They don't set foot on the plants all that often; they spend most of their time on policy issues and any necessary local union negotiations.

The plant managers are chemical engineers, and all but one of them are graduates. Three—known as 'the Docs'—have PhDs. Some of the older managers got their degrees 'the hard way'. They spent the post-war evenings of their youth studying at night school, and then took external degrees through the local technical college. The personnel manager had done this. He had been a plant manager and had worked in R & D (research and development). Like them all he has worked for ChemCo on a number of the Company's sites. But now, in charge of a Personnel team that contains two young social science graduates, he has called it quits. Recognising that he can go no further up the corporate ladder he simply hopes that he can 'carry on doing a good job' and be allowed to retire from Riverside. By contrast, men fifteen and twenty years his junior still live in ambition and hope.

These men are at the hub of chemicals as a 'science-based' growth industry. They spend their days discussing the theoretical and practical aspects of plant technology. The blackboards on their office walls are latticed with diagrams and equations of many colours. But their discussions extend beyond chemical engineering and, of course, financial matters. ChemCo prides itself on its progressive management and Riverside managers are steeped in the verbiage of modern 'human relations'. These men slip easily from talk about how the instability of the phos. plant can be corrected, to other talk about the workers—'the problem of motivation', 'job enrichment' and the like.

The Company leaves the day-to-day running of the plant in the hands of its production foremen, who, between 5.00 p.m. and 9.00 a.m., on Bank Holidays, and at other times when the managers are not around, are responsible to the site shift manager. The foremen, unlike the plant managers, spend all their time at the plant. Their offices are there and they sit in them dressed in their distinctive white coats and site helmets. These offices are quite different from those in the Admin. Block. They lack the same sense of permanence. Some are kept tidier than others but they are all grimy; they are indisputably *used*. They are the focus of a continual to-ing and fro-ing; the fitters for a 'permit to work', one of the blokes to arrange a lieu day, another foreman for a cup of tea, the steward for some information, and so on. In the office—which is 'his' for one shift only—the foreman changes from wellies to shoes and back again, checks lists of names, receives a call on his walkie talkie, fills in reports, and listens to the Tannoy. 'You've got to be a jack-of-all-trades in this job', they say. They have little or no scientific training, but in a crisis in the middle of the night, they are the ones who have to take primary responsibility and who, in cases of doubt, ring up the shift manager or get the plant manager out of bed.

A lot of these men moved down to Riverside with ChemCo from the north of England. These northern men make up just half of the foremen on the fertiliser section, the rest being local recruits. They are older, Company men. They believe in ChemCo and what it stands for. They believe in its past which is their past. When they moved down and settled in the expanding housing estate of Hillsbury, midway between the site and Provincial, they had hopes for ChemCo's future too. Hopes which they linked with their own future and that of their families. But many of them feel increasingly ill at ease with the changes that are now taking place in the Company.

Some 180 men are employed as production workers on the fertiliser section at Riverside. None of them had worked for the Company in the north. They are all 'green' recruits. And although 'local' only half of them were *born* locally, the others coming from Wales and Ireland, the West Indies, London, everywhere. 'They're a mixed bunch', said a foreman from a northern pit village. 'They're a mixed bunch all right.'

When ChemCo started up it had found itself in a tight labour market. It was left with what its recruiting officer described as 'the bad end . . . the cowboys, the bounty hunters'; young men for the most part, who belonged to a generation which had never seen massive unemployment; men who do not readily put up with the discipline of factory work. They moved from job to job, looking for overtime. The quick killing and on again: to the Smoke or up to Brum. They were the despair of the foremen —the northern ones in particular—who remember the time when 'people did what you told them. "Do this" and they did it. If they didn't you could grind them into the ground. Now you've got to be a bit more subtle.'

We thought the older foremen sounded sad about the change. One admitted that he was: 'I'd like to grind them into the ground. Grind my bloody heel into them.' Many of the foremen and the plant managers we talked to certainly voiced such views—but in doing so they were totally at odds in the official ChemCo line on labour relations. This stressed the need to treat these changes 'philosophically', to see them as something to be coped with and adapted to. In the words of a personnel man from the Company's London Head Office: 'Nowadays people are less inclined to, say, do as they are told. They want to be much more *involved* in the things they are doing. And as a standard of philosophy I don't think that's at all bad.'

But the 'cowboys' weren't causing ChemCo too much trouble. What was much more worrying was the increasingly stiff competition that the Company was facing from American and European chemical producers.

From the early 1950s ChemCo has been coping with the difficulties created by being a 'cradle to the grave' employer whose capital, and overall productivity, was inferior to that of its competitors. In the mid-1960s one American worker was producing the same amount of chemicals as 3·4 UK workers, the appropriate manning figures for Sweden and Italy (2·5 workers), Germany (2·6) and France (3·0) also being lower.[1] The Board of Directors decided that things were going to have to be 'tightened up' but it was not until the end of the 1960s that the Company came firmly to grips with its past, and adjusted to its position as a major multinational producer of chemicals. By this time its position was quite vulnerable, as was that of the chemical industry as a whole. In summarising its findings, a 1967 Report[2] which compared the performance of the British and American chemical industries noted that: 'We are confident in asserting that there are real and disturbing differences in manpower usage as between [the two] chemical industries. American output per head is perhaps three times the corresponding figure in Britain. We were able to identify many differences in practices, policies and attitudes contributing to the better achievements in America.' While the report recognised that the real 'solution' for the British industry involved the long-term restructuring of its capital, it also 'found areas of difference where immediate action could be taken to produce significant improvements in the short term. These can all be summarised as requiring the adoption of more enlightened attitudes by all employed in the British chemical industry.' To this were added other, equally revealing, comparisons between the British and European chemical producers. By 1971, for example, each chemical employee in Britain added $9,417 worth of value to the raw materials of the industry, while in Holland the value added was $12,752 and in Germany $14,177. The British firms employed 140 per cent of the management and 150 per cent of the workers used by their continental competitors.[3]

All this information added weight to the discussions that had been going on at Board level at ChemCo throughout the 1960s. Everyone was going to have to change. Managers, foremen, workers, they were going to have to change their approach. The size of the labour force was going to have to be cut over a period of time; the performance of those who remained was going to have to increase. This concern—concern about profitability—led to changes in the managerial structure of the firm. It also led to the introduction of an elaborate productivity deal.

The deal was the product of several years of discussion and its signing was described in the business press as 'a major success in industrial relations'. To quote a senior company official, the New Working Arrangement was 'part of an attempt to change the whole system of work, including the role of managers and shop stewards'. Well, the changes it proposed were not quite as radical as this might make them sound: it was not, for example, the intention to do away with the bosses. What the NWA did was this. It did away with the previous system of wage payment, a complicated mixture of time rates and bonus payments. This was replaced by a form of Measured Day Work. Jobs were to be classified into seven grades by a panel of managers who would follow certain fixed criteria of assessment that had been established by the Head Office staff. Men would be paid according to their grade of work and were to be interchangeable between different work on the same grade. (This interchangeability was construed as job rotation—an additional bonus to the workers.) In return the workers were to receive a large pay rise (at Riverside the average weekly increase was around £5—at that time by far the largest pay rise that any of them had had in their lifetime), and their wage was to be paid as an annual guaranteed salary. In 1970 the annual salary of a 'grade 5 man' on shifts was £1,800. By 1973 this had risen to over £2,200, by autumn 1974 to £2,800—£52 a week. In the summer of 1975, it had risen again to £64 a week.

The agreement also included clauses about the need to 'enrich' work and to 'involve' people in it. In the years that led up to the introduction of the NWA, 'involvement' had become an important part of managerial discourse within ChemCo. Human relations consultants visited the sites and managers were taken away to courses held in country houses or by the seaside. They were also shipped off to 'T Groups' and to 'Workshops'— to return with their heads reeling, and occasionally in a state of shock. The books of McGregor and Herzberg found places on their shelves,[4] and those who were converted to these ideas—men like Colin Brown who, in the words of a colleague, was 'the first one in this place who really got into what job involvement could mean for the system'—began to 'experiment on the plants'. Brown thought of the NWA as 'one great act of faith'; an attempt to do away with 'a lot of the class differentials' within the Company, and to move away from a 'monetary incentive' for the workers.

> 'You can make people work by dangling a carrot but you can't get at what makes them tick so NWA is a genuine attempt by the company to change working patterns. To have for the first time *genuine* productivity.'

Young men who came into ChemCo at that time, more or less straight from graduating with a chemical engineering degree, were told all about 'hygiene factors', 'Mickey Mouse' jobs, 'motivation', 'involvement' . . .

'I came away after hearing all of them talking so confidently and everything and I decided that I had to get into this. I had to understand what it was all about. So I bought this [picking up a copy of McGregor's *The Human Side of Enterprise*] and it's all there. Theory X, Theory Y, it's all there.'

In looking back over those years, the Riverside personnel manager remembers:

'There were pretty genuine feelings that something needed to be done for the sake of providing people with better jobs—all right, we are a commercial organisation, of course there was a return for us, but I think that we felt that it wasn't right to be operating people like this you know; those "Mickey Mouse" jobs, people who stand at the conveyor belt welding two connections together all day long. And we had so many jobs that were, in chemical terms, just like this and they were leading to dissatisfaction.'

This mixture of humanitarian and commercial consideration was a major feature of the deal. As a Company spokesman put it: 'Herzberg's theories, supported by the work of Chris Argyris and others, gave an attractive hypothetical underpinning to the change . . . whilst acknowledging the importance of material factors such as salary, benefits, working conditions, etc. . . . [NWA] for the first time lays emphasis on intrinsic job satisfaction.' Some of the plant managers tended to put the emphasis the other way:

'We had got too many people for what we make and we were going to have to pay a lot more money to workers anyway because we've never been a big earnings company, we've never paid big wages. We're a big company but we've never been in the top league as far as wages go. And there was a need for us to be better placed in the league, if we were going to attract the labour we wanted. So we had to get the money back somehow.'

NWA was the first step in the long-term restructuring of ChemCo's operations. Its aim was to rationalise the system of wage payment and the 'use of labour' (between 1970 and 1973, for example, the manning levels in the packing areas at Riverside, the most labour intensive, dropped by a sixth). At the same time it was to promote the identification of the workers with their jobs and the Company. This was the tension within the package —a tension which points to the central contradiction of capitalist production; the recognition that production is essentially social while at the same time it has to be organised for profit. The trick, and the problem, which faced ChemCo was to socialise production the capitalist way: to bring about a capitalist socialisation. Workers were to be invited to get more 'involved' in their work, to 'self-actualise' and actually to be more exploited. The tensions which resulted from this worked themselves out in different ways and at different times. But from 1970 onward none of those who worked on ChemCo's plants—workers, foremen or managers— was left unaffected.

Notes

1   *The Economist*, 1 October 1966.
2   *Manpower in the Chemical Industry: A Comparison of British and American Experience*, Chemical NEDC, HMSO, 1967.
3   European workers were also paid more, the wages and salaries of a production team in the UK being 80 per cent of that paid in Holland and Germany.
4   McGregor and Herzberg have been two leading figures in the Human Relations Industry. Herzberg's ideas on 'job enrichment' have been particularly fashionable of late amongst 'progressive' managements. At bottom they rest upon a highly individualistic notion of 'human nature'. McGregor's 'Theory X' and 'Theory Y' pose two sets of managerial assumptions about 'human motivation' which are held to relate to different practices. Suffice it to say here that in 'Theory Y' management's stress on direction and control gives way to one on 'integration'. In common with Argyris (referred to below) McGregor considers the employees' 'need' for 'self-actualisation' to be of considerable importance. See F. Herzberg, *Work and the Nature of Man*, Staples Press, 1968; D. McGregor, *The Human Side of Enterprise*, New York, McGraw-Hill, 1961; C. Argyris, *Personality and Organisation*, New York, Harper, 1957.

2
The Labour of Labouring Men

NWA is not just a 'productivity deal'. We see it as a change
programme without parallel in British industry. We want to involve
employees in the creation of new arrangements for doing work in
factories. ... We see NWA as something done together, *with* people
not as something done *to* people.

(*ChemCo press statement*)

The degradation of work brings with it decolonisation of knowledge;
employers do not like the educated, above all the intelligent worker.
Intelligence is prejudicial to output: the conveyor belt operative
and the machine formed so perfect a symbiosis that an idea in the
one had the same effect as damage in the other. Still absence of
mind won't do either: inattention and forgetfulness could occasion
as many disasters as lucid thought; it is necessary *to be there*, a
vigilance without content, a captive consciousness kept awake only
the better to suppress itself.

(J.-P. SARTRE, *The Communists and the Peace*)

AT RIVERSIDE FERTILISER is produced continuously. In a year over
200,000 tons of the stuff leave the site on lorries and in railway wagons.
It is this continuity and the sophisticated design of the whole complex
that the managers stress when they talk about the site. When we first
visited Riverside we were shown around by an old plant manager who'd
been attached to Personnel. We were given an account of the complex
processes involved in the production of ammonia, sulphuric acid, nitric
acid and of the technical difficulties that had been overcome in the
production of fertilisers out of these—and other—ingredients. All this
we found very interesting but as we walked around the site what struck
us most strongly was not this but the noise, the heat, the dust and the
large number of men who were paid to hump one hundredweight bags
of fertiliser.

This sort of situation was not peculiar to Riverside. On six of the seven sites we visited we found that 'control room operatives' were in a minority of the labour force. For every man who watched dials another maintained the plants, another was a lorry driver and another two humped bags or shovelled muck. In fact, about 50 per cent of the work involved in chemical production in Britain is classified as demanding virtually no skill from the worker. Most of the places we visited bore far greater resemblance to Keir Hardie's description than they did to those of Cotgrove or of Blauner. Discussing this with one ChemCo manager we were told that in his view the industry would increasingly be based around two types of work: 'scientific work and donkey work'. We wondered whether this wouldn't lead to the 'donkeys' becoming rather discontented. 'Yes it would', he said, 'unless of course we breed a special race of worker.' A joke of course. But one, as we shall see, with a serious core to it.

Some 180 men labour to produce fertiliser at Riverside. Only 40 of these work in the control rooms, the rest do 'donkey work'—most of them in the Zap and Zap X packing bays. Probably the worst job, though, is in the raw materials store. There, in a shed the size of a factory with a door the size of a large house, one or two men work to ensure that the plants are supplied with the necessary produce. Inside, the air is filled with a thick dust; it's so thick that we had walked past the doorway on several occasions before we realised that men were actually working inside. ICI have a similar store on Teesside where, according to a *Guardian* report,[1]

> Men were working in dust up to 2 ft. deep when a factory inspector checked. . . . There were even fertiliser dust stalactites hanging from the roof . . . and it took a twelve-day shutdown to clean it up.

Conditions at Riverside are as bad.

Sitting in a chase side with a mask on, and goggles which 'don't keep the dust out', one of the men told us how:

> 'You can't see in there. I've been in there and had my gear in forward and tried to look through my windows and with the dust coming down and floating I've had the impression that I am going back and I couldn't understand why. Open the door and I am not even ruddy moving. I am stuck on a pile of rock that's come off the band. I am stuck on it, got the wheel stuck on it and couldn't move.
>
> I felt all giddy. It's definitely upsetting. It's not good for you actually. If you went on continually I think you'd get a bad illness after a couple of years.'

He, like many of the men we talked to, was quite disillusioned with ChemCo—they had come expecting a modern, efficient technological company. In fact ChemCo is all these things. There is more capital laid down at Riverside than most sites of comparable size in the country. But capital needs to make a profit, not make work easier. At Riverside chemical fertiliser is produced at an unprecedented rate, and it is profitable for this production to be serviced by 'donkey work'. To the men who do the work this often seems crazy.

> 'When I came down here I was sadly disillusioned I can tell you. They talk about technology and all the technical bods they've got working for them. Well damn all that. Here we are in the technological age still doing jobs in 1900.'

At the other end of the production process—where the finished product is packed—the parallels with the last century are just as strong. About 140 years ago an observer described the work of labourers on the Liverpool dock:[2]

> These men (chiefly Irishmen) received the full sacks as they were lowered by the crane off the hitch on their shoulders and carried them across the road. They pursued their heavy task during the working hours of a summer's day at a uniform, unremitting pace, a trot of at least five miles an hour, the distance from the vessel to the storehouse being fully fifty yards. . . .

At Riverside a conveyor belt has removed the need for trotting—a definite technological advance. But only to ensure that more fertiliser is packed. The labourers at the Liverpool dock handle 750 sacks a day, at Riverside they handle that many in one hour. At peak rates Zap and Zap X is packed at sixty tons an hour, one ton a minute, a hundredweight bag every three seconds.

The packer stands under the hopper spout at the end of the packing band. He takes a plastic bag off the top of a pile which stands to his right, shakes it open and holds it under the spout. A swift upward motion releases a measured hundredweight into the bag and onto the rollers. All in three seconds. A proficient packer can keep a tight wall of packed green bags going into the sealer and along the bands to the loading bay. Some packers leave gaps. The full bags are sealed by pulling the open end taut, folding it over and feeding it through a heated slot that automatically closes the bag. From here they roll to the loading bay where, at the 'band end', they thud onto the shoulders of the two loaders. If the bags are going 'to road', the two men stack them three or five deep onto the back of a lorry. They catch the bags, turn and drop them. Catch, turn, drop . . . catch, turn, drop. . . . Every *six* seconds. Catch, turn, drop. . . . The 'band end' cannot extend into an enclosed rail wagon so when going 'to rail' there's a deflector which turns the bag onto your shoulder. You only have to catch and drop. But only one man can get into the door of a wagon so they take it in turns. Catch and drop . . . catch and drop . . . . A hundredweight bag every *three* seconds. Warm bags that burn your shoulder; leaving it red raw. In the summer it's stifling. Catch and drop. . . .

In the early years of the site men were signed on by the Personnel department and sent straight to the Zap plant or to the Zap X bagging area. One of the foremen complained that:

'In the early days they'd interview people at the main block and to anyone at all they'd say "Off to the Zap plant." You'd get weedy little blokes sent over here who would have one shift at the band end and it would kill them. . . . If you're going to work on this plant you've got to be able to do heavy work.'

And it is heavy work. The blokes say that the job is 20 per cent boredom and 80 per cent sweat. 'It's a toss up which is the worse really.'

'It's hard work y'know. Catching bags and things like that. I don't like it. I don't enjoy it at all. I think it's a . . . well, let's say it's a boring job. You come in and you do the same routine every day after every day. Well, some jobs you can come in feeling a bit lazy and get away with it, but not this job. You know you've got to come in here with the intention of working. You can't come in and say, "Oh I'm gonna have an easy day today." Y'know; you don't feel up to it today. Sometimes you feel like that but by the time you get in here you've got to throw that away. You just can't feel like that because you know there's no sitting around here. There's a bit of sitting around but you know that you're going to have to *go*. You know when those bags are getting filled you've really got to go, and you can't forget that.'

Off-loading really takes it out of you:

'Every time you take a bag off a lorry you've got to drag it, literally, and then lift it over the side. You sometimes have to do two or three hundred to off-loading and you're stuck up there with bags that are bent and leaking y'know. It's fucking hard work. It's the hardest job in the plant but it's the worst paid. Crazy isn't it? We've tried to put this over to management but they say it's easy. That's not surprising I suppose—they've never had to do it themselves.'

The comparison with the office is both clear and invidious:

'If you work in an office or even in the control room like Alfie you work hard no doubt, but it isn't like the railhead. You're not pushed to the limits like we can be. Y'know? No one wants to go up to the railhead and catch one hundredweight bags for the fun of it. You just think before you start: For this money it's all right.'

And the comparison is often the basis of conflict:

'Well Jack Steele [one of the managers] is not a bad bloke but he doesn't really appreciate the problems of packing; the actual graft involved in the job. The blokes will say, "What the fucking hell does he know about it? He's never done it and he's telling us what to do." And with Steele you just get the same old story all the time. You know: "We're paying you £37 a week to hump bags so we don't want any complaints." It's a bit annoying sometimes.'

And on top of the sweat there's the boredom. They tell you about a bloke who could fall asleep as he worked on the spout and the sealer. They'd put their hands in front of his eyes and he'd carry on packing. 'He'd never miss one.' They talk of becoming remote, detached from themselves and the world they live in. How their minds 'tend to go a bit stale' and how outside of work you feel 'a bit funny', unsure of how to talk to people, uneasy 'when you go out socially'. It's not surprising that they miss shifts.

'I think this is what makes a lot of blokes have a lot of time off y'know. You might not feel *really* sick or ill, but you feel a bit, y'know, cheesed off. And you say, "well I won't go in tonight" and you just have a night off. I suppose it's wrong in a way, letting your mates down, but I can't stick it sometimes. I really can't. I don't know why.'

When they're at work, and not lost in their thoughts, they find themselves
losing their temper. Placid, gentle fathers find themselves behaving in a
way that would be unrecognisable to their children.

> 'I think we're all mad sometimes. Seeing those green bags all the time,
> you see them in your sleep. You're just lying there and you just shut
> your eyes and you see all green. . . . In that situation I think you've
> just *got* to get angry with one another at times. You're working hard,
> catching bags and someone upsets you and that's that. You're getting
> these bags and you're sweating and then you get really angry and start
> swearing. You just blow your top and then forget it in a few minutes.
> That's how it goes . . . in this place.'

Lose your temper, blow your top and wait for the break:

> 'There's no "goal" in this job. That's what no fucker seems to realise.
> When you're packing or loading the only "goal" you've got is the next
> cup of tea.'

ChemCo managers talk a lot about 'goals' and 'motivation'. One of the
main purposes of the NWA was to create, and productively harness,
'involvement in work'. To the packers though, such changes that did
occur seemed anything but radical. 'Job rotation' was introduced. This
meant that instead of being compelled to load for the entire length of an
eight-hour shift, the men were permitted to work as a team, moving from
loading to packing, from packing to sealing and so on. This is clearly
better than doing the same thing all the time. They feel that the shift
passes quicker and two hours of loading is a lot easier to cope with in your
mind than a whole shift of it. The blokes tell you this. But at the same
time they'll tell you that they've always done it, that no one could survive
years of loading. They tell you how they've always tried to share things
around a bit in all the jobs they've done.

'Rotation', then, is necessary for survival, is part of the 'flexibility'
modern management want, but it did nothing for 'involvement'. It
doesn't make them feel *involved* in *their* work. As one of the blokes put it:

> 'You move from one boring, dirty, monotonous job to another boring,
> dirty, monotonous job. And then to another boring, dirty, monotonous
> job. And somehow you're supposed to come out of it all "enriched".
> But I never feel "enriched"—I just feel knackered.'

The fact that the NWA scheme was viewed as a radical departure for British management is testament not to its radicalism but to the overwhelmingly autocratic and conservative nature of factory production. All right, the NWA was a help, but it couldn't prevent men like Joe saying:

> 'You come in here sometimes and you think, "I'd do anything to get out of this." On the sealer you get all sleepy and then on the railhead you get a sore shoulder. You think, "God, what am I doing this for?" But next day you're back. I think all of us are mad. Even when you're at home you see those fucking green bags. Just lie back and shut your eyes and all you see is green.'

They come in, see the plant and they 'can't even describe the feeling. It's just emptiness.'

ChemCo buys their strength. It buys it because it is much cheaper than a machine. It buys it, and when it is exhausted ChemCo will no longer be interested. And the blokes know that packing fertiliser at 60 tons an hour is a young man's job. A foreman put it like this:

> 'We haven't come across the problem of the older blokes yet. I suppose that ChemCo could find them alternative employment. I don't see what employment they could offer though. And if they can't the blokes will just have to leave. They ought to realise this themselves though.'

The men do realise this and they don't look forward to middle age. None of them wants to be packing bags when they're 40. There are one or two 40-year-olds still working on the packing sections and while the younger blokes refer to them for comfort they know that it's no comfort really. They know that they can still do the job but they also know that it's not doing them any good. It doesn't alter the fact that they want to be somewhere else when they're 40. They want something 'a bit quieter than this' for their middle age. And while they are young now, in ten years' time all but a handful of them (17 per cent) will be in their 40s. These men, then, the majority at Riverside, are paid to do heavy repetitive work, 'donkey work'. As work it is little different in content from that demanded of their fathers, for technology and automation have not produced a skilled working class. If anything the opposite is true. During this century the working classes of Europe and America have been systematically *deskilled* by the 'progress' of capitalist production. And with this deskilling (accompanied as it has been by universal 'education' and the stress upon 'fulfilment' in a society of plenty) has come a contempt for work. The only thing that gives meaning to work for these men is the non-work of un-employment. As far as 'job enrichment' goes, perhaps the following quotation from Roeber's *Social Change at Work* is sufficient to raise doubts:

> According to Clark [the man in charge of job evaluation at ICI] the willingness of managers to encourage the radical re-design of jobs was far more important than the grade structure. 'Some of the most enriched jobs I have seen were amongst the lowest grades,' he said, and cited the case of the lavatory attendant at one works. To his basic job of cleaning were added elements that gave him complete autonomy in his area of work: he was given the responsibility for ordering his cleaning materials and the paper and soap needed in the lavatories; he was given the job of making minor running repairs—replacing tap washers and repairing the 'furniture'—and trained to carry them out. I mention this in some ways absurd example because it illustrates well the detailed ways that jobs can be enriched—ways that owe nothing to the complexity of the technology but have much more to do with the completeness of the resulting job and the freedom given to the worker in carrying it out. According to Clark, the result was a far more satis-fying job for the lavatory attendant, who is now a man with complete autonomy in his own work area.

'The main limiting factory to job enrichment', Roeber continues, again quoting Clark, 'is the imagination of the manager.' This, at least, is difficult to refute.

But so far we have only described the 'donkey work'. What of the 'scientific work', the work of monitoring the process technology? First listen to Riverside's site manager:

> 'On a big plane going across the Atlantic the crew don't do very much for long periods of time but, given a set of any one of an infinite variety of emergency conditions, they can spring into action to deal with them under the control of the pilot. . . . If you look at, say one of our modern ammonia plants, they've got to be part of a team, who perhaps for a lot of their time do not do very much. They play cards and so on while the plant is running steadily, but when the alarm goes and the lights flash they can swing into action on any number of a wide variety of contingencies.'

A few weeks after the chief pilot at Riverside treated us to this account of the chemical operative's job, the lights in one of the ammonia plants *did* flash. Some seconds later it blew up. Ten men on the site were shocked and injured and lucky to be alive. A few were in hospital for a period of weeks. One was permanently disabled, another suffered severe nervous tension afterwards and within a year had left the Company. By 1973 he still hadn't been able to sort himself out.

'That was my job stuck in that control room, which is approximately fifteen foot by nine and about ten foot high I suppose. You are stuck in there for the duration and if the plant is running well, reasonably well, then you literally don't see anybody for hours on end. Boredom begins to set in. I think that this is the disease of this type of work. . . . When you know that it's not quite right you do tend to worry about it —although you think, "ah well, fair enough. If it goes, it goes." You know, shut the plant down or something like that—but after four years in that control room the tension, mainly because I was stuck in that square box for such a long time with the ups and downs of the plant and the various things that are going on—I'm afraid that it gradually got through to me, you know, and eventually it started to affect me in as much as my temper began to get very short. Very short tempered. And I found that I was taking it out on my family; consequently it sort of rebounded until in the end I was becoming quite neurotic.'

Terry had been involved in all four 'upsets' that had affected ammonia production on Riverside, and when he talked to us in the company of three other operatives they all nodded in sympathetic agreement. They may handle the strain better than Terry but they experience it none the less, and they understand. Talking to them in the control rooms their eyes shift from your face to the dials over your shoulder. In mid-sentence they will stand up and listen, they move a lever or a knob, listen again and then sit down, but still their eyes are not with you. They find it 'difficult to relax', they tell you that the 'thing about this job is that you spend half your life just looking for trouble'. They also tell of men who came to the job and thought it was a piece of cake, who sat around drinking tea, reading, falling asleep. But the job got back at them, the plant went off line and they left. 'You just can't afford to let your mind wander in this job.'

Most of the control room operatives worked alone. Only in the Zap X plant did two or three workers work as a 'team' in the sense of being in regular face to face contact with each other. The usual shift routine of an operator involves him in coming to terms with working alone. The fore-men realise the problems here. They know that on the one-man plants, 'if one man is unhappy you've got a labour relations problem because he is all the labour there is'. They drop in during the shift for a cup of tea. Talk about their families, about football. They ring them on the telephone just to check. All the blokes we talked to mentioned the problems of working alone as a real drawback to the job. One man raised the issue most poignantly. His wife had died a year ago and he lived on his own. Since her death he had had barely any contact with anybody.

'I come in, have a word with my mate and then—unless anyone rings me up—I don't speak to anyone until I come out again. It doesn't worry me a lot. Mind sometimes I feel as though—you know—"is it all worth it" like. You know, being so lonely. Loneliness is very very bad. It's terrible really. But I'm getting over it a bit now.'

The bloke who followed Tom on the next shift told us:

'You've got to have the attitude that if you don't see anybody for eight or nine hours that's it. If your relief doesn't come in you'll be there for another seven or eight hours again.'

To be left alone, in charge of millions of pounds worth of capital that could blow up in your hands, involves a strain. It's no game, being alone with your thoughts and the noise of the plant. That noise can be a horrible noise.

'You are sat there for an eight-hour shift and everything is running perfectly. You do your readings every two hours and you are tapping your fingers in between whiles. It gives you the temptation to get a book out. You start reading a book and the foreman comes along and says, "you don't get paid for reading, you get paid for doing a job." You say "O.K. So what is there to do?" There are times when you start hoping that something will go wrong so that it breaks the monotony.
You just listen to this noise. It's just a steady drone isn't it? Well, imagine having to sit in this hour after hour watching everything go O.K.'

On one occasion we were, with some difficulty, talking with one operator about the job. We thought we'd like to tape-record some of the things he said. We asked him and he didn't object, so we tried. Our conversation was entirely inaudible. We told him next time we met and he wasn't surprised.

'Sometimes when I come down my ears are tingling—you know buzzing. I suppose they're like that all the time but it's like banging your head against a brick wall—you only notice when you stop.'

So work in the control rooms is noisy and it can be stressful and lonely. But it's not as arduous as packing bags.

During a shift the control room operator on the Zap X plant is able to make himself tea when he wants. He drinks it, and watches the dials; takes regular readings and records them in the log. It's a better job than packing—everybody knows that. But not all the operations are as straightforward or the control rooms as well equipped. One operator at Riverside, for example, is only able to sit down and watch the dials by looking at their reflection in a window. The second operator on the Zap plant works at the top of the shot tower: his job involves him in taking tests right over the top of the tower in conditions which, at the best of times, are very hot and very dirty.

'You know, it gets really hot up there. Once you've got all your equipment on it's fucking killing to go inside there. You say to them: "Look it's fucking hot in there. I could pass out or something." All they ever say is, "It's your job. It's up to you." '

The man who operates the phosphoric acid plant has to watch dials on two different sets of control panels—separated by a flight of a 120 stairs. At least we think that's how many there are. We asked one of the blokes.

'How many stairs are there? Well I've always been told there was about a hundred. I've had time to count them before now but before I've got to the top something has happened. Things change but these stairs will never get any easier will they? You've got to come down them at least once an hour to check your job. Very often you come to the bottom, just get down and start doing your test and the alarm goes and you've got to get back up to the top and see what it is.'

The alarm often goes in the phos. plant. The process there is notoriously unstable. Suddenly it can stop making acid and produce gypsum instead. Slabs of it. So the operator always has to be on his toes. He has to be ready to run up and down the stairs. He has to be able to swing a shovel. And his only help can come from the foreman whose office is two hundred yards away and who can't always be found in a hurry. 'Why they couldn't have designed this fucking thing better I don't know. You're like a flaming yo-yo half the time.' The phosphoric plant is in fact an 'old' plant. Brought on line in 1963 it was designed to produce twelve tons of acid an hour. Over the years the plant was modified and the rate pushed up. After NWA there was a big push to uprate it from sixteen to eighteen tons an hour. The manager tells the operators that no matter what the rate is their job is still the same, that they have to make the same tests; that it should make no difference to them at all. But they all say that the plant goes off the line just that bit quicker on eighteen tons; that the margins are that much finer and the tensions and pressures just that much greater.

The control room operators and the packers came to Riverside with a similar past. The operators were marginally older, but they had all done a similar variety of jobs—usually semi-skilled, or unskilled—usually pretty boring, not always paid 'good money'.

'I used to work in a shop. I was earning twelve pound a bloody week. I wasn't taking home that, that was my gross money: twelve pound a bloody week. I come down here and I'm on, what? Nearly thirty-six quid a week, flat money. So for me, coming from twelve quid a week to three times that amount, I'm bloody glad of the job. You know, no matter bloody what!'

They came to Riverside as 'common labourers' (a phrase from the past that is a part of their heritage and which some still use to describe themselves) and went into the Day Gang or on to the packing lines. Mostly by chance they found their way into the control rooms and trained up on the jobs.

'I just was lucky really to get the job, because since then it hasn't never been so easy to get a job down here. I've got a mate of mine, he's got O-levels and God knows what. Well he's tried no end of times to get in here and he can't. So I think I was probably about one of the last ones to get in just by coming in and asking for a bloody job.'

They all look back at the days and nights they spent on the bagging lines.

'Christ the work there is hard. The only job I was offered in Oxford was humping coal. I came here and humped Zap instead! This was a lot better money like. I was getting more money on the dole than they offered me in Oxford. But the Zap plant was really hard. Y'know I couldn't have put up with it for very long. I couldn't have stuck it y'know if I couldn't have got onto these other plants here.'

They know that their present job, for all the stresses and problems, is 'the best job I could hope for—being unskilled'. They have escaped the tyranny of the bagging line but they live with the fear that it is a temporary release—more a stay of execution than a reprieve. They tell you that they are the 'last labourers who will be running these plants'. The fear of the packer is that his labour power—his physical strength—will not last through his life as a reasonably priced commodity. Similarly the operator who is paid for being able to operate a particular chemical process, is well aware of the transient nature of his skills. These skills 'cannot be taught'— it 'takes years to really get to *know* one of these plants'—but equally, by their very nature, they are tied to the continuance of a particular chemical process. And in an industry dominated by intense world-wide competition —and therefore unplanned and unco-ordinated technological change— the continuance of any plant cannot be anticipated with any confidence. While the phosphoric plant operator protests that ChemCo should have a better designed plant he knows that when one is produced it is not likely to be at Riverside nor is he likely to be its operator.

The operators know the 'projected life' of their plant, and their talk often turns to the technological and market forces that might lengthen this or produce a premature death. They take a keen interest in any mention of future expansion of the site. By 1973, though, they saw little sign of this:

'When I started they were building plants on this site. Every year they built a plant. Every year there were different plants being built. Then suddenly—Bang! it stopped. We don't know what lies ahead. Nobody in this control room knows what he'll be doing in five or ten years time.'

At the time he was drinking tea in the control room with his foreman and the operator from the previous shift who was 'working on' to help with some tests on the plant. Jack (another operator) didn't think that there was any such thing as 'security' any more. Not for any of them.

'Not in this day and age. Then, years ago like, yes. But not any more. Take Rolls-Royce. Obviously they're not going to look after the men; just themselves. You're only secure up to a point here and that's the life of this plant. Where do you go from here? 'Cos you're doing O.K. here doesn't mean that there'll be a job waiting when the plant falls to bits. They're prepared to build a factory but they're not prepared to build permanent, see. You can see that in the materials they use. They're not permanent. This Company wouldn't think twice about building a plant, putting it into production, producing enough to make it pay, get back the price of the building, make a profit and that's it—close down. We could all be made redundant any day—but me, I just live from day to day.'

Albert turned to us:

'Well we've heard some tales here since I've been here. You know, they're gonna shut this down, gonna shut that down. ChemCo works in a very funny way. I mean when they shut the last one down, two weeks before they told them they were gonna shut it down, they took all the blokes out for a slap-up dinner for having a record make, a record production. Took them out to dinner, all on the house mind. ChemCo paid for it all. Comes back and two weeks later they says, "Oh, we're shutting down." Just like that. You don't know. You just don't know from one day to the next.'

But there is more to it still than simply plants closing down and opening elsewhere. A general tendency of capitalist production this century has been the separation of the theoretical and practical sides of production; increasingly concentrating the former in the hands of the controllers. These operators have nothing like the same skills as the nineteenth-century craftsmen. Nor do they have the same identification with their task. While their practical activity, their presence on the plants, gives them some control over their situation, again this doesn't compare with the type of controls that craftsmen have traditionally been able to exercise by virtue of their skill. Practical *skill* has become debased. The division between 'scientific work' and 'donkey work' is increasingly becoming a division between the controller and the controlled.

In all this description of work on a chemical fertiliser site we have, however, left out something important: a tendency which is having an increasingly widespread effect upon the daily lives of working-class people.

The chemical workers that Keir Hardie wrote about worked in Glasgow for twelve hours a day, from six in the morning until six in the evening. At Riverside the men work only eight-hour shifts. But they work them through the day and the night. To work for ChemCo they have to be prepared to travel for miles *and* to work right around the clock.

Everyone has to travel some distance to get to the site: almost all of them live over ten miles away, usually in Provincial. A few live over forty miles away and on one crew there are two men who live 100 miles apart. The Company provides a subsidised bus and Dormobile service. But if you miss it you've had it, there's no second chance. You'll just have to ring in and make your excuses. Really, to work at Riverside you *have* to have a car (or at least have a reliable mate to give you a lift). Not to have one puts hours on your day and makes getting to and from work really hard— hard work in fact. You could just about manage if it wasn't for the shift system but that virtually makes a car a necessity.

The shift system is known as 'the Continental' (apparently it is known as 'the English system' on the Continent), and the men work day shifts ('six to two'), afternoon shifts ('two to ten') and night shifts ('ten to six'). Four crews (or 'shifts' or 'panels') operate a shift rota, based on a four-week cycle. A man who works 'six to two' on Monday will do so again on Tuesday; move to 'two to ten' on the Wednesday and Thursday, be on 'ten to six' for the weekend—Friday, Saturday and Sunday—and be off on Monday and Tuesday, ready for 'six to two' on Wednesday morning. Every fourth week he gets a weekend off work, known as 'the long week-end'. He will finish work at 6.00 a.m. on the Friday and start back at 6.00 a.m. on Monday. For most it means a long sleep.

'This Continental really messes my system about: on the day shift I'll eat like a pig, y'know about five meals a day like. I have a breakfast before I go to work, then I have a big breakfast at work and then I have a few pints before my dinner, then tea, a few pints and chips for supper. Now on "two to tens" I just sleep. I have a big meal before I go to work and some supper but mostly I just sleep. But on nights. Jesus Christ! On nights I don't sleep or eat. Then it's days off to recover and back eating like a pig again.'

The hardened shift men from the north—and others who have worked in the steel industry—reckon to have got used to it. They like being off in mid-week, although they find it a bit strange to be 'the only bugger on the street out mowing the lawn'.

Most of the men dislike shift work: particularly the night shift.

'I hate the night shift you know. I really hate those shifts of "ten to sixes". I can put up with working my weekends—Saturday is just a name really isn't it—but I really hate nights. I don't know what it is. I'm not depressed when I come in here—no more than usual that is—but I get awful irritable with the kids. I won't have the telly on if I'm working nights for example. Because I know that if I'm sat in that chair watching a programme at eight o'clock say, I'll be thinking: "shall I go in?"—"Yes I've bloody got to go in"—"Shall I go in?" It spoils everything. And on top of that you've had it for social functions if you're on shift work. You can never say "Yes" to anything with an easy mind.'

It's not easy to fix up an arrangement for a drink with a shift worker:

'When? A week on Tuesday? Now let's see; no, that's no good, I'm on "two to ten". Then I'll be on nights and I never drink when I'm on nights. (I've enough problems trying to keep awake when I'm sober.) Then it's my long weekend and I've promised to take the wife and kids to her mother's, so that's out. So the best for me would be a fortnight Tuesday 'cos I'll be changing shift from "six to two" to "two to tens" that night, so I can have a lie in in the morning. So let's make it then. Y'know, providing I don't have to work a doubler. You're on the phone though, aren't you. Well I'll let you know if I have to work on. We're not on the phone at home.'

If a continuous process worker works overtime it may just mean an extra hour or two at the end of the shift, but it can mean a doubler. A 'doubler' is a double shift—sixteen hours' work. For those workers like the control room operators who have specific tasks which have to be taken over by their opposite number on the following shift such doublers—in the event of their mate's absence—can be compulsory and extremely inconvenient. To work a doubler on your first shift of 'six to twos', means that you have to be back at work eight hours after you clock off. One bloke told us how during the summer he had worked a doubler on his last morning shift—

i.e. he worked from 6.00 a.m. to 10.00 p.m. His wife was away so he had a few pints, arrived home some time after 11 and set the alarm for 8—in time for him to get ready to go to work in the afternoon. He woke at 7.45 feeling fine and rather surprised. 'Y'know, I thought, "this is great." The sun was shining so I got up, had a wash and went around the corner for the paper. Well the shop was shut. I couldn't understand that but I went down the road to the next one and that was shut as well. Anyway, I was beginning to think it was a bit funny, but it was only when I noticed that the pub was open that it dawned on me that it was eight in the bloody evening.' He had slept for twenty hours, missed a shift without phoning in and let his mate down. Continental shift work does your body no good at all. As Patrick Kinnersley[3] has pointed out:

Recently we've heard a lot about what is fashionably called 'jet lag', the disturbance to physical and mental performance caused by flying across time-zones. In experimental simulations of the London to Japan time shift, subjects lost seven per cent of their muscular strength and five per cent in central nervous system efficiency. . . .

Jet lag is just a short taste of what it's like to be on [shifts], but without the dreary surroundings of a factory at night and in circumstances when mistakes can cost only money—not life or limb. Shift lag is an altogether more serious condition. It affects you every day, every week, every year, for the rest of your working life—if you can stick it.

None of the men who worked on the fertiliser section in 1970 had stuck with one employer in the ten years before they joined ChemCo. Thirty per cent of them had had over four jobs in that time. They came to ChemCo because they needed the money and they'd heard about the summer overtime. They knew it was a pretty secure place to work, that there were no lay-offs or short-time working. They knew ChemCo was a 'pretty good firm' but they hadn't come with the idea of staying. Then at the same time their wages went up, the labour market began to dry up. So they stuck. Stuck with the shift work too. Men on shifts could earn £40 a week at ChemCo in 1972. As one of them put it '£2,000 a year. That's a lot of money if you're an unskilled man. There's not many people earning that sort of money in this area. I wouldn't want to lose this job.' Most of them felt like that. Eighty per cent of them are married with young children, over a third have three or more children. They came in search of money, found it, found a sort of security as well and decided to stay. They were young men with children buying their own homes (two-thirds of them have mortgages, a figure almost twice that of the national average for manual workers). They'd moved around but were settling down at ChemCo.

Some people will say that they work there from choice. Certainly since 1970, when the labour market tightened, those who have complained within earshot of a manager have been reminded that they are free to try their luck somewhere else. It's a strange freedom though, that can be used as a threat, and both these men and their managers know that any freedom of choice they have is illusory. They left school without 'qualifications' and while some of them have been trained in a skilled trade (12 per cent) and others have some clerical experience (8 per cent) they have, for the most part, been offered the choice of a variety of similar unskilled jobs within factories and on building sites.

In the 1960s they'd exercised their 'choice' and moved around a bit. But unemployment had now taken even that possibility from them. They were stuck with ChemCo, and after the NWA increase they were satisfied enough. ChemCo would do. It would have to because, without doubt, it was better than nothing. 'Stuck' and 'have to'; this is the language of working-class freedom.

> 'You're trapped in this job. Every man in this plant now is trapped here, believe it or not. It might seem strange to you, but everyone here *is* trapped. You've got to stay whether you like it or not.'

But for the moment at least it's secure: securely trapped. As one Jamaican put it: 'Man, I sometimes wonder if it was good lucky or bad lucky when I came to this place.'

They've all thought about packing it in: most of them 'many times'.

> 'But you know you've got to think twice about work nowadays. You might say, "well, I'm fed up" and you pack it in and then find that you can't get another job. This is the trouble, see. But this I think is what happens to a lot of blokes down here.'

They want to go, to get out, but they can't because there's nowhere obvious to go. Their frustration is compounded by fear of the sack, and the fear of what might happen in the future, when they're too old to pack bags. Such fears are founded on the reality of the swollen shoulders of the older men and the periodic closure of other plants on the site which have 'run their course'.

'You've got to worry about it because it's where you get your bread, see. You wouldn't worry so much if you could say, "well you can always go out of here and get another job." But I wouldn't like to know what would happen if it packs up down here. When I came to Provincial first I had about three weeks before I could get a job—before I got this job. I wouldn't like to know what would happen now. Probably terrible. I've got an idea you know, about being out of a job. I was only out of one for three weeks but I know it can be really miserable.'

There's not much joy to be had on the dole. And while this generation of workers is much less marked by the brutality and fear of mass unemployment than previous ones (the Welfare State for all its inadequacies is an important political fact) dole money is not much use if you've got a mortgage to pay and young children to care for. So they're trapped at Riverside. They don't like it there. For them, like their fathers, work is something to be endured because, as labouring men, their labour is not their own: it is labour for capital.

Notes

1 At the magistrate's court in Middlesbrough ICI pleaded guilty to a breach in the 1961 Factories Act and were fined £50 (*Guardian*, 5 September 1973).
2 See E. P. Thompson, *The Making of the English Working Class*, Penguin, 1968, p. 474.
3 Patrick Kinnersley, *The Hazards of Work*, Pluto Press, 1974.

3
The Labour of Superintendence: Managers

Economising is the science of the best allocation of scarce resources among competing ends; it is the essential technique for the reduction of 'waste'—as this is measured by the calculus stipulated by the regnant accounting technique. The conditions of economising are a market mechanism as the arbiter of allocation, and a fluid price system which is responsive to the shifting patterns of supply and demand.

(DANIEL BELL, *The Coming of Post-Industrial Society*)

Just as at first the capitalist is relieved from actual labour as soon as his capital has reached that minimum amount with which capitalist production, properly speaking, first begins, so now he hands over the work of direct and constant supervision of the individual workers and groups of workers to a special kind of wage-labourer. An industrial army of workers under the command of a capitalist requires, like a real army, officers (managers) and N.C.O.s (foremen, overseers), who command during the labour process in the name of capital. The work of supervision becomes their established and exclusive function.

(KARL MARX, *Capital I* (Fowkes translation))

IN 1971 THE Riverside site manager was paid about £15,000 a year. Most of the other managers had salaries of £4,000 to £6,000. Judged against the shift foremen's £3,000 or the £2,000 for which ChemCo workers laboured round the clock and worked overtime, this was very good money. Very good money indeed compared to the pay of the great mass of the population who made less than many Riverside workers. But consider what the manager accountants at the top of the big corporations were paid: men like Weinstock at GEC or Callard at ICI, or the ChemCo chairman (then on £50,000 a year). It is highly likely that such people—

over and above their 'fringe benefits' and the future income they've stored up in the form of pension rights—have an investment income from dividends and capital gains. It becomes clear that, compared to the manager accountants, Riverside managers are, quite literally, in a different class.

There is a theory about a 'managerial revolution'. It holds that it is 'the managers' who control industry now; that either power resides in some ill-defined middle level 'technostructure' or (there are different versions) at the top where, because the new men have arrived, profit is no longer the driving force. This theory seems to appeal to some academics and business commentators. Somewhere, there might just be a middle manager who believes it. But if there is, he isn't to be found at Riverside. None of the managers we talked to there was in any doubt that his job was to make profit and that if he failed in this his future with ChemCo was in jeopardy. For whereas management organisation has often been restructured, so that at Riverside managers and foremen have taken on more responsibility, these additional responsibilities have come in such a form that they make these men more closely accountable to capital. The apparent devolution of decision making, rather than resulting in the middle managers becoming an independent power in the corporation reveals them less and less ambiguously for what, objectively, they are; so much (relatively highly paid) labour.

The very process of rationalisation and bureaucratic control to which the superintendence of labour subjects factory workers (though not only factory workers, the same thing is happening in the service sector) simultaneously serves as an organisational device by means of which these managers are themselves held to account. These managers are driven by the impersonal force of capital. And it is of course this very impersonality which gives some credence to the PR men's slogans about how nobody (or everybody) owns the big corporations. But what we want to stress here is that it is now perhaps as clear as at any time in the history of capitalism that the labour of superintendence—the managers and foremen who are 'responsible' for the plants—is itself a victim of this same impersonal force: is a figure on a balance sheet.

Whether managers work in a small 'backward' factory or for a giant 'progressive' corporation, their lives are structured by the imperative to make profit. But in chemicals plant managers often have to cope with complex technology, and complex organisation as well.

Riverside managers talk a lot about 'the system'. Substantially, their job is to ensure that its component parts are most profitably aligned. The grinder manager, for example, is, as he says, always 'juggling'. Aside from 'man management' and technical innovation—and, given his plant is an old one and not designed for the job, the inevitable work of 'mend and make do'—he has to plan the week's production run. He has to specify the quantities of various 'mixes' in advance, then keep the plant running. But demand for particular 'mixes' can fluctuate sharply. This can cause him problems, especially since space in his silo is limited. If a ship loaded with potash docks, his store has to be emptied ready. At such times other managers will make very clear to him that an idle ship loses money. But for technical reasons, to meet their demands could mean that he had to drop 30 tons of his currently—and continuously producing—'mix' on the floor. This will take a bulldozer to clean up. It will also mean lost production, and lost money for his plant. In emergencies he may be able to 'import' particular mixes from ChemCo plants elsewhere—but again this will eat into his plant's profits. It's no real get-out. So, surplus capacity or under capacity he's in trouble. He has to produce continuously for the market. If his plant goes down he's in big trouble, *and*, if his feeder plants go down, *he* is the one who will cry 'Produce! Produce!' to *their* managers.

Ideally, ChemCo in general, and within it the Riverside site, should operate like a computer, with everything programmed in. In monopoly capitalism though, there is still the market to contend with. The working lives of plants can be shortened. They can be technically outmoded in the process of being built. And unplanned shifts in demand can have widespread ramifications for 'the system', even for mundane matters like storage. Take the manager concerned with warehousing:

> 'The selling people tell us they want an order immediately, which means that we've got to completely alter the whole organisation of the job down on the shop floor. It's all part of modern thinking. This is what management, modern management, is all about. Production will want standage, the material handling people will not, so there's a basic incompatibility. The management's job is to be able to come to some compromise, to be able to stand above it all, as it were, and look at things in terms of the overall system. That's why communication comes into it. Modern management therefore is about flexibility and change.
>
> At peak season, like nowadays, in peak season we'll tear ourselves inside out for the customers and that's what Jimmy was doing a minute

ago when he rang me ["that's the system working", he beamed happily after Jimmy rang].'

In one important sense, for all these managers the 'juggling' is the job. Riverside was designed as a technically interdependent system. For example, if certain plants come off line a chain reaction is set up. This not only means that other plants on site have to stop production (or waste their product) but that plants owned by other firms, which the Riverside complex is contracted to supply, also have to stop production. Very obvious economic considerations like these make managers eager to avoid plants coming off line at all, and to get them back on line as soon as possible. Whilst running, given the capital investment at stake, they must run them as efficiently as possible (the same holds for the labour intensive parts of the site. The continuous operation of the capital intensive plants depends on the packing and bagging workers not creating bottlenecks).

'The system', however, is not just a *technical* system. There is also what ChemCo managers call 'the other side'. By this they mean the workers. For just as the plant managers have to work collectively on the technical side of their work, it is essential if the entire mass of labour power on the Riverside site is to be put to the most profitable use that 'the other side' works as one big collectivity too. Short of an explosion or a technical fault which threatens production, 'trouble'—real trouble—means people. Without workers, sophisticated technology counts for nothing.

These managers therefore take 'the other side' seriously. They know that Riverside workers aren't militant but they want to keep things this way. They also want an actively involved and 'flexible' workforce to prevent waste and to make the system run efficiently. This is one reason why NWA came in. Because a workforce which just plodded along and did what it was told to do was no longer good enough. Not if workers *had* to be told.

A by-product of the coming of the NWA was that these managers had to acquaint themselves with a new technical literature—on the psycho-sociology of work. 'You scientific buggers. You're suckers for middle range technical sounding theories', a visiting consultant told them. 'Plenty of diagrams and "theories". You like that don't you?' They do indeed. But they don't get it all from books and courses and they like to add a few embellishments of their own—Army life and experience with their own children are both grist for this particular mill. Moreover their 'theories' make evident both these men's essentially technical frame of reference, and their essentially economic function. 'Human beings', as one put it, 'are our most important piece of machinery. And like machines, if you don't keep them running men will go rusty. You've got to jump on them now and then to make sure they don't seize up.' One manager, pointing to a maintenance marker board, followed the people=machines analogy right through.

> 'Pity we haven't got one for labour. You know, with a column here to tell you which ones are defective, one for those completely u/s, one for replacements. . . .

For the most part this view of workers as things—as people-objects, to be worked on—takes more subtle forms. But that managers think like this is not surprising, in view of these men's technical training and the job they are paid to do, which involves thinking in terms of 'labour costs' and treating the labour power of other men as a commodity.

On the shop floor it's said, about a couple of Riverside managers in particular, that 'They aren't bad blokes. Given that they're managers, that is. They'd do anything for you *personally*.' 'Personally' means letting a bloke borrow your car spraying equipment, or talking to him about what it would be like for his son to do O-level Chemistry, or, providing things aren't too tight, helping him to get time off. It also means not driving it home unnecessarily that you are a manager. But 'personally' or not, these men *are* still managers. The theories of psycho-sociology notwithstanding, they've had to learn the hard way about 'man-management' and how to defend their 'right to manage'. And this means that 'in this game you can either be a bastard or a bad bastard'. ('Bad bastards' are managers who behave like bastards because they *are* bastards. Common or garden 'bastards' are men who find that, as managers, there are unpleasant things they have to do.)

The 'economising' which came to ChemCo in the 1960s was not merely an 'economic' phenomenon. A shift in social technology rather than a supra social 'science', it inevitably involved people. Economic in origin, for it came about to increase profit, economising had implications for the internal structure of the labour of superintendence; for the mode of operation of management; and for the culture of factory life. At ChemCo, as we will see later, it is the older foremen who have been hardest hit in each of these three respects. But all the managers (save for the youngest of them) feel that because of the economising they too have suffered a loss. Hence what can only be called 'the Phil Lancaster legend'.

Phil Lancaster had been promoted to another site before we arrived at Riverside. But his exploits have attained the status of myth. His signal achievement was to start up the Grinder. Since the plant's design specifications were outmoded by the time it went into production this caused numerous technical problems, which were compounded by atrocious working conditions. The men who worked with him on that start up tell how they had to work round the clock and how Phil Lancaster worked with them. 'He might as well have lived on the site', they say. Called in on a Sunday afternoon, 'he jumped right in there, best suit and all, up to his knees in shit.' He had a PhD. But time and again men forgot this in comparing him to some of the 'new'/'modern'/'professional' managers, the ones they say are 'all slide-rule'. 'Phil Lancaster', they say, 'now he was a *real* manager, a man's manager he was.' A university chemist who could get on with people, for the managers, too, he represents a link between the old and the new. Very few discussions we had with Riverside managers about 'man management' finished without some reference to 'the time when Phil started up the Grinder'. 'Phil got the job going.' 'With Phil they'd get the job out.' 'Phil might as well have been one of them.' 'Phil had the human touch.' Phil, it seemed, had everything. But Phil has gone. So to a large extent has his style of management, and not just because the plants are running now rather than being started up.

At about the same time that the NWA came in these managers were experiencing their own kind of 'productivity deal'. They were pushed away from the fumes and rattle of production into the office. 'I've never seen one of them whose shoes aren't scuffed at the back', a long service foreman grumbles—not that they do lounge about all day with their heels on the office desk. But their job has changed. They look more at equations on blackboards now and at figures on sheets of paper. They monitor labour, as a cost—represented in data about turnover, lateness, absenteeism and overtime—and they see the men less. Company policy is that they should plan ahead, make technical improvements, be more cost and profit conscious than before. There's a greater stress on costing and budgetary control—and they like this. As one recalls,

'Two or three years ago you could never see your costs. Now you get the lot. The main purpose is economics. I'm all in favour of it—of the American system where you're given so much money and it is up to you, where you have to see what you can do with it. Things are much better now. You'd be surprised what you can tell from the accounts. I watch them closely for little oddities. If sundries are up I want to know why.'

But if they are very satisfied with their increased and more direct responsibilities for profit making, they miss the shirt-sleeved involvement of being 'down there with the lads'—like Phil Lancaster. Mostly in their mid to late 40s they sympathise, at least to some degree, with the feelings the workers have about young managers who are 'all slide-rule'.

One in particular—Edward Blunsen—was seen to epitomise the new, bright, ambitious, 'whiz kid'. The new type of manager who was increasingly 'passing through' Riverside. Young—in 1970 he was 28—he had come to ChemCo with a 'brilliant degree' in chemistry from a leading university, spent two or three years in the central research laboratories and came from there onto the site as plant manager. There, he determined to put his technical ability to work to make a name for himself—by making profit; often with flagrant disregard for the views or feelings of 'the other side', the men who worked on the plants. Blunsen it was, who talked about the need for a 'special race of worker' fit only for 'donkey work'. He, too, who talked about workers being 'completely u/s' or 'defective'. He called them 'idiots' if they didn't 'understand', and saw them as substantially subordinate to his own technical 'brilliance'.

Of course there have been managers in the past who have excelled technically but 'messed things up on the other side', and Blunsen may be looked at as just a late addition to a long line. However, Blunsen is more than a 'technical man', narrowly defined. Whether he is talking about how much the chairman earns, who in the management structure can assess who for what grade, describing the several little ways in which the grades can be made 'flexible', or explaining how 'loss accounting' works—whatever it is, if it's technical or financial he has the details at his finger tips. In his mind the numerical world is inexorably linked to capitalist rationality—to the accountancy of profit and loss. Production figures, site values, financial estimates for plant modifications and how much they would save the company, these are the staple diet of his conversation, and life. To the other managers he represents, in a far too one-sided way, the direction in which ChemCo and plant managership is headed. For whereas they *are* 'all in favour' of the new economising they *also* know that you've got to 'understand the lads', even if nowadays you don't see them so much:

'There is no good in taking a young graduate who has done a bit of research in the labs and putting him on the plant. They just don't understand the lads . . . they've no understanding of human beings. They don't *manage*. All they want to do is make technical experiments.'

These other managers, then, especially if like Colin Brown they really have 'got into what job involvement could mean', still have a penchant for making what they now call '*social* experiments' as well. And again in contrast to Blunsen, they are not kindly disposed to the world of the corporate suite.

The merely 'social' world is not for them. Here, for example, Blunsen talks with one of these managers, Jack Thompson, about another ChemCo site:

> 'There's lots of invitations all the time. There is a club, a gentlemen's club, a bit like the Free Masons I suppose. Lily ponds as big as that plant over there. All the wives have coffee mornings. You're always going to dinner or returning dinners.' ('They're a load of crawling bastards', mutters Jack.)
>
> 'Mind you, I've got friends at London Head Office who get *no* home life. They're out *every* night, either *for* the Company or with friends *from* the Company. You've got to do that above a certain level. It all becomes a matter of getting together with other companies. With Government people, with people from the Banks and Finance. It's really necessary to know them if you want to get anything done.' ('It's just a gentle form of corruption', growls Jack. 'What a life. Six months of that would kill me.')

To Thompson, a 55-year-old former plant manager (at this time pushed into what was virtually a non-job until he chose to leave) such social trivia—'standing there with a glass in your hand making conversation'—is anathema. 'I can't small talk', he says. Blunsen, by contrast, relishes the very idea of it. Weighing up a colleague's promotion prospects he always takes account of 'the wife'—'that's always an important variable.'

Yet whatever their satisfactions and regrets, and whatever they feel, and whatever they think about it, one thing is certain: the 'economising' which came to ChemCo in the 1960s had very real effects upon these managers' lives at work.

For one thing the management structure has been 'flattened out'. The jobs which used to exist above theirs in the management hierarchy have been removed. As a result, many of them know that their careers have 'come to a halt in the middle'. Too old now to rate as 'whiz kids', they have no place to go. What with children at school or university, mortgages, cars, boats—a whole way of existence to keep up—it's also too late for them to think of pastures new. They like to think they have a universal expertise; an ability to 'deal with' *the* universal-people. But the older they are the more likely it is that other firms will categorise them as 'ChemCo men'—men with a particular, not a universal expertise. Already there have been redundancies (an issue we take up later) but even for those who remain, there is no brooking the fact that to stay 'safe', let alone go higher, means working harder. There are fewer of them, so that they each have to do more work, some managers who hitherto looked after only one plant now being responsible for two. And whereas they like the idea of greater responsibility, it has brought with it greater accountability.

We noted earlier that the technical interdependence of the production process created pressures, and that managers were thereby impelled to control each other. But the performance records which today's manager keeps on his subordinates are a further source of control. By means of these bureaucratic devices the manager himself can ultimately be further exposed to the chill wind of the market. Each manager has a job description and formally specified objectives. Such predefined expectations of performance make failure all the more glaring and cost consciousness all the more important. Moreover, just as each manager holds regular reviews of progress with his foremen, and the foremen with their workers, so he too is subject to regular reviews of progress, about *his* performance with his boss. The 'system' is a bureaucratic system—a system of control. It programmes, monitors and processes the 'performance' of labour, including that of the labour of superintendence, which itself is concerned with programming, monitoring, and processing in order to control.

Of course, barring bottlenecks, labour troubles, unanticipated shifts in supply and demand, leaks and emissions, and urgent phone calls in the middle of the night to say that plant's 'gone down', the manager should lead a programmed, well planned life—one in fact which allows him to plan further. Indeed to 'juggle' successfully, to be able to say 'that's the system working', can spell real satisfaction. But clearly the list of things which can 'upset the system' is by no means short. On any given day few managers can afford to relax, to be confident, as they put it, that 'the system knows what it's doing'. And should a manager make a mistake it can cost him dear.

Today, his 'performance' is indelibly recorded on a personal record card, to be scrutinised and reviewed by managers at the Central Career Planning Department. Any weakness or failure, any 'unnecessary' labour disputes or technical breakdown will be recorded. It will be marked down on his card. These managers are well aware what this can mean. They watched as Edward Blunsen expanded plant capacity but increasingly antagonised the men on the plant—an antagonism that blew up into 'a mess' during spring 1972:

> 'It will go down on his record. One day when he's being considered for a higher job, someone will see it. It may be five years, may be tomorrow, may be twenty years' time, but it will go down on his record. And that will go with him.'

Such are the controls to which the labour of superintendence is now subjected.

The plant managers are well aware that in ChemCo generally 'the dead wood' has been, and is being, cut back. In the last couple of years Jack Thompson has gone. A tradition is ending. For there was a time when every effort was made to shunt managers who had outlived their usefulness into less important jobs, even sometimes into 'non-jobs'. And 'non-jobs' are becoming rarer. Increasingly, older men have it made known to them that they can ask how much the firm would pay them to leave. As the managers put it, 'You can ask your price.' The price being the 'golden handshake', the 'pay-off' that will take them off ChemCo's staff list and into an 'early retirement'.

Given this, some managers find it particularly disturbing when they have to get rid of labour in plants scheduled to close down. George Smith —a manager about whom nearly everyone at ChemCo agrees 'He'd do anything for you personally'—is the prime example of this. George believes sincerely in the NWA 'philosophy' (his term). And in discussing NWA he always wants to get across to workers that the people who 'dreamt it up at Head Office' *really did* care about the jobs men did, 'even though in straight economic terms it should in the long run benefit ChemCo'. (He was outraged when he read a left-wing leaflet in which managers were called 'pigs'. '*Us* they mean', he said to a fellow manager: 'It's *us* they're talking about. I'm no pig. I bloody well *care* about what I'm doing.')

In some ways, like other Riverside managers, he regrets that ChemCo is no longer 'a cradle-to-the-grave organisation'. He knows that '*once a* job at ChemCo was a job for life', and he knows what it means that this isn't so now. He talks about redundancy as 'a moral problem':

'Some of the people further up the organisation give you the hard line about looking after the health of the total system. Of looking after those who are left behind in the system rather than those outside it. I don't know. I don't know what to think about this. You see you find yourself counting. "That's fourteen gone. That'll give a bit of space in the system. One of them's changed his mind—the bastard!" I don't think I'm like *that*—but you certainly find yourself doing it. You can't help yourself from counting numbers. Yet there are men who come in here and sit there in that chair—some of them of course look at it as a new beginning, but others—they just lift up their arms, can't understand it and, for them, it's the end.'

Seeing such things, indeed—as part of 'the economising'—reluctantly being instrumental in bringing them about, can turn a manager in on himself. 'Say it happens to me', says George.

'I'm 48 years old. I joined ChemCo at the age of 24. I've got 24 years' service too. Say I go for an interview. "Ah! Mr Smith, you're a chemist", they say. "A chemist are you?" And there I am, I took my degree in 1947 . . . there are young people just taken their degrees, 25 to 30 years old, can ask for a much lower salary than I'm used to.
    "Ah!" they say, "well, you're a manager are you, Mr Smith? and what do you manage?" And I say, "Well, I've managed this plant now for seven years." "Ah!" they say, "well, where have you managed your plant?" "At ChemCo I say." Now I know the ChemCo system but what about modern innovations they think. "And what salary do you get, Mr Smith? I see, X thousand pounds. Thank you. . . ." So I can understand these blokes when they're 50, when they are sitting in front of the fire, when they don't want to go back north. "Is it going to happen to me?" they think. And then it does. The letter comes. It must be fucking awful.'

Where personal morality and economics collide, George Smith is given to show you he is doubtful and a little confused, even about what his own motives are. 'I don't think I'm like *that*', he says. 'But. . . .' Or 'I don't honestly know.' Or, talking about decisions made higher up, 'I *think* that that's why we did it.' Or, a favourite expression this, 'If you put it in cynical terms of course. . . .'

Yet it would be wrong to think that all ChemCo managers are racked by moral torment. Anyway, whether like some of the 'whiz kids' they delight in quantification and are in love with capitalist rationality or whether like George they dislike 'counting numbers' and hesitatingly inspect themselves for cynicism, they still have a job to do. They are still part of 'the system'. Which is perhaps why, sitting side by side with the site manager, George contains his ambivalence and puts things rather differently. Dr Jones, talking to us with George, was very concerned about production, and about the new human relations:

'I would say we have been very involved, perhaps over-involved, with this sort of thing. We have had innumerable Consultants on the plants. To my mind I don't doubt the theory at all, the theory of Herzberg for example makes a deal of sense. What I doubt is the *application* of it, its applicability to industrial situations. Sometimes you know, I think we spend no time in this place on *work*. We have tried the lot here. T Groups, Job Enlargement, the lot. And I think very few of them, or very few of them we have tried, have made a real impact on *production*. I think the only one that has helped in any way has been Methods Change.'

At this point George joined in:

'James liked Methods Change because it was orientated toward profit, or more obviously oriented toward profit. And he has a point there. Sometimes you do have the impression that we are not here to make fertiliser or chemical or cement at all but to be experimenting with new types of human relations techniques.

The first thing to remember is that we are in business to make money and that management's job is basically production. If all these techniques help then well and good. . . .'

But let's go back to George thinking aloud about redundancy; about the question of who is responsible.

'The thing is I don't think they think it's *me*. I don't think they think it's *my boss*. They think it's *"them"*. But we're *"them"*. But it's not *us*. It's something *above us*. Something up there.'

As he finished this complex soliloquy he gazed up at the ceiling—and lifted up his arms. His sense of confusion is perfectly understandable. In a big corporation like ChemCo business is a complicated business. Yet in a big corporation like ChemCo, business is in some ways still very simple. For when men fail to find any one individual responsible for their fate, and when managers have to make distasteful decisions which conflict with their own often humane inclinations, it can be for one and the same reason: because they are subject to the dictates of an impersonal force—capital.

'Economising' is in some instances highly sophisticated in its mode of operation, in others crude and brutal. But the science of 'economising'—what the American sociologist Daniel Bell calls 'the science of the best allocation of scarce resources . . . [and] . . . the essential technique for the reduction of "waste" '—is capital's 'science'. George Smith, for example, is given to express moral concern about what he sometimes 'has to do'. The site manager is really interested in technical problems. But, as their conversation makes clear, in each other's presence they relate everything back to production, to profit. George said, 'The first thing to remember is that we're in business to make money.' This *is* the first thing they have to remember whether they are 'like *that*' or not. The tighter control, the 'economising', including redundancies in their own ranks, make it clear that the plant managers, like their workers, sell their labour power as a commodity. And in the end—the end as far as capital is concerned—they are told, these human commodities, that they can 'ask their price'.

Politically, at least on first hearing, these middle managers sound clear-headed enough:

> 'The Board are responsible to the shareholders for the profit that they can make on the capital that is invested in the Company. The Board then decides an overall policy in order to make this money for the shareholders. They set up organisations beneath them to run their empire. We run these organisations and are responsible to the Board.'

But in the party political sense they are as close to Labour as Conservative and not really 'political' at all. 'Progressive', in that they have no time for industrial policies which court trouble (they thought the Industrial Relations Act 'irrelevant' and worse), their strategy is to enmesh workers and incorporate their union. As for them joining a union themselves: 'For a manager', they say, 'it's a contradiction in terms.'

They are not, however, without their own contradictions. Part of the superintendence of labour, they are labour. Managers, they are managed. Paid to manage uncertainty in all its forms—economic, technical and social—they are, today, far from secure. A long way from rejecting the wider capitalist system of which their world at ChemCo is a part, their company-fashioned ideological armour is not completely bullet-proof either. And this is not just because of what they experience at work or because they know that redundancy can be 'fucking awful' or because they understand very well *why* so many Riverside workers are doing what they call 'Mickey Mouse' jobs. Nor is it just because, unlike some managers, who exist only to make others work, these men are also directly exploited themselves by virtue of the technical innovations which they make.

The fact is that between 1970 and 1973 the problems of capitalism were such that these managers could not ignore them or entirely wish them away. Their own lives at work were affected by tighter profit margins. They knew unemployment to be exceptionally high for workers and managers alike. Prepared to accept *some* strikes as justified, they thought, in 1970–2, that they had 'got out of control'. The power workers' work-to-rule in late 1970 and the dockers' and the miners' strikes of 1971 affected their own production directly. They were affected, too, by the changing costs of phosphate rock (up to 200 per cent in 1973), of potash and of other raw materials. They were affected first by a definite devaluation, and later by a progressive one. They could not escape knowing that they lived in an inflationary economy. Bombarded by information about the precarious state of the balance of payments, they saw the governments of both parties hopelessly at sea. They lacked an answer, and as far as they could see no one else had one either. As for Heath and Wilson, neither of them seemed capable of 'getting their sums right'.

'Where is it all going to end?' the site manager asked of inflation, of the balance of payments, of strikes. . . . All of them, still without an answer, from time to time ask themselves similar questions. They have learnt enough to know that management's job is to be able to stand above it all; to look at things 'in terms of the overall system'. But what is happening to the system overall—the system which is, and which is not, their system —escapes them.

4
The Labour of Superintendence: Foremen

You men have no business to have your coats off when on duty in your shops unless you are warm. You have no business to take the tools out of a workman's hands to do his work. Your business is to secure results from other men's work. . . . A man cannot work with his hands and at the same time give intelligent supervision to a gang of men, and a foreman who does this is apt to lose the control of the men while he is weakening the confidence of his employers in his abilities as a general.

(Steelmill Manager, Pittsburgh, 1905[1])

The supervisor is the front-line of management. No matter how the company is organised, no matter what title is used, there is always that first-level management position that calls for the direction of the productive employee. Most men at this level are called foreman or supervisor, but whatever their titles, they are members of management. Identified in the minds of others as a manager, they should think like, act like, and perform like the management of their organisation.

This involves knowing the firm's aims and what the firm stands for. It means understanding the goals and objectives of the entire organisation as intimately as the supervisor knows the standards and quotas that exist in his own department. Working in harmony with management, the supervisor becomes a part of this philosophy in word and deed.

(American Management Scientist, 1968[2])

AS EARLY AS 1835 we find Andrew Ure writing in his *Philosophy of Manufactures* that 'it is the constant aim and tendency of every improvement in machinery to supersede human labour altogether.' Quite obviously human labour has *not* been superseded altogether; not even in the chemical industry, which some commentators look to as the modern version of the 'automatic factory'. But the idea of a factory without workers—and this without 'trouble'—has always been close to the hearts of employers. Another idea which appeals is that of workers actively seeking to control (i.e. exploit) themselves. The talk to be heard today—about 'responsible trade unionism', 'worker directors', 'participation', 'autonomous work groups' and 'self-supervision'—can be seen as an expression of this; so too can talk about 'abolishing foremen'.

However, the inner logic of capitalism is such that the men of capital cannot always fully get what they want. A tendency exists, for example, to replace human labour power by the power invested in machines, but this is subject to the proviso that machines are cheaper. A tendency exists also toward the self-supervision of workers, but this too is subject to a most important proviso: that capital must not lose control. Moreover, neither tendency works itself out in an even way across different industries, firms, labour forces and markets. In discovering, therefore, that in the long term ChemCo would like to dispense almost altogether with the labour of foremen we must bear in mind that they may not be entirely successful in this, and that not all firms will inevitably move in this direction (indeed, the trend this century has been toward more foremen, not less). Yet since Riverside management does have plans to introduce a new style and structure of supervision and, as part of the 'economising', has already gone some way toward putting these into practice, it is highly pertinent to consider here what the consequences of this have been *for foremen.*

There are two score foremen at Riverside. The majority, as a manager saw it in 1970, were 'in for a shock':

'They're in for a shock. They're at their limits. In future we won't see any more of this kind of supervision. We'll be having more men with an academic training. . . . *One* man with academic training and the lads could run the job themselves.'

ChemCo's strategy was to revamp the structure and practice of supervision to complement the changes being made in the structure and organisation of management proper. A greater stress on 'self-supervision' by workers was to relieve foremen of some of their duties, a few 'high level' supervisors were to be inserted between the managers and 'the men' and the ranks of supervision were to be slashed. To this end the number of supervisory personnel declined by 30 per cent between 1965 and 1973, and the positions of 'superintendent', 'senior foreman' and 'assistant foreman' ('AF') were erased from the organisation chart. The title of 'foreman' went too. Today, formally speaking, there are no 'foremen' at Riverside and there is no supervisory hierarchy—just 'single line super-vision' and 'supervisors'. None the less, progress toward achieving the Company's long-term objectives is at the moment limited in several respects.

To begin with, there remains what managers regard as a 'surplus' of foremen on site. A big firm like ChemCo is not exposed to the full force of naked market pressures—there is a certain leeway—and in the case of foremen, who often had long experience of ChemCo's 'cradle-to-the-grave' tradition, managers acted considerately. When for example the position of 'assistant foreman' was abolished, the hitherto AFs found themselves made up to 'supervisor'; similarly when two plants were closed their foremen were 'absorbed'. The fact is though that market forces which are held down here tend to pop up elsewhere, and in acting considerately to some foremen, management had only stored up trouble for itself. Sensing that their days are numbered, many Riverside foremen are now watching and waiting nervously. More than this, they are beginning to unionise. And this of course wasn't part of management's plan at all.

The restructuring of supervision has hit another problem too. It's a two-sided problem but it can be summed up in one word—*workers*. For as well as complementing alterations in the structure of management, the changes also anticipated changes in workers' 'attitudes', to be implanted by NWA. Foremen are most resentful that the vast majority of workers simply have not 'entered into the spirit' of the deal. That's one side of the problem. But where workers do co-operate—as in the case of the so-called 'Mobile Operators' which management has created since NWA[3]—this also worries the foremen, and confirms for them that they are being ex-posed to a definite threat.

'Now we've got it both ways', they say, and most certainly they have. They've 'got it both ways' because they are threatened from above with redundancy and from below by the Mobile Ops. They've 'got it both ways' again, because, as they put it, 'we've got more responsibility and—with the sort of workers we've got—we've got the old AF's job too.' For many of the foremen it's a matter of 'they call you "management" and in the end it comes to this. Management's conned us.' What management 'conned' them with was 'single line supervision'—or as they think of it 'a sort of NWA for foremen'. Essentially they are right; they are up against the same economising logic as the workers and the managers—fewer people doing more work, and in the end a reduction in labour costs; this, plus tighter, bureaucratic, control.

It is in fact because of the system of bureaucratic control, and because a certain measure of management control is programmed into the technology, that Riverside is more than usually suited to a policy of 'streamlining' supervision and making 'foremen'/'supervisors' 'the bottom level of management'. Taken together these two factors—the bureaucratisation of control and process technology—do make it relatively less difficult, as managers are wont to say, to 'raise the level of the foremen'. They help to make possible a situation where foremen can follow their managers away from the shop floor and into *their* offices, just as the 'NWA for foremen' holds that they should. Understrappers the 'supervisors' may still be, but they are expected to be low level bureaucrats as well; to collect and process the information which managers need to monitor 'the system' and to run it more profitably.

The bureaucratisation of foremanship has meant for foremen what the bureaucratisation of middle management has meant for managers. Increases in 'responsibility' have brought with them stricter accountability. The foremen have personal record cards now; they too are subjected to regular reviews of progress toward the objectives specified on *their* job descriptions; and as with their managers, every stroke of the pen with which they quantify the performance of those they supervise in turn records *their* progress. The shift from 'physical' to 'mental' labour in the content of the foreman's job has then brought with it some of the trappings of a manager-like status. At the same time though the 'foremen'/ 'supervisors' find themselves starkly confronted by the fact that they are sellers of labour power which is itself even more closely costed and evaluated by capital's criteria. Whereas this hasn't made them into natural allies of the working class it is driving them into the worker-like reaction of trade unionism, for it is increasingly plain that the social niceties of the gold watch ceremony and nostalgic 'retirement' parties are theirs to command.

Yet beyond a certain point it is dangerous to generalise about these 'supervisors'. A definite split is emerging within their ranks; a split summed up in the phrase 'not all foremen are management'.

The majority—the *'traditional foremen'*—are in a falling market. Their technical knowledge is limited, confined to a rule of thumb knowledge of their own plants, and their way of doing things, their 'style', doesn't mesh neatly into ChemCo's reorganised management structure. These men, then, *are* insecure, they *are* unionising, and the 'economising' *will* likely cost them their jobs. Already it has cost them in other ways as well. But politically, technically and in terms of social habit—and in terms of career prospects—not all Riverside supervisors can count as 'traditional foremen'.

'*Management men*'—just half a dozen out of forty-odd foremen—have a style, an ideological stance and a technical ability (though even they lack 'academic training') which marks them off from the rest. These men '*are* management', and in the context of ChemCo's technico-bureaucratic system of control they are harbingers of the future. In the chemical industry the new-style supervisor/lower manager of tomorrow will be a man who thinks, and *acts*, like they do. Or some management and the administrative theorists who specialise in foremanship hope.

The *management men*, confident in their own ability, and of their past successes, are still looking up. They do not feel threatened by the higher wages the productivity deal brought. Nor by the more competent and perhaps more independent workers that could be attracted by a minority of enlarged and better paid jobs. Relaxed enough to let men work without standing over them, they pride themselves on the time they spend in the office. But even though some describe themselves as 'only half-employed' they do not idle their time away. They watch closely their production, absenteeism, labour turnover and lateness records. They share the Company's enlightened management line that the Industrial Relations Act was irrelevant, that Law cannot bring about good industrial relations and in this (in 1971) they differed from the other foremen ('I've always been a Labour man but . . .'). Their view that strikes evidence a failure of *management*—that they are not a result of the unions having too much power nor of communist agitators—also differs from that of most of the other foremen. Most clearly of all though, foremen who 'are management' are characterised by something which marks them out as just that, and would do in most companies, whatever their management's views on industrial relations. They consider their plants to be little companies in their own right—with them the employers. As the management accountants at the top of the big corporations regard their corporations, so they relate to *their* small parts of the corporate world.

Plant managers, as we have seen, are now expected to keep out of the plants and concentrate on technical improvements, costs and major policy. In such circumstances of course—especially since various plants in the Company '*sell*' their products to each other, so becoming companies in microcosm—it is not at all surprising that successful foremen should take on proprietorial airs. One, for example, is given to preface his arguments with the proposition, 'All right, now we're setting up Lunn-Smith (or even 'Nichols-Beynon') Chemicals Limited, now. . . .' Another comments on time keeping in the Zap plant: 'We've got to set a standard. We're the largest employers on site.' These men are under no illusions that they are, or will ever be, 'employers'. But they know that if they are to succeed at ChemCo they must act as if they were. More precisely, they must act like plant-level manager accountants.

Like their managers none of the foremen in this company—'management men' or 'traditional foremen'—have any doubt that the big corporations are in business for profit. 'Management', they say, 'isn't going to give money away. At the top they want profits. They look to Sammy Bell the group manager to get these profits, and he looks to such as us to get them for him.' The truth of this is more urgently borne in on them because the group manager is now just one manager away (only the plant manager intervening).

What makes the management men exceptional is that they actively *search* for more profits. They look for that extra 1 per cent efficiency which in some plants, as they put it, 'could cover the salaries and overheads for a year'. Highly cost conscious individuals, they watch their production figures, check waste, 'get on top of the men', 'get on top of the plant', act not just *for* management but *like* management. Thinking of themselves as employers, they are highly effective agents of capital. Profit-minded, technically competent, 'good with people', such men are well suited to the demands of the new style supervision.

Managers rely upon such men and value their judgment. They are closer to the workers than any plant manager could be and bureaucratic organisations like ChemCo need men in such positions to oil the wheels and to keep 'the system' running smoothly. Management-like non-managers, these men can do little jobs that managers cannot do themselves. They find out what is in the air, chat up shop stewards, assess their strength, look out for likely lads. So: a word here to a worker of some authority on a shift with an 'awkward' West Indian—'What are you going to do about him then? It's about time he got the sack and was finished from down here . . . you get some of your mates together and make a few complaints': a pertinent question there to an applicant for a job on another plant—'would you put up for steward if you got the job?' A special remit from Sammy Bell about another steward, a 'trouble maker' —'I don't care how you do it but get rid of him.' In such ways these men act as management's unofficial arm. Nothing new about these techniques of course. But these men are chosen because, though still in a way 'in the middle', they have let it be known (to management) that there is no room for doubt which side they are on. Also because they are already a part of management, at least at an informal level.

'Socially' some of the other foremen felt so out of place at the firm's Staff Club that they formed their own 'Munich 1972 Club' to save up for a trip to the Olympics and enjoy themselves fund-raising in the meantime. Of the staff dances one complained, 'It's all managers.' Of the various other official–unofficial activities, 'They're all *their* activities—photography, drama and that.' Management men don't feel like this. Anyway they don't appear to. Outside work it's sometimes golf, sometimes sailing, and sometimes with a manager. It would be difficult to think of anything that could be more different from the social activities of some of the old style foremen. ('Had a great night last night,' said one of them. 'Bloody great!' 'Company-do, was it?' we asked. 'No—Grand Order of Moose— Piss up.')

If a foreman is aiming for higher things he needs to convince management that he can 'mix with anyone'—and 'anyone' of course includes management. But not least he has to spend time thinking how to advance himself. Few ChemCo foremen think of their present job as part of a still on-going career. It would be nonsense for them to do so—the jobs are just not there. Yet the management men think like this. Being successful, they are also consulted by ambitious workers on how 'to get a white coat'.

Alan is ChemCo's management man *par excellence*. Very bright, by far the best foreman as judged by both management and men, he thinks a lot about promotion. Significantly, perhaps, he holds to the same neatly self-validating theory about promotion common among managers themselves. 'The most successful', he says, 'are those who don't stay in the same job long enough to have their mistakes found out'—though, like them, he appreciates that to do this today you have to move on *fast*. But over and above this he has another theory. He is apt to illustrate this with well rehearsed anecdotes, for example about his Cycling Club days. 'Once you get behind you've got to go faster to catch them up. That's what it's like in life, see.' Another favourite example is that of the man who developed boils and was therefore able to grow a beard with holes in it.

'Everybody knew him. Promotion no trouble!' He rubs his point home by reference to the Welsh Rugby team:

'They come from Swansea, Cardiff, Newport—but not many from the Valleys. Now they could get forty or fifty from the Valleys to play in the Welsh team. And it's the same with life. What you've got to do is distinguish yourself. Distinguish yourself from the mass.'

With his large, detached, expensively furnished house and a small boat to go with it, Alan has distinguished himself all right and he makes no bones about it. An ex-shop steward (half the Riverside foremen were once shop stewards) and, as he tells it, a militant one, he has no illusions about how organisations work. No illusions about capitalism either. He was once schooled in politics by a Communist Party convenor. Now a disillusioned socialist he learnt his lessons well. And humorous as some of his stories about promotion may be, they come from the mind of a man who has thought seriously about how it is won. 'Have you ever thought how vicars get to be Archbishop of Canterbury?' he asks. 'It doesn't happen by accident, y'know!'

As far as promotion goes, Alan and the few others like him, have already figured out the odds. 'There's two shift managers about to retire', says one. 'Charlie Fell and Alan will go into these. That'll leave two jobs over there. And they're thinking of moving over to Area Supervision anyway—someone like me looking after two plants. . . .' He's right of course. This is indeed what the managers are thinking and men like this are in tune with their thought, and are capable of bringing it to fruition.

There are, then, highly competent and successful foremen at ChemCo who feel secure in their jobs. Young men for whom 'the money's bloody good'—and could get better—who, when asked about the 'early retirement' of a colleague, assert confidently 'It doesn't worry me. . . . If you're valuable to the company they'll look after you.'

Obviously enough these men are *not* 'employers', and they are in a different class to the real manager accountants. But they, a tiny stratum, may be able to compete if and when—and they think this will happen—the day of the graduate foreman arrives. They *are* sure that they *are* valuable and that they *will* be looked after. But ironically this is just how the traditional foremen recall feeling when, upon first becoming foremen, they crossed the class divide. They have found since, though, that capital's need to accumulate makes it but a poor respecter of its petty servants. And now, as the traditional foremen feel the effects of the economising, they are much more concerned to hang on to what they have got than to advance their 'careers'.

Most of the *traditional foremen* are in their 40s, often over 50. Many are northerners brought down for plant start-ups and they have been with ChemCo long enough to see the system change. As they see it:

'Before, it was a family sort of firm. Then we had all this economising. It started with the Directors and came right down to the shop floor. We became a Yankee-type firm. The iron fist began to show. Instead of the manager being someone who knows the blokes personally, a manager was a manager. "You must economise"—we have that all the time. It knocks a lot of pride out of the foremen. We had all these managers straight from public school. They knew their chemistry but they didn't know their men.'

The traditional foremen themselves, then, are critical of the very changes in their job that management and their manager-like colleagues value so much.

By no means free to use their increased power arbitrarily, they find it difficult to carry off the new style supposed to go with it. There is no difficulty now in amassing material to 'throw the book' at troublesome workers: time-keeping and absence records, detailed reports of any disciplinary action, and copies of the annual reports made out on each man see to that. But this is a bureaucrat's way of doing things. These men feel a certain spontaneity has been lost. 'When I'm bollocking a man', one told us the first time we met, 'I always bring him in the office. I'd never do it out there in front of his mates.' But though they know what *management*'s line on supervision is, they don't always live up to it in practice. This foreman and a couple of others in particular, are notorious for bollocking in public, even for blaring it all out over the Zap Tannoy. This is indicative of the way they have adjusted to the new style supervision generally.

For these men, to be a good foreman is to be a 'good bastard'. Like their managers, many say that as to being a bastard or not there is no choice. Again like their managers, they regret their lack of 'involvement on the plant'. But these foremen, even though they don't stay in the office for as long as they have been told they should, feel the loss much more acutely. Whereas their managers (and the management men) appreciate the increased control of the new accountancy facilities, the traditional foremen, like their workers, have a quite different view of the way their jobs have been 'enriched'.

It isn't just that 'with all the paper work that goes with it, it's more like a clerk's job now'. After all, managers don't care much for the paper work either. Rather they feel that from the mid to late 1960s onwards, they have been on the receiving end of 'all this economising (which) started with the Directors and came right down to the shop floor'. Managers call them 'good ChemCo men', and this they may be. But these foremen remember what ChemCo was like before it became a 'Yankee-type firm'. A dozen little things remind them that this is no longer their world. The economising not only knocked a lot of pride out of the foremen, it led to a re-definition of what a foreman was. And as far as they are concerned, doing things the new way is not really being a foreman at all. Being a *real* foreman takes 'character', an understanding of men, a kind of flair, a gruff warmth, the hardness of a man's man. Foremanship—real foreman-ship—is an Art. 'It's the old kidology', they say. Not of course that the 'management' men are beyond using this as well, but, given the choice, these men would much sooner exercise control by way of tricks and bluffs and shouts. They cannot stop doing it anyway—changing the reading on a gauge to make men believe they are under pressure; spurring them on by belittling their ability; claiming to have seen other men do better with no trouble—'*He'd* piss through that.' Also, buying the lads a pint. ('Harry', his workers say of one of them, 'is the biggest bloody liar I know—a good bloke, mind.' There's no telling whether Harry knows that everyone sees through his colossal lies—but it would warm his heart to know they call him a 'good bloke'. For him, as for the others, being thought a '*good* bastard' matters.)

They share with their men something of a common culture—and some-times, too, something more than this. For example, following the intro-duction of NWA one of their new powers was to determine which workers were competent and adequately trained to move from one grade of pay to another. In one case one of these foremen rapidly promoted everyone to the highest grade. Their pleasure was only rivalled by his pride in doing right by the lads, and maybe by his hope they would repay him if ever he needed something 'extra' from them. ('It makes my blood boil', a manager said.) Then again, one plant has a shift that works reasonably smoothly because, as one of those in the know put it so succinctly, 'Ted [the fore-man] has got something on all of us—and we've all got something on him.' Dribs and drabs of Company property flow out the gates, sometimes by the foreman, quite legitimately, signing chits; sometimes by judicious use of nods and winks.

Just as the managers like to think they are good on 'the other side' so, above all, these foremen believe themselves to 'know' people. To know there are times to swear, times not to; times to turn a blind eye, times to bollock; men to speak to in one way and men to speak to in another. Managers regard them with some affection. 'A good bunch of lads aren't they?' The foremen in turn help perpetuate a mythic past. Managers are part of the furniture of their lives. They plot their working lives in terms of the managers they have had, how they were interviewed by them here, what they said about them there. 'He came to the plant I was on when he started. A real gentleman he is', one recalls about Dr Jones, the site manager. Some managers—in particular Phil Lancaster—are their folk heroes:

'He'd roll his sleeves up and work with us. Right away. A great manager he was. A real man's manager. I worked in his team on start-up. . . .'

Through the tricks and the bluffs and the shouting these men still find 'satisfaction' in their work. But, looking back, their open good humour reveals more than a tinge of regret. They look back to 'Phil Lancaster's day' and, often, beyond that to what it used to be like, up north. This harking back to the past is partly a reaction to the rise of the younger 'all slide-rule' technically qualified graduate managers. But to hear them talk about the 'economising' is to understand that what hurts them, personally, is the passing of a culture of which they are part. A change which is strongly linked to the prospect of redundancy and to the fact that 'seniority' now counts for little against the strict canons of 'efficiency' and 'productivity'. At Riverside some of these older foremen have no better salaries or perks than men twenty years younger, perhaps even local boys they have brought on—people 'with hardly any service at all'.

Added to this, they feel that workers at Riverside are not like they used to be in the north. Talking to them about this they tell you that these blokes have always had it 'soft'. Since the war they think there has been a rise in confidence among workers generally. And they put this down to 'education'. Quite a few cannot fathom out their own children—'O-levels he's got—*O-levels!*—and doing jobs like that! He went to grammar school *for that.*' 'It's the modern generation,' they say.

'They haven't the same pride in their work the old men had. In the old days the control room panel would be spotless. Now they won't even clean it—spread cigarette ends all over the floor.'

But even without the 'new generation', the tauter working methods, and the greater willing compliance that is needed from workers today mean that they cannot be treated in the traditional way. 'Foremanship' has changed and some of the foremen have changed with it. 'When I came here I was a hard hat', one says, 'but I've become a humanitarian.' All the same, it still sticks in their throats that 'up north, if you ask someone to do a job he'll do it. Here it's a question of "it's not my job".'

A couple of them have had their jobs made as secure as jobs can be. 'Charlie's been with us now for forty years', his manager says resignedly. But even though management does its best to 'stand by Charlie', he—a 'senior foreman' in a firm that no longer has 'foremen' and has '*single* line supervision' to boot—is still 'a bit of a nuisance'. Strange detours have to be made on ChemCo's organisation chart on his account. Managers don't like this—at least they'll be pleased should he 'decide' to go. And so will those foremen who, but for him, really would be single line 'supervisors'. For them he's 'a *bloody* nuisance'. They envy him in some ways, too. They envy him his job security *and* that he was made senior foreman at a time when it really counted. For in Charlie's day to get a white coat *was* to join an 'aristocracy' of labour. The old foremen used to wear bowler hats, they tell you. And 'you'd have to call them "Mister".'

At Riverside today, the old status distinctions which management once used to divide and rule are being swept away—again by management—in order to try and increase profitability. Division is being reimposed by means of 'grading' now: rule, ideally, is through the 'supervision' of 'management men'. For supervisors it's 'education' and, above all, performance that will count in future. Not a few of them feel that they've 'missed the boat'—or indeed the flight, for 'poaching' by foreign firms has taken some of their former colleagues off to hot climes far away. 'I had the chance once', they tell you, 'but the wife. . . .' They know it's too late *now* to 'make a packet'. They also know that it is too late now to *ever* get a job like Charlie's; *and* that, anyway, 'the foremen then and the foremen today is a different kettle of fish'. This is partly because the job has changed but it's also because 'it doesn't *mean* what it did'. 'People down here', the ones from the north tell you, 'just don't appreciate what it used to mean to get a job with the firm up there, let alone get a white coat.'

To *be* somebody, the foreman needs the social backcloth of the manual working class. But these men tend to live tucked away in Wimpey houses on 'mixed' but predominately 'white collar' estates. They work the same shifts that their manual workers do, and despite the 'office work' get dirty. Hundreds of miles away from 'home', they lack the audience required to confirm to themselves that they have indeed distinguished themselves from the mass.

Here they are then. Stuck. Stuck with ChemCo because it represents their entire experience of industry. Stuck because demand is falling for the particular brand of supervision they have to offer. Stuck, too, in a part of the world where they don't feel they belong. Stuck in a system where, though they have more responsibility than most of them ever dreamt possible, they have cause to regret that in the past, up north, 'the foreman used to *be* somebody'. And to top it all, their workers know just how to add insult to injury: 'what sort of foreman is it', they ask, 'who has to travel three hundred miles to get a white coat?'

'Some of them you can see ageing', one of the management men says of the traditional foremen. For working at ChemCo so long, working the Continental which means going to work when others sleep, and moving away from family and friends, has conspired to make the rest of these men's lives residual. Not feeling at home at home, the very demands of their work which bring them satisfaction have, in other respects, cost them a lot. Charlie, who has been with ChemCo the longest, has talked it over with his wife. 'After all these years', she said, 'you wouldn't be happy anywhere else.' And both of them believe that he *has* to stay on at ChemCo in order to keep alive. But the fact is that ChemCo itself is no longer what it used to be. Even the traditional perks of being a ChemCo trusty—like 'putting a word in' for someone—can count for nothing now. This is not just because of the stress on qualifications but because the 'modern generation', including some of these foremen's own children, have seen what working—even for ChemCo—can mean:

'When she left school I told my daughter that I could get her a good job with the firm. "Thank you Dad", she said, "but I've seen what that place did to our home. You being down there all hours of the day and night. I'm not going to give my life to ChemCo as well. I'm going to get a bit out of life." '

'Perhaps', he added, 'she's right.'

Others tell of the six foremen who retired on another site and how not one lived to draw his pension twelve months. They know this isn't all that unusual but at their time of life—in a world where 'you're too old at 40'—'it makes you think'. And what with managers 'straight from public school' (though actually they're not) and workers who don't seem to care (not like these foremen always felt *they* had to anyway) it makes them wonder what it's all been for.

To get established as a foreman was something of a struggle. Not least for Bob, who was one of the 'lucky' local lads who the northern foremen brought on—

'I came here as an operator then I went training Assistant Foreman. The plant manager used to say to me, "Get a white coat on" and I'd say, "I'll put one on when I'm monthly staff." I'd have looked a right fool. White coat one day, off the next. The lads would have said, "Ah, they've found you out. Back on the other side today is it? . . ."

At the beginning they thought that I was still one of the lads. They thought they could get away with things. Had to put your foot down a bit harder. . . . You'd say to a lad, "Do this for me" and he'd say, "O.K. Bob, I'll have a cup of tea first"—probably remembered that that's the sort of thing I used to do.'

To be a foreman, however, is to find yourself the centre of a struggle. This was something Bob learnt (and made clear to 'his men' who had once been his mates) early on.

'And I'd have to say, "Do it *now*." I'd say to them, "*Look*, this is my *iob*. I've got *my* arse kicked. Now, *you're* getting *your* arse kicked." '

A great deal is being said here about what 'promotion' means for workers in factories. About how difficult it can be to get started. How it has to be made clear you are not 'still one of the lads'. Also, having done this, what it might mean to have to take that white coat off. This brings us to those foremen who have taken the full brunt of change already.

In practice there are very few cases at Riverside of foremen being put back on the plants as operatives. But there are cases where men have been shifted from one job to another to help 'absorb' the surplus of foremen on site. And for some of those who have been faced with a choice between redundancy and a transfer, the latter course has proved the crueller. Doug, for instance, was moved to a new plant when his old one shut down. He had not set foot on it before, and therefore knew much less than the men about its everyday running. In fact the men were in a much better position to make decisions than he was. As far as they were concerned he was an overpaid incompetent, and one who was in a job that they all knew they could do better. By the end of his first and only month he had a nervous breakdown. On the last day four or five men sat round 'killing ourselves laughing' when *he* tried to run the job. Later, sickened by the whole episode, men reflected that Doug's position had been 'just impossible'.

Sometimes it happens that a man knows full well he just cannot do his new job. Herbert—who moved to a more highly automated plant—was a case in point; a case which underlines that even apparent 'promotions' can take their toll in stress and strain, and which explains a phrase which ChemCo managers and foremen use a lot: 'you never get rid of your best. . . .' He had been with Phil Lancaster on the Grinder start-up. He worked hard then, continued to do so, and got his white coat. But after spending all his working life in ChemCo in the Grinder he was transferred and given different, more technically demanding work. His new plant manager, Edward Blunsen, went out of his way to train him. He spent many, many hours with Herbert. But as another foreman reports: 'Herbert's eyes just went round and round.' And as he said himself: 'I left school at 14. All those long words. I haven't the background.'

Although the men resented that he had come in over their heads they were sympathetic. But they thought him not just lacking in competence but dangerous too. He became absent minded:

'About two in the morning the alarm went. Nothing happened for a long time, then we saw Herbert come out of the foreman's office. He walked toward the plant. When he was half-way he stopped in front of a steam jet. He couldn't hear the bell. He stood there for a couple of minutes. A good couple of minutes. Then he turned round and wandered back. The bell was still ringing.'

In the end Herbert was relieved to be offered a lump sum and go. After all it was more money than he'd ever get his hands on any other way, and getting off the job did bring peace of mind. ('I'm Herbert', he smiled pleasantly when we first met him. 'I'm the one they're getting rid of.') He was even a bit sorry for Jim, the new foreman transferred from another plant to take over his job. A plant operator remarked:

'When Jim first came over he told me he'd come to sort out the plant, him being a senior foreman. "*That's* what you think is it, Jim?" I thought to myself. "*You're* on the way out the gate, mate." '

Pretty soon Jim too was glad to go.

'I've been taking the job home with me. That's something I've never done before. But now I'm looking forward to a change. And it's a nice little sum I've got. And there'll be the pension. And with little job I've got at about twenty quid a week the wife and I'll be quite happy.'

Taking Jim from his old well-worn job and putting him into a new situation lost him sleep, injured his pride, made him so sick of it that he had *had* to leave. The long-service foremen took note, as did the workers. 'That's another on his way', they said, not without relish either. On Blunsen's plant they had seen plenty come—and go—before. Their supervision consisted almost entirely of foremen who had been 'promoted' from other plants and they had long past ceased to give them the benefit of the doubt. A couple of them, some conceded, were competent. But no one would go further than this. So the operators either ran the job themselves without the unhelpful 'interference' of these foremen—'*we* have to *teach* them the bloody job', they said—or they simply belittled their ability. Usually they did both. They laughed at the entries they made in the log book and at the mistakes they made on the plant. They despised the way they 'grovelled' to Blunsen, allegedly told lies for and were used by him. 'It's not the sort of thing any man should do.' 'They're shit scared', they said. And there can be no doubt that when Herbert and Jim left the remaining foremen were very worried indeed.

'I've been told that I'm all right for at least two years', one of them said. A long way this from 'a job with ChemCo is a job for life'. And others asked pertinently, 'If, as they say, Herbert wasn't up to the job, why take *two years* to get rid of him?' Why indeed? Was it to reward his hard work in the Grinder? If so, was it only management's kindness that was keeping *other* foremen in their jobs now? And if so. . . .

Fortunately Jim got another job outside the factory. It wasn't what he was used to, but in a way he had been lucky. 'A process supervisor', as Herbert said, 'has no skills—not that you could categorise.' Herbert himself had been offered a job on another site, or 'a lesser job as operative on the present site'—or a lump sum. Greg, the men's steward, had suggested Herbert ought to try for even better terms. 'Why not get onto the Foremen's Association secretary?' he asked. 'I can't', said Herbert, 'it's Jim. He's the one that's getting my job.'

'What would you have done?' he asked as he went off in search of unskilled work elsewhere. When we last heard of him he was sweeping up at a local sweet factory.

In the same year that Herbert and Jim went, one of the management men, Alan, was made up to shift manager. The traditional foremen knew there was no chance whatsoever that they would follow in his footsteps. Everything pointed to the contrary, to the fact that one day they would follow the path just trodden by Herbert and Jim. Who? and when? these were the vital questions now. For if anyone was threatened by the rationalisation of which the NWA was one part and the reorganisation of management another, it was the traditional foreman and in this situation it has become increasingly clear that the Foremen's Association isn't up to the task of protecting their jobs. The workers they supervise aren't slow to spell out what they think is really happening:

'What this Mobile Op. business is about really is, they're looking for someone to replace the supervisor. They want someone to make decisions. From the actual job description of the Mobile Operator there's no reason why any number of blokes—any one of at least a half a dozen of us—shouldn't get the job. It's to do with supervision this. You mark my words.'

During the three years that we visited the site the foremen were subjected to innumerable indignities. Although 'well off for working men', they felt that the advantages of the 'white coat' were being substantially reduced. Their wages aren't all that much higher than those of a top-grade operator prepared to chase overtime and they know the 'staff status' is not what it was. One or two of them compare their position with other supervisors in the area.

'Well, I've a friend at Nostik [which is just down the road] and I can keep in pretty close contact with what is going on in that plant. You see we are in the same situation. The supervisors there put in for a rise.

Assoc. of Scientific, Technical and
Managerial Staffs

Most of them were in the ASTMS. They put in for a rise and pressured management. I was following it pretty carefully because we put in for a rise the same time. The Company was saying, "Have faith, trust us" and such things but I was getting a bit sceptical and I'm even more sceptical now. They got 11½ per cent at Nostik, we only got 10 per cent. Yes, I'm getting very sceptical of the Company altogether. When NWA was being put in they were saying, "It's important, get it in, let's get it done." It's important for them then you see, because it's the pay roll. With us nobody is pushing them.'

More and more of the foremen came to see the sense of what Henry had been telling them for years: that 'without a union we've got no backbone'; that 'though supervisors are not being *forced* to go, they *are* going'. And that

'The Company can look at it their way and see us between them and the shop floor. But we can look at it our way. And looking at it our way, we're losing out.'

By 1972 most foremen knew beyond doubt that ChemCo was too big to be handled by an Association: 'It's run on family lines', they'd say. 'It just can't push the company and that's what we're going to have to do now. Push back a bit.'

'You get this great force coming from above and the pressure coming from below. The job's getting bigger and we're not getting the rewards. The management think they can treat us how they like but they'll find out how militant men can be.'

And to an extent they did.

The Company commissioned a census of all its staff to determine their feelings on the question of unionism. They found well over a half of the supervisors and technicians to be in favour of union membership—a majority that contrasted with the handful of people above those grades who wanted a union. This fact came as a surprise to the managers at Riverside. Frank discussions with the foremen we have called 'management men', and some less than frank talks with the other foremen, had led them to believe that there was general opposition to trade unionism for supervisors.

Indeed, the 'management men' really were against it. Their eyes turned upwards toward success, they were sure that those who fell by the way-side could expect no better fate.

'Herbert was never any good. I'm not worried. It doesn't worry me at all—though it would worry a lot. If you're valuable to the company they'll look after you. He got treated well, I think. In the Steel Industry or the Mines he'd have been kicked out long ago.'

They had a jumble of reasons:

'I get along without it O.K. I don't see how I could benefit—perhaps if I were off with injury for a long time. As far as pay rises are con-cerned if the blokes get one we do—we're leaning a bit on the union probably. I don't like ASTMS—Clive Jenkins is a big mouth and a big head.'   ↳ CEO ASTMS

But, essentially, as 'part of management', they thought their bread was buttered differently.

Support for the union came from the foremen who felt most vulnerable and who now had no hope of advancement—the men we have called 'traditional foremen'. It also came from the less well paid 'local lads' who the traditional foremen had brought on; men of whom they said 'they lack loyalty'.

Foremen say of their workers

'They've got a big shock coming. They think the firm's a soft touch. Well perhaps it is. But they don't realise that if I sack any one of them I can slap an advert in and get six men to fill that job next day.'

But they've had more than an inkling now that the managers have 'a shock' in store for *them*. In terms of money they say that 'the only thing that . . . bothers me with regard to salaries is the differential between the supervisor and the mass.' But this *does* bother them. For although they earn more than the workers (there are some anomalies where workers, on the Continental shift, earn more with their shift allowance than do some foremen who work days and receive no such allowance), the differentials aren't so great now as they once were. It makes them wonder whether they really have 'bettered themselves', and got off the factory floor. When they're honest with themselves, though, they know that 'this is the best job I could have hoped for'. They know that they have 'a good standard of living' and that all in all they've 'done pretty well'. It is the prospect of *losing* all this that threatens—and worries—them most. For they know that at their age they cannot hope to get another job remotely as good. To go back north would be to go back unemployed; they could probably get work around Provincial but it won't be what they're used to. They know that Herbert could only get a job 'on the brush'.

When we first went to the site in 1970 we were told by one of the more 'senior' foremen, who, like Jim, then called himself a 'company servant', that

'I'm like a stick of rock with "ChemCo" stamped right through. This Company doesn't owe me a bloody thing but I owe it a lot. It's given me *security*.'

But things change very quickly—so quickly in fact that even this man's loyalty was tested. Two years later he told us:

'I think the Foremen's Association is good enough really. Because they are more in touch and they can do things right away. But if the majority wanted to form a union then it would be O.K. by me. I'd join.'

Another foreman, his close friend, agreed.

'I think that there should be a union. You should have someone to go to for help. I don't believe in strikes—no supervisor does—but I think we do need the protection that we could get from a union. I'd still want to negotiate my own salary with the company but if you got moved from a job or if you got the sack it would be good to have a union on your side.'

The new 'economising' had pushed these men this far, but the majority were prepared to go further still. For they were coming to see that capitalist rationality cuts right across the idea of personal salaries and personal loyalties: the 'new rationality' meant for them a change in the 'character' of ChemCo and the culture of the factory.

'I think the supervisors are going to have to have some representation. As it is now the firm can do anything it likes to you. They say our salaries are a personal thing between us and the firm but we've got no chance. We get what we're given. You see in the past the foreman used to be somebody. The foreman today and what he's going to be in the future is a different kettle of fish.'   Transport and General Workers' Union

One took out a ACTSS card (the supervisory section of the TGWU) and as others followed him they thought about their past.

> 'I am a believer in unions, I always have been. If they are going to do something for you. I remember though, as an Assistant Foreman, that we had to be in a union but had no representation whatsoever. Now that's not unionism, I don't think there is any sense in being a member of a union which has no representation. If they [i.e. ChemCo management] requested us to join on this site, I wouldn't hesitate. If they requested us to join and were giving us representation, I would be pleased to be a member of a union.'

One of the ironies of this situation is that the managerial strategy of increasing profitability by both *rationalising* the production process and seeking to *involve* the workforce in that process has led to the disaffection of the one group whose involvement was unquestionable. What these men now want is not 'involvement' but a union. Because they think that a union will give them a voice. They want something with teeth that will gain them some advantage. But this is not a complete break from the past. They want a union but they don't want strikes, and they don't want to be 'lumped in with the workers'. What they want is *protection*.

> 'There are two unions we could join, there is Jenkins' union and then there is a section of the T & G, the Supervisory section of the T & G. But I think I prefer Jenkins' union. If we were in the same union as the men, there is always a worry on my mind that if the men go on strike they may force me to go on strike. Now ChemCo has always been a great Company, there is no need for strikes with this Company.'

Their demand then, was for a sectional organisation, separate from the workers. No one talked about setting up a common cause with the men they supervised, nor did any one consider starting a union campaign on the site. To quote their most militant spokesman:

> 'I used to get a bit bitter about everything, but I'm resigned to it now. I come to work for ChemCo and I either get out or I stay. If I stay I

must accept the system 90 per cent and try to get things a bit better. Since NWA we have been making ourselves heard more and on the whole I'm very satisfied. After roughing it around all my life I look at where I am now and I think I've probably done all right. Yes I think I've done all right for myself.'

Mostly they avoided any possibility of antagonising the manager and waited to see if the Company would 'instruct us to join'. The Company was in a difficult position. As the personnel manager at Riverside saw it,

'The Company is riding two horses. On the one hand they've said to supervisors, "You're part of the management team" but on the other hand they're going to have to allow them to join a union.'

The notion of a 'management team' and with it the Foremen's Association hadn't to be lost. So the door was opened to unionism—but only slightly. Those foremen who were interested in joining a union were invited to take up membership of the supervisory sections of the already recognised manual unions. These unions would represent them if they felt they had a grievance but they wouldn't be granted 'negotiating rights'. As always the question of salaries would be a personal matter for the Company and the individual to agree upon. As one plant manager—George Smith— put it: 'If you wanted to be cynical you could say we've done very well out of it.' So too had the established manual unions with their increased memberships. But one of the foremen who was most strongly committed to trade unionism decided not to join: 'I'd only join if there was one super- visory union with *negotiating rights*. This thing doesn't go far enough for me.' It was a halfway house, and while the foremen were prepared to accept it, it's doubtful if the situation will stay like this for long. Because things really are changing. The 'traditional foremen' really are men of the past and the new rationality is fracturing the idea of a 'management team' just as it brings a new one into existence. They find themselves caught. On the one side are 'the modern generation of workers'; on the other an increasingly demanding, 'economising', management.

In the case of the traditional foremen it is very plain that culture is not politics.[4] Many of them and all those from the north (half of whom came from mining communities) have a strong line in socialist rhetoric. For example, they glorify the Jarrow march and the General Strike. But this is always to let you know how bad things were then; to underline, too, how much they have had to struggle, and how easy it is today, especially as they see it, 'if you have the education'. And of course within the factory they use their working-class culture to cajole and—as management would say—'motivate' the men they overlook. These men vote for the Labour Party, 'always have done'. But in 1970–3 they saw as much good in Heath as they did in Wilson. Their horizons are limited. The worlds of the board room and of high finance do not enter their thinking much. And when they do—in the guise of 'economising'—their resentment takes on a cultural rather than political form. A mythical conception of earlier generations of the working class is clearly part of this, but myths about ChemCo are equally important. The low wages, the Company's anti-unionism are forgotten; what they regret is the passing of ChemCo as 'a family firm'. They resent 'Yankee' ideas. They are saddened that, with the advent of the reign of the accountants, the 'Gentlemen' must give way. As George Orwell thought of England, so they, the subalterns of industry, think of ChemCo: a family with the wrong members in control.

Their resentment is directed not at capital and capitalism but at the progress manual workers have made since the war. Their politics lends itself to support for an authoritarian state machine to be used against unions that 'go too far' and against the 'greedy' (affluent) and 'idle' (unemployed) segments of the working class—the class which produced them, and which has been the source of much which is meaningful in their lives. As workers some of them travelled 300 miles to get a white coat; wearing it, they've been on site 'all hours of the day and night'. They feel they have had to sacrifice a lot—particularly of their home lives—to get where they are. That it has all turned out as it has only feeds their hostility toward the 'greedy' and the 'idle'—to those who 'don't know what it is to struggle'. For now these traditional foremen are on the way out. The 'modern managers' of this 'modern factory' are revamping the image and style of the labour of superintendence; planning ahead they don't want to make provision 'for any more of this type of supervision'.

Notes

1 Editorial comment, *Iron Age*, 6 July 1905. Quoted in Katherine Stone, 'The Origins of Job Structures in the Steel Industry', *Radical America*, vol. 7, no. 6, 1973.
2 Bradford B. Boyd, *Management-Minded Supervision*, New York, McGraw-Hill, 1968.
3 Forty per cent of the Mobile Operator's time was to be spent covering for foremen. Of the remaining 60 per cent, 40 per cent was to be spent covering two control

rooms and 20 per cent on what, with justice, the blokes call 'shit shovelling'. These highly graded Superworkers—who sometimes hold ONCs, with a minimum of O-level being looked for by management—span 'donkey work' and 'scientific work'. Their arrival underlined to the foremen the extent to which technical and supervisory work were becoming interconnected. (We visited another fertiliser complex where a similar grade of operator had been introduced, managers referring to such men as 'our commando unit' and 'our shock troops'. As at Riverside, foremen—and workers—were far from enthusiastic.)

4 See Theo Nichols, 'Labourism and Class Consciousness: The "Class Ideology" of Some Northern Foremen', *Sociological Review*, November 1974.

5
Capital's Division of Labour

IN THE PAST four chapters we have offered a description of what work is like at Riverside and of the different ways in which workers, foremen and managers feel about it. In this quite a lot of emphasis has been given to the 'culture of the factory'. But that 'culture' does not exist independently of class relations. Here therefore, and by way of conclusion to Part I, we want to briefly comment, in a more formal way, on the structure of these relations; on the forces which underpin daily life in this 'modern factory'.

Go to the Riverside site and you will see workers watching control panels, workers driving trucks and workers humping bags of fertiliser. Basically, what there is to be *seen* is the on-going operation of a *technical division of labour*—a division according to technical specialism (in which, let it be remembered, the numerically largest 'specialism' is that of *unskilled* labour). Much discussion about the division of labour in our society is limited to this one aspect. So, in the case of process technologies in general, and of the chemical industry in particular, we find sociologists following Blauner's lead and stressing that physical drudgery is giving way to a new type of 'meaningful' work. In optimistic vein it is even sometimes suggested that the chemical industry represents the shape of an already emerging future; a future which will bring a new dignity to what is euphemistically called 'blue collar work'; which will see a reduction in so-called 'alienation', and so on. Views like these may afford some comfort to their authors, but their relationship to reality is questionable. At Riverside, for example, the packing and bagging operators do very much the same sort of work to be found on traditional assembly lines in technically less 'progressive' sectors, and the jobs in the control rooms, while easier, can hardly be said to have produced a 'new type' of worker.

However not all those who concentrate their gaze on industry's technical division of labour are optimists. Many people are only too ready to argue that, given a particular product, the technical division of labour must of necessity take the form it does now. To paraphrase this sort of view: yes, men do boring jobs—but that's just the price we have to pay for cheap agricultural produce, washing machines or whatever. (We leave aside here the gratuitous insult that's sometimes thrown in for good measure, about some people liking boring jobs; also, for the moment, the question of *who* the 'we' are who have to pay the price.)

Now neither Blauner's vision of hope, which equates increased automation with reduced 'alienation', nor that vision of despair (or complacency) which holds that things must be as they are at present, take much cognisance of the *social division of labour*. Yet in any mode of production the technical division of labour exists in relation to a social division of labour. And in capitalist enterprise the relation of the social to the technical takes a specific form; a political form in which technology, which properly understood is the organisation of people's labour, exists to serve and augment capital. For it is not a 'technical' reason which explains why so many people at Riverside work as appendages to machines; it is not a 'technical imperative to co-ordinate' which explains the specific objectives which managers are paid to seek; nor is it 'technical' considerations which rule out the possibility of workers organising work in their own interests. No more is it the case that simply because plant managers have 'technical' knowledge such abilities must always be linked to the interests of capital.

Certainly in any mode of production, given the existence of specialised training, some men will be more technically competent to solve certain problems than others. This is so obvious as to hardly require stating. But something else which should also be obvious is often ignored. For concern with the technical structure of complexes like Riverside can all too easily obscure the fact that they were not even designed to make chemicals, but to make chemicals for profit. The reality is that their division of labour is capital's division of labour, and this effectively sets limits to how far the organisation of workers and their jobs can be altered, and by whom. It sets limits to the sharing of financial and technical information. Above all, it sets limits to who can be safely allowed to make decisions, because for management to permit the balance of power to be tipped in favour of workers could be to threaten the entire purpose of the enterprise. Ignore all this, and very likely it will seem as if everything must (for apparently 'technical' reasons) stay as it is now. But once see the jobs men do and the way they are organised as means to a highly sectional end, private profit, and the possibility emerges that, outside of a divisive class system, things just could be organised differently; that technical knowledge could be something to be shared and put toward a collective purpose; that the management function could be rotated—and not merely (as at Riverside today) the work of humping, filling and stacking one hundredweight bags, the driving of trucks and suchlike; that, in a different mode of production different definitions might prevail about what constituted a 'reasonable' job, or what constituted 'reasonable' conditions; and indeed that different answers, arrived at by different people, could be given to questions about 'technical' imperatives, and whose interests technology should serve.

Technologies, job specifications and skill requirements are not developed or imposed extra-socially, outside of a social mode of production. And the capitalist system divides and socialises, enriches and impoverishes, upgrades and degrades in the interest of capital, not labour. Recognise this; consider the likely priorities; and there is little mystery about why, for Riverside workers, the NWA—heralded by management as 'a change programme without parallel in British industry'—meant no fundamental change at all in their power of decision making or conditions of work. Profit—the sort of profit with which industrial capital is mainly concerned—is not that which comes from buying certain things cheap and selling them dear. Such activities are not ruled out, but the profit which interests industrial capital is the profit which comes from buying a most peculiar commodity, human labour power, putting it to work and exploiting it to produce a surplus; thereby accumulating the wherewithal to continue the process and accumulate further. The surplus goes *to* capital. It comes *from* the working class. To look at a factory or site like the Riverside one, to see only the inter-linked nature of the plants, or only the way everyone on site is in some way or other working, or to see first and foremost differences between those who perform mental and physical labour, or to see managers only as men who 'juggle' without asking to what end—and without seeing them as implicated in political, class, relations—is to miss this entirely.

The problem is that to look at the world through 'technical' spectacles is often to enter into a naturalistic fallacy whereby things which happen must always happen as they do. And this even though there is nothing 'natural' about men doing the work of machines, nothing 'natural' about millions of people being effectively deprived of technical competence, nothing 'natural' about the largest class of the society being denied control over the product of its own collective labour and the means of its production, and nothing 'natural' about the domination of human labour power by the power of capital. Of course it *is* natural, but in quite another sense—

that is, given an international capitalist economy—to expect that when a corporation's profits come under threat it will tighten management control; and, depending on its particular situation, including the 'industrial relations' situation, will resort to explicitly coercive measures, like redundancy, and/or more 'progressive' ones like 'job enlargement', 'enrichment' and 'participation' in order to more effectively harness productive labour to capital. This is why it is no cause for surprise that ChemCo, a firm famous for its human relations policies, should have shed 15 per cent of its national labour force in the early 1970s. That it did so affected both workers and the labour of superintendence on site (most especially foremen) even though Riverside's product markets were not so tight as some others in the corporation, and even though Chemicals was not hit as hard as some other industries.

Riverside employees were also affected by other policies of a long-term nature which were also intended to more closely, smoothly and predictably subject the entire operation of the enterprise to the accountancy of profit and loss: thus, the further institutionalisation of management–union relations (which we come to in Part III); the detailed specification of manning levels and the duties of manual workers; and the bureaucratisation of the management structure itself. All this, the process of 'economising', of which in reality redundancy was just another aspect, was indeed nothing other than a working out in a particular context of the 'normal' profit seeking tendencies built into capitalist production. Yet it is noteworthy that 'economising', with its heightened stress on the unnatural basis of evaluation of the relations between men, ensnares the evaluators along with those they evaluate: the managers along with the managed. What then does this tell us about management?

Foremen and all save a minority of managers are, like those they manage, clearly non-owners of the means of production. They are also wage earners; more precisely they are 'salary' earners (as at Riverside are manual workers). However, neither this nor the fact that managers are managed, and supervisors supervised, makes them as some would have it 'part of the working class'.[1] Nor can this be said to be the case simply because managers sometimes perform productive labour by the direct application of their technical skills. (So did some of the early capitalists and so indeed do some of the owner managers of the present day.) True, looked at one way, the position of managers such as those at Riverside underlines the important extent to which labour in our society is divided against itself. But to leave matters here is to fail to make plain that, in a society which makes a commodity of almost everything, including the services of supervision, labour is divided against itself by capital, and that in this division management stands on capital's side.

It may be that in specific situations—for instance, where everyone in a factory is threatened by unemployment—managers will put their technical knowledge at the disposal of workers, and fight with them. But this does not mean that an alliance between workers and managers is likely to constitute a viable basis for fundamental political change in capitalist society.² In fact, as we have seen from the example of the 'traditional foremen' at Riverside, such alliances are by no means an automatic response, even given the threat of unemployment. As to mangers, whatever their uncertainties about 'politics' in the conventional sense, in the politics of production they act for capital. In short: whatever their yearnings to sniff the noxious fumes of production and 'to get in there with the lads', their *raison d'être*, as managers, is to plan and to organise, thereby to better exploit the labour power of others. In a sense everyone employed at Riverside labours for capital. But the managers and also the foremen (whose culture is in some respects 'working class' but which they use against their class of origin) are paid to be capital's agents. Lowly agents perhaps, most definitely not 'capitalists' in their own right; but none the less agents of capital, not labour.

Three things about labour for capital then:

One, and generally: in a capitalist mode of production the technical division of labour does not exist independently of the social division of labour (class relations). It is a function of capital's division of labour; it is no 'natural' manifestation.

Two: capital's grip is tightening on *all* those employed. At Riverside, whatever their factory position—workers, foremen, managers—the rationalisation and 'economising' affects them all.

Three: minor modifications to jobs cannot—and at Riverside have not—vanquished the social division of labour. This holds for workers and foremen and managers:

Riverside workers: they perform essentially the same function in the technical division of labour, despite the talk of 'enrichment'. A tiny stratum has been inserted to perform higher level technical and minor supervisory work. But the majority have not had their skills up-graded. For many, work remains degrading. In the social division of labour they remain, unambiguously, working class.

Riverside foremen: as a small top stratum emerges—'men with academic training'—the majority find themselves perilously situated: on the way out, or down, back to the working class whence they came.

Increases in responsibility have meant tighter accountability. They remain the subalterns of industry; to be more exact, of capital. Riverside managers: as they see it, they are beneficiaries of the process which confers on them greater responsibility. But for them, as for the foremen, increased responsibility has brought stricter accountability. It is becoming increasingly clear that they are themselves sellers of the commodity labour power, *and* that they must act as agents of capital.

Notes

1 See, for example, the influential book by Anderson which identifies Marxism with the view that American society is divided into 'capitalists'—4 per cent of the population—and the rest, the 'working class'. C. H. Anderson, *The Political Economy of Social Class*, New York, Prentice-Hall, 1974.
2 A view which seems to be gaining support within the European Communist Parties and the Institute of Workers Control in Britain. It is in this context, for example, that Topham has celebrated British Leyland as a situation in which 'former supervisors and managerial workers make common cause with manual workers to affirm the values of cooperative production against the authority of private property and market economics'. (Tony Topham, Introduction to Serge Mallet, *The New Working Class*, Nottingham, Spokesman Books, 1975, p. xiv.)

Part II

Individuals in a Class Society

IN PART I, *Labour for Capital*, we looked at how workers *and* foremen *and* managers have been affected by corporate capital's drive to accumulate. Later, in Part III, we will look more closely at the relationship between 'management' and 'men': 'management' being paid agents in the service of capital and the 'men' forming part of a very different, and potentially explosive, force—the working class.

In this book we are trying to say something about social classes; about the forces which fashion them and the ways they are changing. This means taking capital seriously. For the growth of the multinational corporation, the increasing proportion of the population who live only by selling their labour power, the migrations of people from one part of the globe to another—none of this can be understood without taking account of the importance of capital's drive to accumulate and reproduce itself. Capital is the great driving force; one which drags in new sources of labour, which expands new technologies and makes others obsolete, which both creates and destroys opportunities. In the face of national and international capital, 'custom' and old ways of doing things can come to count for little.

But to say all this is not to say enough; for to talk of capital is to talk of a social relationship—a relationship based upon the exploitation of one class by another. Social class is about how people exploit and are exploited and also how they understand this. To split off the one from the other— 'exploitation' and 'understanding'—as if they are in some sense separate parts of society, is to misunderstand both. If social class means anything at all it is to be found in the expression of the forces we have just talked about in the real lives of real people. To talk of 'class-consciousness' is not to indulge in abstract theorising but to talk of the ways in which people come to understand themselves and their position in society and in history through their concrete experience of that society. In Parts III and IV we look in some detail at some of these concrete experiences and the sense that people make of them. There, however, we will be concerned to make generalised statements about groups of people at Riverside—to concern ourselves with a collective consciousness; a consciousness which, although present in the minds and actions of many of the people we talked to, takes on a presence, and a force which is greater than the sum of their individual consciousnesses. Yet trying to do this we do not want to lose sight of the people. Of the fact that the people who share the experience of working for ChemCo bring to that situation different experiences, different styles and the marks of different cultures. For while they are all produced socially they are produced as different people.

Here, therefore, in Part II, we want to concentrate on individuals; to briefly indicate how the forces and tendencies we mention in various other parts of the book are brought together in different—and similar ways—in different people. It could be objected that this concern of ours to present 'people as people' is irrelevant to the question of how society is structured. There is some sense in this. If, for example, directors of industry were recruited from a generation of miners' sons this need have no effect upon the exploitative nature of our society. Certainly there is a danger of mistaking 'culture' and 'opportunity' as the essence of capitalist society. But there is also a danger of going too far the other way; for it is a matter of historical fact that miners' sons do not generally become company directors, and this fact does have some significance for the way miners (and chemical workers and chemical managers) understand themselves and this society. People are not the *simple* product of the forces that work on them. People are not 'the effect' or 'the cause' but both one and the other at the same time; and the way they produce their lives out of what is made available for them is important, for them and for other people.

6
Lives in Process

MICHAEL KENNEDY, HAROLD STEVENS, Billy King, Tommy Robson, John Baird; these are just five people whom we talked to from time to time over the first three years of the 1970s. Three of them are workers, another a foreman and another a plant manager. The first four work on the A shift in the Zap plant and the manager, John Baird, worked there too before he was moved to another plant. Five men, then, who were in contact with each other, who do different jobs and who came along very different paths to Riverside. The three workers are separated by age—the eldest being twice the age of the youngest—by the fact that they were born in three different countries and by much else besides. But they work together on the Zap plant, supervised by Tommy Robson, the foreman from the north of England. A 'mixed bunch' in many ways. People from and with different worlds, but people we think it worth while to listen to. They aren't 'special people' or people we think have anything more special to say than anyone else; nor are they a 'representative sample'; they are simply five of the two hundred we talked to about their work, their lives, their futures and their pasts.

Michael Kennedy

Michael Kennedy was born in the west of Ireland in 1927. His father was the local policeman until he bought a farm of his own—'not a big farm, more of a small farm'. Michael was one of fourteen children and all but four of them were forced to emigrate. Today he has a brother in Canada and a sister in America. 'The rest of us are over here—scattered about.' He tells you how he really loved farming but that he only worked on the farm for a few of his boyhood years. The farm wasn't big enough to support the whole family and so his father arranged for him to take a labouring job—cutting peat:

'It was a job, working in a peat bog. It was a government job and I was there working on a machine called a collector. They used the peat for the power stations and at one time it used to be cut by hand, but they got the machines in because it was a terrific amount of turf they had to cut: a terrible amount. The machines would go down about eighty feet you know—I suppose the same as coal really—and I was on the machine. Eighty tons, that was the weight of it, and it had a crew of twenty-one men.'

He found it a very hard job; and the money wasn't up to much either. By that time his brothers and sisters and several of his friends had gone to England so in 1950 he followed them—to London. And there he got himself a job on the Underground.

'I was working with, what were they called, a linesman, now a linesman doesn't seem a lot but actually he was a qualified engineer. What we were doing was connecting all those cables up to the live rail, you see, and there was a head man in charge, but he didn't do no work. Anyway I worked there and you had to work a weekend of nights, you know Saturday and Sundays and I wouldn't work nights then like. Well you wouldn't work nights now would you? Not when you're young! Oh I had a job to get out of there because they wanted you to stay on and on and on. London Underground was pretty good concerning the type of work, but the money wasn't much good so I went to the buildings for better money like.'

'The Underground' was the only 'permanent job' he had had before he came to work for ChemCo in 1966. During the fifteen years that intervened he had worked for 'umpteen building firms' in London and around the country. He worked hard and sometimes he managed to save some money. At one time in the early 1950s he had £300: when that job was finished he went 'straight to Ireland and I didn't come back until it was all spent'. When he did come back though he found it difficult to get a start on the buildings and so he ended up as a dustman—and almost a permanent job.

'When I got back I had nothing and this bloke was working on the dusts. He was an old Cockney bloke, actually he was driving. And I said, "I am badly stuck, how about a job?" And he said, "come with me." So I stuck it out for three weeks and it was a great number. But I couldn't stay long on it. I said to this bloke, he was a Cockney you know—all Cockneys, they are great blokes to work with, great men for the pub and all things like that—well I said to him, "there is a lot of worms on your back man." "Far back from my neck are they," he says. "Crawling down from my neck?" "They are coming up to your neck", I says. "Well", he said, "you should see *yours*," he said, "have you got no experience of this?" And I said, "No. And I am not going to do it no more", and I went. I couldn't stick that no more, I had to get out of that.'

Apart from the worms it was 'a good number'. The basic rate wasn't too high but on certain runs they'd be given tips 'and no matter what it was, whether it was a pound or a sixpence it all had to go into the little bag in the driver's cab. And when we had all finished we would divide up that money. Equal shares. And sometimes after a day I got five or six pounds out of it; and plenty of beer as well.'

But the worms were too much so he went back on the buildings, again in London. It was there that he met the girl he wanted to marry. She was from the Provincial area so he moved down and they got married in 1955. He continued to work on the buildings, sometimes travelling twenty miles to work for twelve hours before returning home in the evening. He refused to work on the lump, he always worked 'on decent jobs', always with 'proper firms'. He worked on power stations and laying gas lines and on flyovers and motorways. His longest job lasted three years and eleven months but it, like the rest, wasn't a 'permanent job'. It was a job that ended with redundancy as soon as the work had finished. Sometimes he found himself 'made redundant before anybody else because I wasn't friends with the foreman'. But usually things worked out 'reasonably well'; these were the days when there was always more work if you were prepared to work hard and travel around.

But increasingly he found the jobs he was offered involved sub-contracting on the buildings—'you know a kind of lump labour—and I couldn't afford that, not with a family, you know with the girls, so I thought it best to try to get a job. Well, I was getting on a bit, so I thought I could do with a bit of a permanent job like.'

He had the chance to work in a local smelting works but he turned it down after talking in a pub with one of the workers who he had known from 'a way back'. 'He said to me, "don't start here. The heat here would kill you man. This is a cruel job Paddy and I'm getting out of here as soon as I can." ' So he tried 'the ChemCo place' and in 1966 he started there. On the bagging line in the Zap plant.

'I started in August about three years and five months ago. I didn't think that I would be here that length because, believe me, you may not think it but this is a hard job. When you go up there at night time loading those trucks, when you are on 60 tons, on 55 tons, even on 50 tons and you have to load 3 trucks and you are punching them out—I am telling you boy, you knock some sweat out of you. If you get a really warm night—do you remember about four months ago, we had really warm weather—well honest to God the sweat was pouring off me.

When I came here first I thought it was really hard work and the machinery was absolutely hopeless too. It is only in the last year or eighteen months, well say eighteen months, that the machinery down here is going well at all because it used to be terrible, man, out there at one time. You couldn't walk the shed with broken bags and all the bloody bands cutting out and causing pile-ups. Well, it was blummin' terrible and no matter where you worked you would probably say to yourself, "I don't feel like working but I have got to work", to try and get something out of it, and you might say to yourself, "well this might be an easy shift" and Lord God it never stopped, although it was only cleaning.'

It is a bit easier now. The machinery is better, there are fewer break-downs and so the breaks can be planned. But still:

'You have ten minutes to smoke and when the smoking's done you catch bags. You've got to catch them on your shoulder mind, and you'll check say, 240 bags. And you're catching them like this every day of the week. Right through the year. *You* count how many bags you catch in one month, in twelve months. . . .'

It's hard work. You don't get sacked on the spot at ChemCo. You don't have to go home dirty, you don't have to work out in the wet. There are good showers and a good canteen. It is a much better job—a 'permanent job': the sort of job Michael needed for a while when his family was growing up. He has four children—all girls. And his main concern is to give them a good start in life.

'Because my belief is that kiddies coming up now in the present day, they don't get much of a chance—not with all this unemployment and with all the struggles all over the world. I have been lucky. I've done all right out of labouring. Not great, but all right. But if I had sons, I'd do everything in my power to get them trained in some way—if it cost

me my last penny. I would never let them go labouring on any job.
But anyway I've got four girls and I think the same with them. Education is a great thing. I don't understand it but the wife is a great one
for these things. I was never well educated. I never went to nothing;
only a National School. But two of my girls are at the grammar school
and the youngest is going in for the exam next year. The oldest one
is teaching her now and I hope that she will get through. Up to now,
for the last fourteen or fifteen years, I try and give them every chance
and see them through all right—as far as I can.

And to do that he has had to work for ChemCo. His children and his
family—and not the pseudo-satisfiers of the new human relations—
provide the only purpose for his work. But as he works he reflects upon
his life. He thinks about 'the buildings'. There were good things about the
buildings.

'For one thing you are started at 8 in the morning and you finished at
6 in the evening, and you had proper meals, you know. And then if
you had to work overtime you only worked until 8:00 p.m. I haven't
worked on a building site yet that hasn't been like that.'

He thinks about money and overtime.

'I am a terrible one for overtime you know. It is wrong really but I am.
Bloody greedy I suppose. I don't know. I know it is ridiculous talking
about overtime but it is true enough that if you don't work overtime
you won't have nothing, will you? I know the unions are trying to cut
down hours. They are talking about a forty-hour week and that. But
it is all right for them to talk about it, isn't it? But the likes of us blokes
down here; trying to run a car and, you know, keep a family going
pretty well and all of that. We have got to work overtime. Yet I can see
it is wrong in a way.'

He also thinks about being Irish:

'I think now that I feel just the same here as an Englishman—although
I didn't at first. But Ireland you know: I go over to Ireland every year
because my Mother and Father are still over there. I go to see them
with my wife and the kids. We go for a month. I don't take any time

off during the year and then I take a month all in one lump. Well I go over there to the farm—my brother-in-law has taken over now like —to see them all. I don't think I'd ever go back to Ireland to live. I always go to see the family, but when they are gone I suppose that I will finish then. I'm not a turncoat. Don't get me wrong. It is just that financially I'm better off here. This is where I've had to make my life.'

And living in a 'free society':

'I've been thinking about this a lot; and I'm not just talking about England but I'm talking about the whole British Isles. They say it is a "free country" but you don't have a hell of a lot of say. The only way you can have any sort of say is through somebody else. Well take for instance when you are working through the union. It is always through someone outside—your councillor I suppose you could call him.'

This feeling of always being told what to do worried him more and more as the unemployment figures began to rise. He worried about what could happen and the way some of his mates talked did nothing to ease his concern.

'Terrible. It is terrible to hear a lot of blokes telling about men being on the Labour Exchange in Provincial. Going down there to that place and drawing money and all like this. People laughs at them. People say that they are lazy which is all wrong, and it is happening. And I know two blokes in particular and they are down there because they had to be down there, they can't get work and they are tradesmen, they are welders and they can't get work. They were years working in and around Provincial and it's all wrong. It is terrible the way that blokes talk about them, but I don't know what is to be done about this unemployment. It is very bad. I don't know what is going to happen to the likes of me to be quite honest with you. Because after all I am an Irishman and people, if they do rear up, you can't do a lot about it can you? It is bound to affect me, it is bound to affect me and it is bound to affect say Poles and even coloured chaps, it is bound to in times to come.'

And he knows that he is getting old. He tells you how 'I was working on a farm before a lot of the young blokes here were born.' He was 44 when we last talked to him. Many blokes—who'd never even met him—

told us 'there's this strong Irishman on "A" shift'. But he was beginning to feel the strain of those years on the band-end.

'Yes, you want to be a fit man to work here. Well I am pretty old but I would claim to be as fit as any man here. I used to be a fair runner in my younger days. But this *is* a young man's job. No doubt about it. No shamming. After a few years if I am still here I am going to put in for a transfer to an easier plant. That is my future. That is what I have planned. I have said nothing at home but I am just thinking about things, you know. But on the other hand if the buildings come back in full swing again I think I would go back there because I always got on well on the buildings. But I have said nothing at home.'

Harold Stevens

Harold Stevens was born in Barbados in 1941. His father owned a small farm and he arranged for Harold to be trained as a stone mason—'what do you call it here? Bricklaying and things like that?' Increasingly, though, he found it difficult to get work in his trade, or any work at all. He worked in factories and on building sites—and he cut sugar cane. 'You'll be in a job today, tomorrow you go home. You see what I mean? That was the trouble in the West Indies.' Finally, in 1962, he got what he describes as 'the travelling urge'. By that time most of his friends and the relatives of his generation had emigrated—mostly to Britain but some to the USA as well—and he had a brother and a cousin living in Provincial. He decided to follow them.

'I wanted to do a bit of travelling like. To see different things and different ways of living. I think it's necessary. But when I decided to come over here, my old man said, "Don't go." You know he has worked hard, got a good position, and I had learned my trade. So he wanted me to stay—to stick it out there like. But I said: "Everybody's going over there. Why can't I go and have a try and see how it goes." Well he said, "You'll be back soon. It is cold over there" and all that you know. But I told him that I wanted to have a good go at it.'

So in 1962 he had a go. The Barbados government operated a scheme which assisted emigration to Britain, so with the help of that and the encouragement of letters from his brother he moved to Provincial. He was amazed by the factories, the houses, the lights—by the whole fabric of metropolitan urban life. His clearest memories of that time are of the difficulties he found surviving as a single man in a big city.

'You won't believe this but when I first came over here I couldn't cook an egg. I couldn't do anything. You know my old lady and my sisters they'd done everything for me. . . . I go to work, I come home, I get my dinner. Just like that. I finish my dinner and I have a drink. Everything is put on the table there. It was great . . . but you travel, and you do more things for yourself. I don't regret it.'

He learned to cook—if.mostly from tins—and he learned what it meant to be black in a white man's world.

'When you go on a bus I used to find it. I would sit on a bus in a seat by myself and nobody would sit next to me. No white man would sit down by the side of me. Not until the bus was really full up and sometimes then people would prefer to stand up rather than sit by the black man.'

But his biggest problem was finding a job. He searched the town for work but it took him four weeks to get a job. He remembers the experience as being 'really miserable'.

'When I first came, I had a hard time getting a job. I try a few places but, you know, they say they always have no vacancies. I tried to get on the buses first. I went to the Labour Exchange and they said there was a vacancy in the buses and they gave me a letter to send me up. And when I go up there, the chap said, "Well, there is a vacancy but the trouble is, you got to put your name on the list and then when we get to your name, we'll call you up." '

He waited and heard nothing. (The local bus company was later found to have been operating a colour bar on certain of its jobs. Faced by criticism the local TGWU officer defended himself in the local press: 'Because we are trying to run a responsible union without interfering in policy matters we are accused of discrimination.') Meanwhile his cousin had started work at ChemCo. He told Harold and got him fixed up with the opening of the Zap plant. He started as the only 'coloured bloke' on the shift.

'I was the only coloured down here at the time. There wasn't no coloured blokes around and I had a hell of a lot of trouble because the blokes used to be really awkward, you know. They'd try to pick fights and things but there was two blokes on my side which is what I can say, Alf in the control room [the shop steward], and another bloke on D shift. Well they said to me, "don't care" like. I was so hurt first like, I decide to pack it in. I did hand in my notice and there was an assistant foreman on our shift, he's gone now. He said to me, "Oh, care for no man." And the manager came in and said, "Well, I'll have a word with them." Well, it was getting used to it I suppose. After a bit it changed but it was rough for about the first two years. It was a bit rough but I think you got to get nerve really.'

He got his nerve. He ignored a lot of the 'nigger jokes' and the taunting; and he turned his back on men who wanted 'to pick fights'. In this he was helped by white men like Alf but more so by the arrival of other black men from the West Indies. (When we talked with Harold in 1970 a third of the men employed on the Zap and Zap X packing areas were black.) Over the past years they had stuck together, helped each other, returned jibe with jibe and developed some 'jokes' of their own. In all this they were helped by the idea of an international black movement; by the presence of Mohammed Ali and the West Indian cricket team. In 1971 the tour of Garfield Sobers' West Indian team was followed with avid interest and with wild jubilation as the colonialists were defeated at their own game.

By 1970 Harold was finding his life in Britain much more pleasant. He had married a Jamaican girl three years earlier. They had managed to save enough money to put a deposit down for a house. Harold had saved by working doublers:

'When I first started working down here I did a lot of overtime. I did too much in fact—we were saving for a house then you know. I really done too much. I was really sick—I was dying so I decided to pack it in. I was getting trouble with my stomach and everything. Ear ache, head ache, back ache. I tell you I was dying here. Cos you know I was single then and I was still living on my own. When I'd done a doubler, I'd go home and I had to have a rest. You know, I never had time to cook a meal or anything like that. It was terrible.'

But he managed to save the money and get a house. Only for the Corporation to purchase it compulsorily and knock it down to build a road. 'One year we lived in that house. Now we live in a flat. My wife wants to buy another house. But something like that—it makes it hard the second time.' The compensation money was soon gone.

At ChemCo in 1970 there was no black manager or foreman. Neither was there a black control room operator or co-ordinator. Harold had worked on the Zap plant longer than anyone else, and few workers at Riverside had been with ChemCo longer than him. But he still worked on the packing line; and he still disliked it. He feels that 'it nearly drives me mad sometimes'. He talks a lot about seeing green bags for hours after leaving the plant. He describes his job there as 'boring', 'routine', 'useless', and 'bloody hard work'. What he would really like to be is a control room operator. He had spent some time in the control room with Alf and he'd learned how to run the plant—certainly to Alf's satisfaction. He'd quite like to do the job permanently but he knows that to do that—to become a control room operator—he needs to be put on the formalised training scheme. The blokes on the shift have put it to him that he should approach the foreman, ask him for more time training, ask about the possibility of an operator's job somewhere, ask about being made into a co-ordinator. But he won't *ask*.

'Not for that type of favour, I don't like that type of favour at all. Other types of favours, I don't mind. Like asking for a day off or something. But where the job is concerned I don't think I'll ever do it. I've been seven years and never asked yet. I mean, a bloke said to me, "Oh, you've been down here so long you should be co-ordinator, or something like that. Blokes come here after you and they're made co-ordinator." I said, "That's the way it goes. If the foreman don't think I'm good enough, then that's up to him. I'm not gonna beg him." And this is it, see.'

Harold sees the foremen as 'firm's men'.

'Well you see I come to work and do a day's work and get paid. They come to work to do a day's work too, but it's just not the same with them. They're not prepared just to let things go along like. They're always pushing. Production—that is their interest more than anything else. They try to tell you about safety and things like that. Well they might be interested in safety. Nobody likes to see a bloke get into an accident. But, I think if they get their production going and things like that and the job going all right, that's their interest. As far as the blokes are concerned, I don't think they care much about you really. This is my feeling, I might be wrong. But I've been here this long and you see things. For instance, say we on sixty tons an hour, something happen, one of those bags break. None of these foremen, none, none of them, like to drop the rates, none of them. When you are on that rate and the band's stopped for a minute you get a bollocking off the foremen. Even if you miss a bag on a spout, they're shouting. Things like this. Ah, it's never right. And this is why you get these accidents because on this rate blokes, you know, they're rushing. This is it, see. And I think as long as everybody's going in there smooth, and their production's going up, I don't really think they give a damn.'

And production favours the rich:

'The rich man always gets the most benefit. What I reckon—what I feel is that everything should be shared equally. And I think a lot of blokes feel like that too. I just don't think the workers get enough of it. I think we're worth a lot more for what we do down here. I reckon we're underpaid. Everything should be shared out equally.'

Frequently he compares the shift work, the pressure for production, the pressure of living in Britain, with his earlier life in Barbados. If he misses anything it is the sense of enjoyment; the loss that comes with working day and night for 'The Man'.

'I think it's more work here you know. It's all work in this country and then when you're at home it's boring—because on these shifts everybody else is at work. You don't see anyone to chat to. You just drive around and get fed up. But in Barbados you stay at home ten months and it doesn't bother you. You know, you chat with someone, you go on the beach . . . anything.'

He thinks a lot about Barbados. About leaving. About who he is, where he belongs and if he'll ever go back for good.

'We think about that. You know about when you get older. You say, "we will go back to our country and relax and enjoy ourselves" because, you know, you come here, you work hard and I suppose most of us have it in mind. But sometimes I think it's just a dream, because you might not be able to save enough money to go back there and live over there. You'd still have to get another job. So I suppose it is a dream. It's like thinking about winning the pools or something like that.'

In 1971 he and his wife took a holiday to visit their families in the West Indies. They saved up and took presents back for everyone. 'It cost a fortune you know. Because when you go home—you go to a different country and return—everyone thinks "he's rich now". They don't know, see. But that is what they've got in their head. And everyone expects something.'

Everyone was pleased to see them but what left a lasting impression on Harold and his wife was the high level of prices in the West Indies—that and the poverty and the unemployment. This experience had chilled their hopes of retiring in their country.

'When people ask you, "why did you leave your country?" I just think now that it was necessary. It was just necessary to leave. That's my opinion. Because over there you haven't got a decent job. You can't even earn money to buy shoes and clothes. It was just necessary. It's given me experience and things like that too. I've learned a lot about places that I would never have learned if I'd stayed. And that's it. I haven't any regrets. You know I'd like to see my parents again before they die—or before I die. But apart from that I'm happy. I suppose.'

Billy King

Billy King was born in Provincial in 1948. His father worked on the buildings and he raised Billy and three other children in a small terraced house in the 'downtown' area of Provincial. 'It's a bit of a slummy area. They're knocking it all down now; and not before time I'd say.' Billy remembers disliking school as a small boy; he remembers failing the eleven plus and some wasted years in a dilapidated secondary modern school. He didn't like the teachers or the school or 'anything else about it. They didn't teach us anything. They just weren't interested in us and we just wanted to leave.' He left when he was 15 and his father managed to get him fixed up with an electrical apprenticeship.

'It was a sort of small firm like. They trained you and you were the sort of tea-boy, errand-boy and everything else. I didn't mind that too much, but the money was no good. I was getting three pound a week and there were lads my age on the buildings getting three times that much.'

He married when he was 17 and with that decided to get a job as a labourer on the buildings. For the next few years he 'just chased the money; you know the highest bidder, that sort of thing'. He moved from job to job, worked long hours and earned 'good money'. But by 1968— when he was 20—he had two babies to care for and he was beginning to feel the need for security. As he put it, 'you've got to grow up fast when you've got kiddies to think of.'

'Well, you know, I was working all over. Start a job one week; start another the next week. You know the sort of thing. Well that's all right when you're a single man but with the wife and the babies I began to think it would be a good idea to get myself fixed up with something a bit steadier like. Well I had a mate who worked down here and he told me that the basic rate was only sixteen pound but that the overtime was there for the asking. But it was the security that really decided me, you know ChemCo being such a big firm, treats its workers well sort of thing. My mate told me like: "Nobody gets the sack from here." And you can't imagine ChemCo closing down can you?'

So he came to ChemCo to work, with the rest, on the bagging line. He found it hard—though no harder than carrying a hod on the buildings— and boring. 'It's just donkey work. The work is made for donkeys not for men. If you've got any intelligence at all you'll want to get off that bagging line.' And by 1970, when we met him first, he was quite determined that he was not going to stop on the bagging.

'I'd like to get involved with this firm. I'm on the outside looking in and I think I should get on the inside looking out. Blokes imagine they can't do it, so they don't try it. I know it's a minority but some blokes do get on from back streets. I don't want to be doing this when I'm 40.'

Like everyone else he wanted to get off the bagging line, and at Riverside there were only two places to go—into the control rooms or up to supervisor. Both moves involved 'promotion'; in each case you had to prove to the 'higher ups' that you were worthy of a move. Billy realised this. He scoffed at the blokes who thought that 'long service will be rewarded':

'Not in this day and age it won't. This Company is a forward-looking company. You can see that. If you're going to get on in this place you're going to have to prove yourself. They're not going to be promoting any dumbos. Some of them in there [the mess room] don't think about these sort of things at all. I think about them a lot. You know about what this Company wants; about how it works. A lot of them though, they just come here to pack bags.'

He was critical of many of the foremen too—and for the same reason. They hadn't realised that ChemCo had changed either:

'I don't rate many of the foremen—except Alan and Charlie Fell of the ones I know. They don't seem to fit into this type of firm. They tell you how they've been here for twenty, thirty years. Well I think perhaps they've been here too long. Really though: they are piss poor. They can be very two-faced and very weak. Instead of working out what needs to be done and being firm about it they try to make people look fools. You know the sort of thing: talk about people behind their back, spread tales about people. I wouldn't behave like that. If ever I got into a position where I could, I'd throw it up at them. To my way of thinking they're the wrong sort of people to be foremen in a company like this. And what are they after all? Gash hands who came three hundred miles to be made up as foremen. It really annoys me. Particularly when you see how they behave. They like to show you their power. Not like a manager. They don't have to let you know. They're a better sort of bloke by and large. They take a fairer outlook and weigh up the situation. They're not *personal* like these fellas.'

What Billy knows—what he has worked out in midnight conversations with Alan and one or two of the other 'management men'—is that he will have to 'draw attention to himself' if he is to get ahead at ChemCo. Alan's account of the bicycle race made a real impression on him.

'He's right you see. When I came here I was well behind wasn't I? Just an ordinary labourer; and that's what I still am, I suppose. And that's what I'll always be unless I make something out of being here.'

In 1971 he stood as a Works Council representative. None of the other blokes wanted the job and although they had a good idea why Billy wanted it they voted him in. From then on he attended monthly meetings in the Administration Block along with the other representatives, the site manager and several of the other plant managers. He found it a 'good experience'.

'You know, you find out a lot just by listening to how they talk about things. They're all educated you see. They're all real engineers with degrees and everything else. They know what they're talking about. You take Dr Jones [the site manager]. Well he must know just about everything there is to know about these plants. And he's a real gentleman.'

So Billy had got a bit on the inside. He also played for the Riverside cricket team and he felt that that helped too. It helped to single him out and also to satisfy his real curiosity about managers—who they were; what they were like; whether or not they drank pints. 'I'd never met a manager before I came here.'

In 1972 he applied for a job as a trainee operator on the acid plants. He wasn't successful—in fact no one was appointed. This disappointed him quite a bit; but he was more puzzled by the questions they asked him in the interview:

'It really took me aback, you know. I did these tests like and I really expected them to want to talk with me about what I'd written down and such like. But they seemed to be more interested in talking with me about the union. Well, I've nothing against the union and I said so like. They seemed pleased about that and then they asked me if I'd consider standing as a shop steward if I moved onto the plant. I thought that was a very funny question to be asking at an interview. See, this firm is very crafty. They like to use the shop stewards. I've seen that. They try to make the steward the foreman and things like that. Well I don't think that's right. I definitely want to be a foreman but I don't think it's right to be the foreman and the shop steward.'

Throughout 1972 he noticed more and more funny things. More ways in which the firm was being crafty.

Billy was not too keen on the West Indians. He tells you that he doesn't mind them but that some of them are 'a bit fanatical'. He was particularly sensitive about their reaction to the defeat of Illingworth's Test team:

'Some of them are really *arrogant*. I expect you've come across that yourself this summer down here. This summer especially. They say, "We're going to smash you." *And they really mean it.* It's the same when Clay fights. It's just the same. Sometimes I think they're a bit more prejudiced than we are.'

He's 'got nothing against them' but feels that he 'can't get on with them'. Like most of the white people we talked to at Riverside he comes out with the occasional derogatory, racist, comment. The management know this and in the middle of 1972 Alan approached one of the blokes on A shift (Jack); Billy told us the story with some astonishment:

'You know Mathew? Well he's disliked down here. There's no doubt about that. He's not a very nice person I don't think. Even the West Indian fellas get fed up with him. And I think the firm's been trying to get rid of him ever since he started here. The foremen hate and detest him. That's the truth. Well Alan had the cheek to call Jack into the office the other day. And he said, "What are we going to do about this Mathew then?" Well, Jack like wanted to know what that had to do with him. So Alan said, "It's about time he got the sack and was finished down here isn't it?" Well anyway Jack said that that was nothing to do with him like—you know Jack hasn't got any time for Mathew like but he didn't know what that had to do with him like. And do you know what Alan said? He said, "It's about time you got some of the blokes up together and made a few complaints about him. You know—get rid of him." Well Jack really told him then. "Look," he said, "if you haven't got the nerve to sack him don't expect us to do it." And that's right you know. It's not up to us to go around getting blokes the sack. They're a bit that way here. A bit artful, a bit crafty.'

By this time Billy's view of 'the inside' was becoming a bit jaundiced and he was more and more unsure of what path to follow. He had found his interview for the operative's job a chastening experience—'and then they didn't appoint anybody to the job'. He'd seen a film about Japan on the television and this also had made a great impression on him:

'It's really terrible over there. The pollution is terrible and the unions are really weak. You know you just have to live for the Company.

The Company more or less owns you. It's like it was here about fifty years ago. You've got a situation there where you've got young fellas with university degrees doing jobs that the likes of me do over here. In a few years time there will be a revolution over there. Bound to be. But it's happening here too actually. All the new operator's jobs in the Pharmy plant were advertised for people with qualifications. And this new Mobile Op. job here. That's the way it's going.'

Did this mean that we too were heading for revolution? He thought not. The British people 'wouldn't stand for revolution'. But nevertheless 'it's getting pretty bad here'.

When we last spoke with Billy he was still talking about the idea of getting on with ChemCo; the idea of becoming a foreman and moving—with a company assisted mortgage—to the new estate where almost all the Riverside foremen lived. But he'd lost his sense of certainty; and even at 25 he was finding the bags getting heavier. As we left he told us that:

'The most important thing though is to get the mortgage paid off on this little house that we've got. So that I can get a quieter job than this when the kids grow up.'

Tommy Robson

Tommy is a big man and his white coat makes him look even bigger. He stands in his boots, his white coat billowing open, hands in trouser pockets, helmet on the back of his head and all shift long—'he's *murder* on Nights'—he shouts abuse or laughs. He tells many drinking tales, of drinking seven pints in twenty minutes after the 'two till ten' afternoon shift, of how 'no weekend passes without a piss-up in our house', of how his little lad likes a Guinness with his Sunday dinner. Everyone rates him 'a character'. 'Have you seen Tommy yet?' managers would ask us. 'The salt of the earth, Tommy.'

Born into a family of coalminers in 1921, he spent his youth in a northern pit village: 'thirty-six families and thirty of them related. We knew everybody, everybody knew us.' His father died in the pits when Tommy was 10. He went straight from elementary school down the pits himself. After the war he joined ChemCo as a process worker. 'Up there ChemCo was *the* firm.' But sixteen years later Tommy was still on the shop floor: 'Up there you had to wait for someone to die to get a white coat.' So when his boss asked him if he'd mind going south he says he replied, 'I'll go where I'm bloody well told to go. . . . I was only here seven months and they made me foreman.' He looks back on the Riverside start-up as 'a great time. The Royal Hotel, that's where we were—you wouldn't credit how much ale there was. Suitcases full of brown ale, bought it with us we did. Ring a bell and you got a little flunkey with a tray of sandwiches. Bloody great! And work—it wasn't like now. Have you heard of Phil Lancaster? . . . But the hotel—like lords we were—not that the wife knew, mind.'

His wife was unsettled when they first came south. But Tommy winks about this now. He reckons the 'nice little house' (which the Company helped him buy) and especially the blow air central heating and the phone have done the trick. 'I tell you though', he says, 'when we first came here there were two prices in the shops. One for us and one for the locals. And it's not like up north, next door never speak. Mind', he adds, 'if they don't bloody talk to *me*, I don't bloody talk to *them*.'

'It's not like up north'—that's one of Tommy's abiding themes. Jokes, lies, politics, sport, strength, human dignity, women, drink— whatever it is, Tommy always makes his point by reference to differences between the north and south.

Tommy likes to let you know that he's a canny lad. Canny with the blokes too. 'Hello, Fred', he shouts, as the previous shift comes out of the shower and off home:

'Hello, Harry. Hello, Billy. *Hello you miserable bugger.* (I always talk to him like that. He'd think there was something wrong if I said "Hello Jack. How are you?") Hello, Sam—how's the garden? Hello, Steven. (Nice bloke him, wife's very ill.) All right, Mac? Don't keep her waiting y'bastard! Hello, Mitchell—What? Not working a doubler? Hello, Ted. . . .'

'You see', he says in the middle of this performance—a performance which Fred, Harry, Billy, Jack, Sam, Steven, Mac, Mitchell and Ted understand very well—'you've got to know how to approach people. . . . In the old days a foreman knew everything about his workers. How often they had their leg over. The lot.'

As a foreman Tommy doesn't hold back on the shouts and bluffs and threats. But he likes to 'do right by the lads'. He'd be hurt if at a fundamental level he didn't have their respect—even though they are southern, 'don't know what hard work is', and 'haven't seen children go bare-foot'. 'I've not seen a site like this one for thieving', he says. 'Mind', he adds,

'I could leave a pound note on my desk—yes, with the bloody door open —and it wouldn't move. It would not move.' When occasion arises— which is not very often at Riverside since there's no company club with a bar and people rarely meet off the site—he enjoys buying the blokes a pint. In spite of all this comradeship though, he thinks they're all bad workers, and bad trade unionists to boot. He complains that they don't do the job properly, they don't go to Branch meetings, they lack solidarity. Not like 'up north'. 'Up north, if anything happened the others would support you—that's unionism.' However, this doesn't mean that Tommy wants his workers to go militant.

As he sees it, 'a good shop steward should look at every problem in two ways. He hasn't got to be one-sided. He works for ChemCo, ChemCo doesn't work for him.' He doesn't want unions that 'go too far'. No 'reds'. He thought the 1971 Industrial Relations Act 'essential' because 'We've just got to stop having so many strikes.' 'People have just got to pull their bloody socks up *and work*.' The north, the past, the working class and hardship are all one to him. So, he celebrates the rigours of 1926; has a real soft spot for miners; evaluates all current struggles against the *real* struggles of the past—or 'up north'. But feeling that current industrial actions fall short of the tragic dimensions which characterised those of the past, he rejects them. He sees them as 'stupid', or 'bloody minded'— nothing to do with *real* trade unionism.

He's a mixture, is Tommy. 'The working-class man is a bloody fool to himself', he tells you, 'and that includes me.' Watching the blokes hump bags he tells you that 'bandwork is archaic in this day and age'— only to go on and on about how the southerners have got it 'soft'. One day, talking about the 1930s and his Dad and uncles in the pits, he'll be telling you 'unemployment is a great evil'. Next day, complaining about spillage in his plant or absenteeism or lateness he'll rage: 'these buggers need a bout of unemployment'. But given the severe contrast between his childhood and the 'affluence' of the south of England in the early 1970s there's a sort of sense in all this. Because things have changed. Not just in terms of 'affluence' either. For although it is important to him that 'in the old days the difference between the staff and payroll was tremendous', other things have changed as well. There's the workers' 'different attitude of mind'—there's also the blacks, who are 'going to take us over'.

Tommy doesn't put things in official Company language but the nuances of ChemCo's recruitment policy are not lost on him.

'I don't want a fucking industrial psychologist to set me an exam to find the men I'm after. They've got to be physically capable of carrying one hundredweight and mentally capable of normal straightforward arithmetic. I want them wanting to settle down, married, wanting regular work, not just six months. I wouldn't take a single bloke, I can tell you that. You have a job to get the bastards to work. Their time keeping is bad. They regularly have one off for the Queen. If they've got a bit of stuff they're off. A married man may have a bit of stuff on the side, mind. But he's still got to come to work, his wife kicks him out.'

But ask Tommy what sort of workers he gets and he's likely to give you a one word answer—'Niggers!' 'I'm not colour prejudiced, mind', he tells you, and 'there's no trouble down here. But you find with these Jamaicans that they spend their time sleeping, or hiding. They'll do anything to get out of work.'

We were talking to Tommy one morning in the company of one of his mates, another foreman who had come south, and a fellow fancier of budgies. ('I go round to see his budgie now and then', Tommy told us, 'like a fucking eagle it is.') 'There's coloureds everywhere', his pal said, 'I'd never seen a coloured before I came down here—down here I'm more like a bloody Colonial Chief.' 'Like Powell says. Forty per cent coloured, there are', Tommy chimed in. 'No', we said, 'Not even four.' 'Look out that bloody window', they said. We did. In ten minutes seven West Indians passed by and one white. At this Tommy was off—onto 'young kids with more money than sense', 'beer like piss', and workers who 'don't know what work is. Not like up north.'

'I don't want to run people down but where we come from was a depressed area. The sort of bloke you got up there was far superior to the blokes you get down here. You've got to drive a man down here to get anything out of him. You don't seem to get a proper team spirit here. In the north if you gave a man a job to do he did it, you didn't have to go back to find out if he'd done it or to tell him to get a move on, you knew that he'd do the job as well as you could. You didn't have to drive him but you've got to drive the blokes down here.'

Tommy would prefer to be back in the north. Sometimes he wishes he'd never moved, but as he says, 'I've made my bed.' He'll stay in the south, but he isn't happy with it. He 'goes back' four or five times a year and always spends his summer holidays 'up home'—according to one of his mates 'in a bloody big club'.

He's a man who went where he was 'bloody well told to go', by ChemCo. His service now spans a quarter of a century. On the Wimpey estate where he lives he is culturally uprooted; for it's true that neither his neighbours nor his workers know what it once meant, up north, to get a job with the firm—let alone a white coat. But he is loyal to ChemCo still. At least, in 1970, when we first met him he tried very hard to convince us of this. 'I've seen quite a few changes in my lifetime, I can tell you', he'd begun, and he went on to explain that he was a 'supervisor' now. Cursing 'all this bloody paper', pointing out that 'you've got to be a bit more humanitarian nowadays—not a bad thing, mind', and complaining about his 'soft' undisciplined workers, by way of conclusion he passed his damning verdict on the few local foremen who he and his mates had brought on: 'No bloody loyalty.' As for foremen being in a union, he'd had 'no time for that'. As he saw it then 'nine out of ten times management will move in the direction that the Foremen's Association would like them to. So I don't really think that there's a need for a union for us supervisors.' But that was in 1970.

Every year which passed brought news of a heart attack that had befallen another foreman with whom Tommy had once worked, or of yet another foreman who had 'decided to leave'. Increasingly the 'Company-do's' he went to in the Royal Hotel were retirement parties for other foremen like him. Men who'd come south to get a white coat. As far as his manager knew, Tommy was still a loyal Company servant and was still 'stamped end to end "ChemCo" ' in 1972. And so he was, as a supervisor of workers. But this is just why his workers delighted in calling him 'shit scared' when they found out that Tommy, now aged 52, had joined the supervisory branch of the union—*their* union, and the union Tommy had belonged to before he thought he'd left the likes of them behind him. Tommy faced things out in rumbustious style telling what he'd do with the money which he now foresaw ChemCo would one day thrust upon him, and the amount of which he hoped the union would fight to increase. Ocean cruises and that big club up north figured prominently in his plans: 'A big lump sum,' he'd say. 'Bloody great!' No one really believed him though. Because he'd put too much of himself into ChemCo for too long to feel at home—even up north—without also being on the job. When that big lump sum runs out Tommy will be on the dole. And, not working any more, he'll be plain 'Tommy Robson'; at best, 'Tommy Robson who used to be a ChemCo foreman'.

Tommy still tells you that 'ChemCo's been a great firm'. But it's not what he's got in mind for his little lad. 'Airline pilot. Footballer. It's his life, mind. I believe in that. Anyway in the end I don't suppose it'll matter a damn what I say. But not here. Not now. I don't think so.'

John Baird

John Baird is in his mid-20s. His father is a senior civil servant, and his brother joined the Foreign Office in 1965. John was educated at a direct grant grammar school, took science subjects at A-level, and 'did all right'. He had always expected to go to university—'it was just automatic really' —and he chose chemical engineering 'because it seemed to offer the prospect of a good career'. He took his degree—'did all right again'— and then went to ChemCo 'because of the money they offered'. In 1971 following a short period in research he arrived at Riverside as plant manager. 'They asked me to apply, and I did', he told us. 'So, here I am. Two years out of university with a wife, a house, a plant and £3,000 odd a year.' Feet on desk in his new office, he looked relaxed enough. He could have chosen differently—and compared to his workers he did have choices to make—but it appeared now as if he had always been on route toward his present job, or one like it; a position of some authority, and relatively well paid.

In the first few weeks John had 'felt a bit out of it' when talking to his fellow managers, the jargon of Management Science not then being his to command. But new to the job, and until recently 'an outsider', he claimed to find 'just being in industry really interesting'. He watched closely how other managers coped, thought about what the job meant for their lives, and about what it could come to mean for him. Workers on John's plant had had five, ten, or even twenty or so different jobs by the time they were his age. At 30 years old they'd been working for fifteen years and, with very few exceptions, had got as far as they would ever get. Yet young managers at ChemCo are apt to invest the age of 30 with an almost magical significance. As they see things, anyone—any manager— who is going places is expected to be on his way by then. Although John claimed he wasn't ambitious ('not really') this got him to thinking about being 30 himself—

'The way I look at things is that when I'm 30 I don't want to be looking back and saying "Damn, I wish I had done that when I was 25." You know, when you're thirty with a wife and a couple of kids in tow the things you can do are quite limited really. At the moment I'm all right. I've got a good salary. You get a really bloody good salary with this firm. . . . That's the problem I think, you just can't leave.'

He worried for a time that he really would end up with regrets; he even wondered whether he'd simply 'sold' himself to ChemCo. 'Money isn't everything', he said. But being involved in technical problems (*'real* technical problems') brought him a lot of satisfaction. Maybe his fascination with the technical didn't extend quite as far as he liked to suggest— 'You know', he told us once, 'when you go abroad people say, "look at that beautiful cathedral" and I say "Yes, look at that beautiful cathedral", and then they say, "Look at that *smelly* old chemical works." But I'll say, "No, look at that *beautiful* chemical works. Let's find out how it works" ' —but it was not long before he arrived at a point where, in his own words, 'I think I must be too interested in it now to try something else.' Apart from solving technical problems, he'd also come to positively enjoy the variety and hustle and bustle of the plant manager's job; a job in which, according to John, again with some exaggeration, 'you're really on the go all the time':

> 'You know, you come in and clear your desk. Go to a meeting. Come back. Go over to the plant. Do some more work on your desk. Then you're back over on the plant. You're on the go all the time being a plant manager.'

Making mental notes of the necessary do's and don't's, he spotted early on that it could be dangerous for a plant manager to get too involved with the technical side of things, even in career terms. 'He was just *too* bloody good', he said of another manager:

> 'Too interested in the job he was. Had a double First. Thought nothing of going into Sammy's office, saying, "Look here", and working out three lines of equations. Equations all over the board! I think they thought, "Get rid of him for Christ's sake. He's too hot to handle this lad." So he's plant manager somewhere else now. . . .'

After six months' experience though, John Baird himself was becoming slightly concerned about 'getting too involved'. Despite his talk about 'beautiful chemical works' he wasn't really bothered about 'becoming one of those all slide-rule merchants', nor about damaging his career because of this. What he was thinking about was the prospect of his whole *life* becoming a mere adjunct to *work*. For what had happened to other young managers, like Jack Steele, had given him pause for thought.

'Take Jack Steele. He just *lives* the work. You know, he has just *become* it. You see him outside, even at home with his wife and kids, and he is not as much at ease there as he is in the work situation here. I think it's a pity if you lose all interest in things except work but perhaps it's inevitable. I don't know. I don't really. Perhaps it will happen to me. Perhaps that's what you've got to be to be a plant manager. . . .'

In John's case, such over-involvement still remained a future possibility; something to be coped with if and when he felt definitely threatened. From the moment he took over the plant, however, he had found himself confronted with something 'strange' and 'eerie'; something which, whilst it didn't lose him sleep, did represent 'a puzzle'. A little embarrassed, but wanting to talk about it, he put it to us like this:

'When I go down on the plant I know that they react to me differently. You know, it's all right in town—if you meet one of them in Provincial. You are just another person there. It's all right. They talk to you as an ordinary person. But I don't know what it is—but down there on the plant they don't react to me as if I was one of them.'

On one level John knew this shouldn't have puzzled him. But it did. He really did find it 'rather disturbing that, as far as I can see, just because you are a manager workers treat you differently'.

At 25 years old, workers *were* strange to John Baird. Part of another world. He had been brought up in a quiet village in Surrey. Before he came to Riverside most of his life had been taken up with his family, school and university. Neither this nor the two years he'd spent in research had done much to bring him into contact with the realities of factory life. 'I just drifted into it really', he told us, and so he had: drifted into university, drifted into chemical engineering, drifted into becoming a ChemCo plant manager. The workers on his plant had also 'drifted', but the tide that ran against them—that impelled them to the point where they 'chose' to work at Riverside—was not the tide that he caught. His had been a comfortable drift, and continued to be so—until, that is, he first fell foul of a shop steward.

What took place was far from being a major clash, and it happened at a plant meeting where, as John himself admitted, he 'wasn't expecting any trouble'. As he recalled it—

> 'I said, "Well, let's all get down to this. Let's all pull together" sort of thing. "Let's work it out face to face." I think it *was* going really well but then I saw what an experienced shop steward could do. He said, "Why haven't you negotiated with me on this? It's in the agreement. You must negotiate before you introduce any changes. . . ." And I was saying that there were a number of *reasons* why I hadn't negotiated, and I was listing the reasons. But I was just trying to be *reasonable*. And the more reasonable I became the worse it got. And oh, he had a field day really. I really just didn't know how to cope with it. And I coped with it very badly. The upshot of it was that he said that all the shifts were very disturbed about it and they wanted an answer by Monday, or else.'

Faced with this, John scurried round to find an answer by the Monday. It was only later, when he had the chance to see another plant manager in operation in a similar situation, that he came to see the error of his ways. From this he says, he learnt a lot.

> 'Colin [Brown] went up to the steward and said, "What's all this mularky?" "We want a decision", said the steward. "Well you can't have a bloody decision", he said. "You'll have a decision when *I* say so." What he was doing there was saying that *he* was the plant manager, that *he* had the authority to say to do these things. And I think you've got to have the ability to say that to a steward. That's what *I* had lacked. That's what I'd been unable to do because I hadn't had the experience of dealing with shop stewards in these situations. And I think if you're going to be a plant manager those are the sort of things you've got to be able to do.'

This incident, and others like it, made it patently obvious to John Baird that the book on 'Theory X' and 'Theory Y', which he'd once bought to 'bone up' on the language that ChemCo's modern managers used, was no adequate guide to their practice. But it *also* taught him something about power—his power—and this made a far deeper impression than any book. Before he went to Riverside John had never really had to think about power. Since he didn't see its consequences it was, in a sense, inconsequential. Something not central to the functioning of this society and work. But, 'in industry', and now a manager, he had had to learn that capitalism is not a 'reasonable' system; that a manager cannot afford to forfeit his 'right to manage'; and also that to manage other people—people who sold their labour power to ChemCo, which is one good reason why they didn't relate to him 'as an ordinary person'—he had first to manage himself.

John was still learning—finding out 'the sort of things you've got to be able to do'—when, in late 1972, he was shipped off to manage one of ChemCo's northern plants. 'Queer lad. Not a bad kiddie, mind', the steward commented in an almost avuncular way as he recounted yet again his version of the day he'd had John 'going everywhichway'. John Baird, for his part, had no doubt that his stay at Riverside marked an important chapter in his life. As he said a few days before he left: 'you could say it's been something to put down to experience really.' But what he will really do with this experience—experience which, combined with yet another experience and the position he occupies in the factory class structure, makes him different from Michael, Harold, Billy and Tommy—this, however, remains to be seen. 'You can either be a bastard or a bad bastard', Riverside managers told us. One thing's for sure: John Baird—a reasonable enough bloke who told us once that all he wanted was 'to make myself useful'—won't be much use to ChemCo if he fails to grasp what they mean.

Part III

The Politics of the Factory

IN THE INTRODUCTION we noted that in writing about the chemical industry, the sociologist Robert Blauner referred to 'a secular decline in the workers' class consciousness and militancy'. He argued that this decline was a consequence of the industry's advanced technology and the 'economic prosperity' enjoyed by its workers. We hope that so far in this book we have done something to distinguish the chemical worker from his sociological stereotype. We also hope to have made clear that advanced technology—involving, as it does, massive concentrations of capital—does not take away the pressure for profit; and we want to devote the rest of this book to a consideration of the effects of this upon the people who work at Riverside: first, in Part III, by looking at the question of trade unionism and militancy in the context of the NWA deal, second, in Part IV, by placing the 'affluence' of the Riverside workers—and foremen and managers—within the context of British society. A society of commodities which is itself driven by capital's drive to accumulate.

To begin with we see no reason to assume that any particular 'technology' will automatically rule out industrial conflict and struggle. In fact it is only possible to argue such if the 'technical' aspects of the division of labour are split off from their social, class, base. The makers of chemical plants employing 'process technology' have always realised that their workers could give them a lot of trouble if they were well organised and in recent years the Electricity Generating Board (and the rest of us) have learned this fact very well. Advanced technology—in and of itself—doesn't solve the issue of power or of economic rewards.

But the fact remains that the chemical industry—compared with, say, the engineering industry—has been remarkably free from overt industrial conflict in the past decades. Partly—as we shall see—this has had to do with the structure of working arrangements within the industry; and partly too with the way in which the companies have been able to operate a system of national bargaining. But perhaps most significant of all has been the approach of the companies themselves. Operating in the steadily expanding post-war market (and not so affected by the short-term economic fluctuations as the engineering firms) they have been particularly conscious of the need to preserve 'good industrial relations'. Bob Edwards saw this clearly in 1945 when he wrote that the chemical companies had 'no illusions about the disastrous consequence for the chemical industry, and the effect upon profits that would result, from the existence of sharp antagonisms . . . because chemical processes depend upon the continuous nature of production'. And that: 'For this very reason extraordinary care has been applied to labour policy . . . so as to prevent the development of a strong, militant trade union organisation amongst its workers.' This is equally apt today: if anything it is much more the case now than it was then. For what Bob Edwards made clear is that 'integration' is no neutral—or 'natural'—social process. It is a definite managerial strategy: and since the war management has grown more sophisticated, not less.

One of the main purposes of the next chapter is to examine the strategy of integration within the context of the most 'modern' of giant international corporations. Taking Riverside as an example we look at the way in which management relates to trade unionism and attempt to incorporate it within the rubric of the 'new philosophy' of NWA. We look at the effect of this upon the development of trade unionism on the site and upon the militancy of the workers. In all we are trying to argue four things.

(1) that management seeks to incorporate the union, nationally and locally; and that this, plus the important extent to which the union exists 'over the men's heads', and plus the fragmentation of labour—which is the other side of the technical 'integration' of the site as a chemical complex—poses real difficulties for rank and file organisation;

(2) that the liberal progressiveness of managerial corporatism is limited, both in terms of actual management practice, which contains an element of cynicism, and in terms of the ambivalence which characterises workers' views about the type of trade unionism which management seeks to foster;

(3) that despite Company practice and ideology, and in some ways despite the union, men act—and to a degree informally organise—against work, and the management which directs it;

(4) that such informal organisation itself makes evident a tension between different conceptions of 'trade unionism'; and more generally, that these differing conceptions of what trade unionism is, and should be, correspond to different ideological traditions within the working class.

7
The Management Strategy

AT RIVERSIDE, a technologically advanced chemical complex, most of the men employed as manual workers performed heavy, repetitive, boring work. Deeply unskilled work—packing and stacking bags of fertiliser. Here, and at ChemCo generally, it is clear that the new (scientific) skills associated with advanced chemical production are not concentrated on the factory floor but rather in the hands of the controllers—the better to be put to the end of capital accumulation.

The tendency for capitalism to *deskill* the work performed by the working class has been a central one. Marx wrote about it in the nineteenth century and more recently in the USA Harry Braverman has argued that the history of capitalism is synonymous with 'the degradation of work'.[1] The controls that particular groups of workers were able to obtain over the work process by virtue of their skills and their detailed knowledge of production, served (with the onset of the machine age) as an important impediment to the development of capital.[2] At the turn of the century in the USA 'Scientific Management' provided a force to attack these controls. Jobs were broken down and detailed specifications of performance and responsibility allotted to each subdivided task. This radical extension of the *division* of labour became the bedrock of job design in the twentieth century.

But this was not the only tendency. Skill is not essential to control. It is possible for unskilled workers, subdivided into routine repetitive jobs, to use their collective strength to oppose capital. Such opposition has been another sporadic feature of capitalism during this century. So job design (work degradation) has had to be supported by a strategy which deals not with the *job* but with the entire *labour force*. For just as the capitalist brought about the detailed labourer the better to control the job, so today the most progressive agents of capital seek to incorporate trade unions in a web of centralised procedures and to fracture in various personal and impersonal ways the potential unity of what is essentially *social* labour. All this to seek to make effective an increasingly broadly conceived capitalistic imperative to control.

One of the first things that the managers we met at Riverside wanted to talk to us about was trade unionism and the state of unionism on the site. 'There is not a militant on this site', said one of them knowingly: 'some hotheads but no militants.' He was clear that this was in his interests and in 'the interest of the Company' and that one of the main tasks of management at Riverside was to keep the situation this way. In this, as we shall see, they had a lot going for them.

To begin with the question of 'militants'. If we mean by this workers who have had some experience of dealing with management; who have learned how to stand up to them and how to protect their rights and the rights of other workers; who have learned the need to plan a strategy for dealing with management, the need for meetings, for leaflets, for *organisation*; if this is what a militant is, then it is clear that there was no such man at Riverside. If these men had anything in common it was a near total lack of contact with organised shop floor trade unionism. They had all worked in a variety of jobs—some 'good', some 'bad'—for a variety of often small employers. They had moved around a lot, sometimes they'd taken out a union card, sometimes not. We talked with only two who had taken any active part in trade unionism before they came to this site— both of these men were shop stewards.

So the workforce at Riverside could not draw upon any traditions of militancy from within its collective past. These men had come from far and wide to an area of England that has been remarkably free from confrontation and industrial strife during this century. They live in different parts of the area, travelling on average some twenty miles to work. Few of them meet a workmate outside work and at work they are split apart too. They work on separate plants; plants that are separated by a half mile or so, which have different car parks, different changing rooms, different managers. Their existence at work is so separate that none of the workers that we talked to on the acid plants knew *anyone* who worked on the Zap plant. Moreover within each plant the workforce is further fragmented by the Continental shift. Only a quarter of the workers who work on a plant will be there at any one time. Almost all the people we talked to who said that they had 'friends' at Riverside found those friends on their own plant and on their own shift. Taken together the plants and the shift system broke a workforce of almost 200 into a series of very small groups.

One of the men on the Zap plant saw the situation like this:

'The big problem is there's no contact between the plants. You don't know what the other hand is doing type of thing. We're becoming a bit friendlier with Zap X since we've been working overtime over there. But there's no *social life* with this plant. There's no social life in work. It's a pretty off hand plant to work on really.'

All this has obvious and very real consequences for the development of 'militancy' at Riverside.[3] A factory militant relies, above all else, upon the collective strength of the workers. This collective strength has been asserted in the past through slogans like 'one out all out'; through the strike and through blacking—the practice whereby workers collectively refuse to do a particular job or piece of work. At Riverside much ran against the development of such a collectivism. Men on one shift who decide to refuse to do particular work find that it is done by men on another shift who they never see. Such action could of course be co-ordinated through meetings held off the site at the union office in Provincial but the shift system also makes these very difficult to organise. At any one time half the labour force is either at work or asleep while the other half is preparing to go to work or getting used to being at home.

Now these problems aren't insuperable ones (we know of one site, for example, where for a time two men regularly came to work an hour early and left an hour late so that they could talk with the people on the other shifts and establish particular working practices) but they are significant. They create difficulties for collective organisation that aren't encountered in engineering factories that work for one shift a day. And the conjunction between this fragmentation and the experience of the workers who came to Riverside placed ChemCo's management in a very strong position. When it came to changing things, to planning and co-ordination, they were faced with a divided labour force which, by the standards of many British factories—certainly those which hit the headlines—could be considered 'docile' and 'unsophisticated'. Certainly if management had wanted a quiet life they could have had it at Riverside. But that quiet life fits very uneasily into the rationality of monopoly capital. Riverside's management was under pressure throughout the 1960s—but particularly toward the end of that decade—to increase the 'performance of the plants'. And this meant that docility was not enough. In deciding to embark upon the change of attitudes that the NEDC had held to be so necessary for the industry, ChemCo's manager accountants therefore sought to 'motivate' their workforce toward higher productivity. They also rethought their approach to trade unionism. So much so that at Riverside management became directly involved in making the union on site.

The personnel manager at Riverside explained the situation like this:

'They're *still* very equivocal about unionism at Roxborough [ChemCo's oldest northern plant]. Really they don't want the buggers in the place. You see ChemCo has traditionally avoided unions, preferring its own system of consultation through works representatives. Christ, my old dad was a union man in the pits and "Works Representative" for him was a form of abuse.'

But at Roxborough, and elsewhere in the Company, they *had* to have 'the buggers' in the place.

'We've had to change. We can't rely on those methods any more and I think this is a better situation morally. Now we have to battle for the minds and wills of the men.'

The NWA and the negotiations which led up to it were central to this battle of wills, and the issue of trade unionism played a central part in all this. It is worth reminding ourselves what was involved in the deal. Partly the deal was about ideology—the negotiations contained strong and clear statements by senior management about the need for new attitudes, the need for commitment, for a 'revolution' in the social relationships within the factory. We have already seen something of the reality of this 'revolution' but it is important to point out that such a message was regularly put across to the workforce at Riverside during the years that we visited the plant. An observer of another British chemical firm during the 1960s noticed similar tendencies.[4]

In regard to employment at British Chemicals, the firm claims that 'from the outset British Chemicals attached the utmost importance to the well-being of those who worked in it, recognising that prosperity would be neither deserved nor achieved without the goodwill and co-operation of all of them'. A company booklet speaks of close standing relations with trade unions. . . . The point is made that British Chemicals has contributed significantly to the growth of the British economy and balance of payments . . . a weekly newspaper . . . includes news of improvements in welfare and retirement benefits. . . . There is mention of attempts to 'push responsibility down the line'. Links are made between productivity and personal effectiveness. . . . [A speech by the Chairman asserts] 'that the needs of the Company and the needs of individuals are interdependent. It is clearly the Company's duty to give opportunities for everyone to make the best of their own abilities and thus get more satisfaction from the work that has to be done. If this can be achieved, then all of us benefit twice—by increased personal satisfaction and by the increased prosperity of the Company—which in turn will enable us to measure up more fully to our other inescapable responsibilities—to customers, to shareholders and to the nation itself.'

At Riverside things were much the same. The site newspaper came out every two weeks and its editorials touched on similar issues. They pointed to the Company's profit sharing scheme as evidence of the fact that 'no one person owns ChemCo'. They argued that the modern corporation serves the interests of *everyone*. That the NWA deal with its stress upon co-operation provided the basis for a new working relationship that would produce more chemicals, more wages, more profit—for everyone. (It was just this argument that ChemCo used in full page advertisements in the national press when, in 1974, it was threatened with nationalisation by its inclusion in the Labour Party's alleged list of likely companies. A threat which—predictably perhaps—has come to nothing.)

The NWA deal, then, was closely bound up with the continuous production of ideology. But there was much more to the deal than this. Central to the agreement was the establishment of a *national* wage rate. On the introduction of NWA all grades of workers in the Company were given a large increase in their basic rate of pay but at the expense of losing all locally agreed bonuses, premium payments and the like. The deal did away with all *local* wage negotiation and replaced it with a centralised, national structure. From then on all 'money talk' was restricted to the conference room in London. In addition to this the agreement established that all jobs in the Company would be graded (on a scale from 2, the bottom, to 7), each job grade carrying a fixed national pay rate, with a fixed maximum addition for bad working conditions and with a fixed national shift allowance. The stress in this part of the agreement was upon the isolation of local, shop floor organisations from the collective bargaining process. Such organisations were seen to have a role on the plant-based consultation and productivity committees; but they were, in the Company's view, to be the administrative adjuncts of the deal.

For management, then, the presence of trade unionism was seen as a central aspect of the NWA. ChemCo's new approach to unionism was rooted in the 'battle for the minds and wills of the men'. Trade unionism was accepted and the pressure was on to mould it into a functional part of the corporation. NWA marked the quintessence of corporate rationality: within it, ChemCo, having rationalised its own management structures, set about rationalising the structure of trade unionism as well.

In 1967 very few people who worked at Riverside were members of a union. A branch of the TGWU had been established in 1962 but the branch secretary and the shop stewards from the Zap and Zap X plants were promoted to foremen in 1963, for some time after which there was very little union activity on the site. The branch secretary's job, for example, lay vacant for a while until it was taken on by a man who'd come to ChemCo from the Army.

> 'I came from the Army you see and there you were told to do something and you did it. I went to the chemical industry and I was told that you are expected to join the union. I knew nothing about unions but I thought, "I've got to have this job and if that's part of the job I'll join." As it turned out only 20 per cent were in.'

Having joined he decided that 'if I was going to be in something I wanted to have some say in it'. So he attended the branch meeting—and was elected branch secretary.

Men who worked on the plants in the early years remember that 'the union' was badly organised, they remember the stewards who were promoted, they remember trying to join and then giving up.

> 'I never joined. I was going to join when I first came here like. The shop steward had given me the forms to fill in. I filled them in—I thought I might as well like . . . [but] . . . he wasn't a very good shop steward and nothing came of it. He couldn't have sent them in. So when he gave me another lot of forms about a year later I told him what he could do with 'em. I said I'm not bothering like. Well, when the firm started stopping it, I joined then.'

The 'firm started stopping it' when, as part of the preliminaries to NWA, a 'check-off' arrangement was agreed between the Company and the union at national level.

There are arguments in favour of the check-off. It ensures the preservation of the closed shop—at Riverside it brought 100 per cent of the production workers into the union—and it saves shop stewards a lot of routine work while avoiding the problem of members falling into arrears and collectors absconding with the funds. But the check-off also makes it possible for the members to lose an important contact between themselves and the union organisation: with the check-off the union due can become more of a tax than a contribution to an on-going labour organisation. Such considerations have led many well organised shop steward committees to resist the introduction of such schemes, preferring to retain the traditional method of payment through collectors. At Riverside the check-off was welcomed. The District Officer told us that 'management was very keen on the idea and so were we. With the closed shop, you see, we have the ability to discipline our members.'

The closed shop was enforced at Riverside by an agreement between the Company and the union. (Management gave an assurance that while they wouldn't absolutely refuse to employ non-trade unionists new recruits would be told very clearly what was expected of them.) Those who were shop stewards at the time welcomed the agreement because it established the union at Riverside and saved them a lot of work. But it also ensured that no widespread, active, recruiting campaign ever took place on site. The union was established without a struggle and this meant that for many of these workers (as for an increasing number in the country generally) their *first* contact with trade unionism came through the personnel officer and a weekly deduction on the pay slip. Alan, a foreman well schooled in union politics, saw this quite clearly:

'After the closed shop was introduced I would say the union collapsed completely.'

A strange, but by no means unique, situation.

A union in name only, a paper membership, was not however enough for ChemCo. Given the contrasting difficulties of management by fiat and mass meeting, the very implementation of the NWA rested on the involvement of the union. It was to this end that workers' representatives —shop stewards—who were going to be packed off to productivity and consultative committees, were elected. Foremen were instructed by their plant managers to seek out 'likely material' on the plants and encourage them to stand as shop stewards in the coming elections. In this quest it became clear that while the management ideology of the 1960s differed in important respects from what had gone before the differences were only of degree and not of real substance. The 'management men' amongst the foremen talked often of the 'new role' for shop stewards within the Company. They'd stress that foremen and shop stewards have comparable functions—'they've got their job, and we've got ours and we both have to follow procedure'. One of them told us that:

'A good shop steward is my friend. He's a good man to have on the plant. You see, he knows the procedure; he knows just how far he can go and how far I can go. Oh yes, a good shop steward is my friend. He's an asset.'

But in reality—and this is not all that disguised here ('an asset' indeed)—when looking for workers to sponsor for shop steward, they acted on the view of the old-style foremen, for whom 'a shop steward with ChemCo should be a Company man'.

It is undeniable that ChemCo management exercised an important—and even determining—influence over the way in which the trade union organisation developed at Riverside. Of the six shop stewards who represented the men who worked on the fertiliser plant only two had been in any way active in trade unionism before they came on the site. These two (Alfie Grey and Greg Andrews whom we will look at in more detail in Chapter 9) were elected as shop stewards a few years before NWA was introduced. The other four had all been encouraged to stand for the office by their foreman, and two of them soon became the 'deputy fore-men' (standing in during the foreman's absence) on their section. Managers tell you that the District Officer first made contact with the site on their invitation. They privately boast that many of the shop stewards were their nominees. They justify all this with the language of 'participation'; with talk of the new style and the new modern corporation. But in its practice this ideology is inevitably flawed. When they talk of 'participation' they don't mean 'equal participation'; nor does trade unionism imply equal rights for all. In their view—a view that is firmly established within the structure of corporate capitalism—'participation' and 'trade unionism' are inevitably subordinate to the need for hierarchy and the need for profit. The need for management to manage.

Many trade unionists would accept this view and a lot of trade union officials act on it regularly in their daily lives. But the fact of the matter is that the establishment of organisation amongst workers on the factory floor always poses a *potential* threat to both the authority of the corporate hierarchy and to the accumulation of profit. This potential was well understood by the management at Riverside; as it was by the foreman who insisted that 'the unions shouldn't rule the roost'. For while they are clear that trade unionism now has an important role to play in the future of ChemCo they are also clear that it must be a particular type of trade unionism. 'Real', 'responsible' trade unionism. Their fear was that in setting up some form of collective organisation amongst the workers in the plants they might be preparing the ground for *militancy*. In short they were clearly aware that they could be playing with something which if not exactly fire could turn out to be too hot to handle.

The dangers were always there, right from the earliest days of the NWA negotiations at Riverside. For though the foremen were instructed to take care in approaching *sensible* people their judgments weren't infallible. One or two of the stewards, while not 'militants', were certainly not quite what the management had in mind. These men began to take the language of 'participation' seriously; as they did Jack Jones' talk about a union run from the factory floor. All this meant that Riverside management didn't get things all its own way. The introduction of trade unionism and the NWA revealed some clear flaws in management's 'labour relations system'. In 1970 the personnel manager explained:

> 'Five years ago if I had a problem I knew I could call in the full time officer and he'd get me out of it—he'd get the blokes back to work, tell them what to do or whatever. I feel less confident about that now.
>
> The full time officials at the local level have become paid lackeys. I've heard that term used. You know they're just leading the blokes in the direction they want to go. That's where the power is now— those few hundred buggers out there. *Before* the full time officer used to lead them by *telling* them where they were going. He can't do that now.'

But, although not entirely happy about it, he saw this as part of the challenge of 'the new philosophy'. The problem was to ensure that the workers used their union and their participation 'correctly'. And this problem was greatest during the phase when NWA was being introduced at Riverside and when the workers and their representative had—to use the language of participation—'heightened expectations'.

Under the deal the newly elected shop stewards were given facilities to meet every Friday in the Admin. Block to discuss problems associated with the introduction of NWA. Stewards who were not at work at that time would be paid by the Company to attend these meetings. The stewards understood those meetings to be theirs as of right under the agreement. The management accepted this but became very worried when the stewards refused access to the personnel manager. This worried them because they felt that 'they'll not be using those meetings to discuss our deal. Those buggers will be discussing the union in them. It's just not going to be very constructive.' But the managers put up with the meetings until NWA was fully operational; until the plant productivity agreements had been ironed out and all the jobs on the site had been graded. Once this was done Sammy Bell argued that, 'the Friday meetings are now simply an unproductive use of time.' From then on stewards were no longer allowed to meet each other in 'Company time', except in meetings with management. The deal had been implemented and participation and consultation were to be the rule, but they were the rule only within the context of the power of management—their right ('responsibility') to manage in the interest of capital.

The management at Riverside had to make sure that trade unionism existed on the Riverside site and that the NWA deal—'our agreement' as they called it—was introduced without causing trouble for themselves. There is no doubt they were successful in this. Riverside workers were not 'difficult'—and not experienced—like men on some recalcitrant plants up north.[5]

There were some problems but it all passed over quietly enough. After the Friday meetings ended there were no further meetings of shop stewards; in fact there was very little communication at all (aside from informal and chance meetings) between the stewards on the various plants. The introduction of trade unionism and a shop steward system had caused a few ripples in 'the system' but basically it had left the workforce as fragmented and disorganised as before. In fact the introduction of the grading structure added a further dimension to their fragmentation. But before we look into the dynamics of this new situation it is important to establish the *extent* of the fragmentation and isolation of the workers and trade unionism on the Riverside site.

On one occasion in 1971 we met one of the shop stewards off the fertiliser section and asked him what he felt about the Company's plan to close down one of the largest plants on the site. We had heard about this about a week earlier as part of a casual conversation in the corridors of the Admin. Block.

'I didn't know that. Redundancy over there. Well that's the first I've heard of it and Tommy [the foreman] hasn't said anything and he is usually the first one on anything like that, he's terrified of losing his job. That's the first I've heard of that. And they are closing? They are shutting the plant down.'

We were to be involved in several incidents like this one and they all point to the fact that the introduction of trade unionism on the Riverside site hardly affected the extent to which the workers on each plant existed separately from each other.

This lack of contact between the plants is compounded by a near total isolation from the workers at the other ChemCo sites in the country, and from the central, national organisation of their unions. (Something like 60 per cent of the Company's labour force is concentrated in two areas in the north and these are the centre of union activity.) To take a further example. After the NWA negotiations the national officers of the signatory unions put forward a counter-claim which attempted to use the Company's talk of 'involvement' and 'participation' against it. In a detailed document the union negotiators asked for more money and also more information about profits, sales, investment plans and so on. They argued not just for improved jobs and promotion opportunities but for worker directors on the Board. Now these are hardly revolutionary demands—even so they were rejected by ChemCo—but they do provide some platform for organisation around the issue of profit and the purpose of chemical production; matters of course which management had been careful to keep out of the NWA negotiations. As such this document could have been important for union propaganda on the plants. The fact is that it never reached there. Most of the stewards and almost all of their members had *no* knowledge of the negotiations. In fact we were responsible for distributing copies of the documents on the site. Men on the fertiliser sections had simply never heard that their union was demanding 'worker directors' at ChemCo. All they knew was that there had been 'something in the pipeline' and that out of this there would come, as there always did, a pay increase.

These comments of ours—about how 'we told them' about this and that—are not, we should perhaps add, meant in a self-congratulatory vein. We make them simply to emphasise the extent to which the Riverside workforce is fragmented and isolated internally in time and location, and externally in relation to the national union and other sites. Organisation at Riverside is, in a real sense, a near monopoly of management.

A lot of a manager's time is taken up with talking; at Riverside a lot of this talk had to do with how best to deal with 'the other side'—what to say to a disgruntled worker, how to handle a steward with a legitimate grievance. In all this ChemCo had been concerned to train its managers in a particular 'style'. And the central purpose of this style was to ensure that the prerogatives and power of management (and thereby capital) were retained in a situation where their subordinates—the workers—had to become 'involved' in ChemCo; to be given certain rights.

In this situation the idea of managers and workers combining together in co-operation to make—so to speak—*One Big Collective Worker* may be a useful shot in management's ideological locker but it is nowhere near the reality of things.[6] The co-operation—the collective work—that is achieved at Riverside and elsewhere is achieved in the context of an implicit understanding that only certain sorts of things are possible. When this understanding is broken management 'asserts its authority'— its power becomes explicit. Workers (and managers like John Baird) have learned this; they have learned that in a capitalist enterprise there is a limit to reasonableness and co-operation. And this limit is not set by some innate proletarian consciousness; or by some pathological refusal of workers—or managers—to co-operate. It is not simply a matter of 'changing attitudes'. The limit to reasonableness is set by the fact that the logic of capital (a logic which counts bags; forces managers to 'count numbers'; assesses profit and loss) is not the same as (and only reflects in a *deformed* way) the experience of the workers.

Most managers realise this. They may cope with this realisation in different ways—thinking of the workers as 'children' is one way—but what they know is that there is no easy route from explaining profit figures to the workers to obtaining 'motivation'. What they know as well is that they—as capital's subaltern class—are paid to serve the interests of capital and that unless they serve them well they face the sack. As men—intelligent for the most part—whose working lives are intricately bound up in these conflicts, they know the score. And because of this—because of what the score is—their 'industrial relations' are tinged with subterfuge, bad faith and, most of all, cynicism.

One or two of the managers at Riverside prided themselves on their cynicism. Edward Blunsen was the most open in this respect. 'It's a hard world' was one of his favourite expressions. But, interestingly, in his emphasis upon hardness and in the very openness of his cynicism and ambition he failed to capture the essence of the ChemCo management style. Playing the abrasive Mr Heath (with more than a touch of Enoch Powell in his case) it passed him by that, at ChemCo, Harold Wilson was a far more appropriate political mentor. And it was to prove his undoing. It is appropriate here that we should be linking management style with politicians, for politics—factory politics—is a central part of these plant managers' job. There's the 'juggling', as we called it in Chapter 3, where we were mostly concerned with the technical, co-ordinating, aspect of the function they perform. But they also know the value of the empty phrase, the nod and the wink, the pat on the back, and the occasional kick in the balls. And the most skilled of them put all this together in a highly professional performance. A performance so good that it appears real. A performance that is directed toward the *hegemony* of capital; the dominance of a particular view of things over all others. For these men are dealers in ideology.

The chemical plants at Riverside are small, as are most plants in the industry. Not small in terms of the capital employed but, compared to, say, the massed workforces that characterise parts of the engineering industry, small in numbers of men. Despite the fact that managers have been pushed off the plants into the Admin. Block, then, it is still possible, relatively speaking, for them to 'know their men'. And it's important that they do—precisely because so much capital is at stake. The 'professionals' know this and they devote a lot of their time to the 'personal' side of things. They know too that trade unionism has become a necessity; that it is better to 'have it in' and clearly established along agreed lines rather than be involved in perpetual arguments about a 'closed shop', 'non-union workers' and so on. They accept trade unionism and a lot of them will say that they 'agree with it'—providing it's 'properly set up'. It's part of the 'new approach' and they know that they need to give a lot of personal attention to the men's elected representatives—the shop stewards. The institutional level relationships between company and union being fixed, what these men engage in at plant and site level—at an individual level—is manipulation. Here we find the 'old kidology' that the 'traditional foremen' talk of, revamped in the language of 'modern' human relations; a 'revolution in industrial relations' played out in the context of 'modern' manufacture.

It was just this relationship between the old and the new that had escaped Edward Blunsen and was to prove his undoing. 'Young', 'vigorous', 'clear-headed', 'profit conscious', 'scientifically trained', most certainly 'talented' and 'ambitious' and 'competitive', he was—in some ways—everything the rulers of this society are apt to bemoan British managers are not. Crystal clear where he wanted to go—workers reported that he'd told them he wanted to get on the Main Board—he still, however, hadn't got the style right. He might have got away with his abrasiveness in a small, up-and-coming cut-throat operation. But not at ChemCo. ChemCo plant managers *don't* thrust their power in workers' faces. They try *not* to let the iron fist behind the velvet glove show, and they certainly don't tell workers that 'a man with a good manager doesn't need a union'. Riverside managers play it 'firm but fair'. They push and jostle workers and stewards, they 'jump on them'—but their overall strategy is to seek to enmesh workers, to bring about a situation where they don't have to be *driven*. While they might *think* of workers in the language of engineering they also go to great lengths to relate to them 'personally'.

Sammy Bell, the group manager at Riverside, is perhaps the best of 'the professionals' on the site. Every month, for example, he makes a 'CO's visit' to each shift. It takes place at the same time every month, everyone knows he's coming and everyone's prepared for him. He knows this too. For him, though, it's a way of 'making them jump' and 'keeping them on their toes'. But this is just one side of Sammy Bell. He can play the hard man; march around issuing instructions to his supervisors, spotting things which shouldn't be there and things which are missing; losing his temper. Yet in his office—particularly in his regular meetings with 'my shop stewards'—he's much more amenable and accommodating. 'A lovely cuddly teddy bear' is how his secretary describes him. And while the stewards don't take their loyalty to him this far there is no doubt that they *are* loyal to him; that they like the way he is with them and that they look forward to the morning they spend with him each month, in his office discussing 'problems'.

Experienced managers know that 'the office' is their territory. Desks, chairs, secretaries, coffee (and biscuits), telephone calls: these are all part of their world—not the world of the shop floor. And they know how to use this world against shop stewards. Many shop stewards have been overwhelmed by, and sucked into, the world of the office; edged along by managers who tell them how much more 'reasonable' they are than the 'average worker we employ'. And those who resist such talk, try to push a different point of view, find 'their flow' cut off at key moments by telephone calls or by secretaries with letters to be signed. Sammy Bell was the master of the office. Other managers told us repeatedly of how inexperienced shop stewards go to see him with a grievance and come out of his office—having got nowhere—'full of smiles'. They smile fondly as they tell you this. And they smile even more when they talk about the way he 'takes the stewards on his knee'—taking them out to dinner after the odd meeting and buying them drinks at Christmas. For them Sammy

Bell is the supreme artist. They watch him and if they're wise they try to learn from him.

Colin Brown, for example, says that he's 'learned a lot from watching Sammy', and he's Riverside's system-thinker *par excellence*. For him 'the system' matters; NWA was 'an important step in the right direction'. He reads avidly from the pages of the new psycho-social theory books. He talks—endlessly so it seems—about the 'new philosophy'; the 'problems of motivation'; the 'new role of the trade unions'. But Brown—like the rest of the managers—has a job to do and in his performance of this job there is no doubting that he has a very astute assessment of what is needed to keep himself—and ChemCo—at an advantage. The men who work on his plants tell you that 'he always tries it on—always'. There's 'a lot of spoof in him' they say. And Brown delights in his 'spoof'.

'Every man is born to do something and my function in life is to manage and I've just got to manage. I think this is a problem that most managers have failed to get to grips with. Now take an example. As far as I can see any man who takes on the job of shop steward wants his ego boosting. But you've got to boost his ego in the proper manner.

Now if I get a bit of trouble—now take an example, perhaps of a serious case of a man who has been perpetually late. Now, I'm the manager, and it's my function to manage. It's my function to discipline this particular man. But I have to deal with the steward. So, what do I do? I take the shop steward aside and I tell him that in half an hour's time this man Smith is going to walk into this room. That I'm going to stamp and bang the table and tell him that I'm going to put him out on the road.

Then I'll say to the shop steward, "and what *you* can do will be to intervene at this time. Make a case for the man. And we'll agree to let the man off with a caution."

Now the man comes in and I bang the table and the steward says, "Come on, Mr Brown. Couldn't you give him one more chance?" I relent. The shop steward gets out of the meeting with the man and says to him, "I've got you off this bloody time but don't expect me to do it again." You see, the shop steward gets his ego boosted. He gets what he wants and I get what I want. That's what good management is about.'

It's Brown's function to manage. Like the rest of them he does 'bang the table', and occasionally he does make threats to put workers out on the road, but his main strategy is to get the steward to work *with* him. This is what the new stress on psycho-sociology is for. 'Democratic leadership', he told us once, 'is the only way. But you'll know that, won't you? Psychologists have proved it with children.' Well, there are 'children' and adult workers, and there's 'democracy' and democracy. In Riverside's democratic family there's no doubt who plays the role of understanding parent.

Equally there is no doubt that in their practice of the 'new industrial relations' Riverside managers are involved in what is often a cynical relationship with the people they are dealing with. To put it at its hardest, they are involved in the manipulation of other people. This is a problem for people (like us) who try to understand them and people (like Riverside workers) who have to deal with them, for the defining feature of manipulation is precisely that it isn't declared for what it is. Self-deception and bad faith are structured in. So much so that it is often extremely difficult to separate the appearance from the reality—the shadow from the substance. Difficult, one suspects, for them too. For while these men recognise—and are critical of—the manipulation which goes on at the higher levels of the management structure (Jack Thompson's 'gentle form of corruption') they draw back from recognising it in themselves. For them it's 'a game'; more a matter of 'being good with people'.

But what of the workers in all this? They, after all, were 'the object of the exercise'. NWA and the new management was all constructed with them in mind. How did they react to being unionised, being consulted and represented; what did they make of the new participation?

Well, they were quite glad to be in a union. With very few exceptions the men we talked to felt that at one level 'you need a union'; that a union was important 'to see fair play for the working man'. Brian, for example, claimed to 'disagree with unions' but recognised that:

'You've got to have them. You've got to have them for protection. To protect the workers against that one man doing something stupid. If you didn't have unions you could get that type of firm that would twist you round their little finger.'

Without a union, they say, 'lots of firms would take advantage'. Without a union 'they'd give rises when they want'. Without a union 'we wouldn't really get anywhere'. More than a few of them have experienced workplaces where there is no union. They tell you that 'If you take away the power from the union I think things would just deteriorate.' They don't doubt the *necessity* of trade unions; but they are not happy with their experience of trade unions at Riverside.

We should remember again that very few of the men had had any close relationship with trade unions before they came to Riverside. They had read newspaper reports of strikes in the car plants, seen mass meetings on the television, but they'd never been a part of such activity. A lot of them felt that unions—though necessary—had 'too much power'. A lot of them agreed with the Industrial Relations Act. Jimmy was one:

'Yes, it's a good thing because some unions—not those here—are getting out of hand. They've caused chaos, struck for practically no reason at all . . . they're wrecking the country in the long run. They may be going against the management in particular but it all comes back to us, to the working class eventually, in higher prices and so on. And if the country's not doing well, we can't be doing well. If the country's doing well, in the long term we can gain out of it. All these strikes only affect the nation as a whole in the long run and if this Act can stop a lot of it, I'm all for it.'

But at Riverside it was a different story. There the criticisms he and most of his mates directed against their own shop steward were precisely the opposite to these. Jimmy felt that:

'Down here the stewards aren't militant enough. We've got a steward but as compared to those on the docks he's nothing. They don't even count down here. I think this firm has got them all tied up.'

He complained, for example, that when the Company mechanised a part of the bagging operation, the men weren't consulted or even told about it until after the event.

'I don't think they consulted the union at all—they wouldn't bother to consult Alfie Grey on it—whereas if they had a real militant shop steward they'd get his views on the subject . . . they seem to have Alfie pretty well tied up.'[7]

They complain too about the grading structure that was established under NWA. The management established the criteria against which each job was to be graded and it became apparent—as it later became in the case of the foremen—that responsibility for capital equipment rated much higher than physical effort or appalling conditions. The phos. operator (who had to negotiate those hundred-odd stairs throughout his shift) was placed on a lower grade than the leading operator on the Grinder.

'I can't understand it. I mean we have to take all these tests and we have to look after the control rooms. I can't see what he can be doing over there for the extra grade. I can't see that he can be doing more work than the likes of us here.'

This directs our attention to the question of *who* decides how much physical work is involved in a job. A packer on the Zap X warehouse describes one situation:

'We've got a job in here that's got high physical content and yet there's other jobs on this site that have been judged with more physical marks. We just don't understand it because if anybody is ever unloading a lorry, you know, unloading say, a twenty tonner, they just know what you're talking about. You can do two or three hundred ton off-loading and if you're up on the top and two or three of those lorries come in—with bags bent and they leak—well, we try and put over to the management that it's hard. They say it's easy.

Now I put it to them once and I'll put the same thing to you. I'd like you to give me an answer as well because if you've got a twenty ton lorry—this is no trick question—If you've got a twenty ton lorry and you've got four men off-loading that lorry, two men on top passing down, one on each side, and two men on the floor, how much tonnage has been handled?'

Well, you've got ten tons each side of the lorry, multiply by four presumably.

'That's the first honest answer I've had, because I say that to them, and they say, "Of course, it's *twenty* ton." It's *not* twenty ton because that man on top of the one side has pulled off ten ton. You know only twenty ton *on paper*. And do you think I can convince anybody about the actual tonnage handled? If you do ten of those lorries in a day, *each man* would handle a hundred ton and yet there's only five hundred ton in through the store being booked in. And yet I can't get them to. . . . They say "a hundred ton, four men, twenty-five ton each". And that's what their physical rating is on—it just seems as though we were robbed.'

A lot of the blokes we talked to shared this feeling that the grading system, and the mechanism of establishing grades, was a part of management's world, not theirs. And the same went for the assessment of 'conditions money'. Fair or not, it was an established fact and the only action open to the workers who felt severely wronged was to apply for their job to be reassessed. But they soon learned that very few of those who put in for regrading were successful.[8]

In this situation the men knew that they could get representation through the union but increasingly they began to feel that the representation that they had achieved through NWA was not particularly effective. Some of them talked to us about a dispute they were involved in before NWA was introduced. There had been a disagreement over bonus payment (these payments were of course abolished under the new agreement) and the men insisted that they wouldn't work unless they were paid what they felt they deserved. Colin Brown was their manager and they were informed by the foreman that Brown was not on the site—he was in London at a meeting. So they decided that that was that—they refused to work.

'As soon as we stopped Henry [the foreman] was off ringing the Admin. Block and old Brown was down here in five minutes. In he came, through the door, and right away he started the management psychology bit. "Why did *you* stop?" he said, pointing one of us out. But one of our coloured lads got him! "Let's get this straight", he said. "*We all stopped!*" And we got our back pay that afternoon.'

They remembered this issue because it was one of the few occasions on which they knew that they had won out against Colin Brown, his 'spoofing' and his 'psychology'. Usually they didn't know if they'd won or not; always suspecting that they'd probably 'been had'. That they won in this case was largely due to the fact that they were able to pit their direct *collective* action against management. The whole aim of management under NWA was to prevent or stall the use of such action, through the use of 'consultation' and 'participation' and through the regular meetings with the shop stewards. The manager accountants had had it figured to have their cake—binding the union to agreements at national level—and eat it—dealing with local union issues as a series of isolated, individual, problems.

Most of the workers we talked to at Riverside felt that the stewards weren't their men, that they weren't as trade unionists should be. Past promotions from shop steward to supervisor had not gone unnoticed and for those with short memories it was kept alive by those shop stewards who doubled as 'acting supervisor' when their foreman was off the plant. As the men saw it:

'It's a bloody big temptation, isn't it? If you can get a secure job and about £10 bloody more a week than you are getting. I know a few people that have turned it down, but in the end they've got them like. This company is very clever my boy. Very clever indeed.'

'Consultation' was seen as a further sample of such cleverness. The regular meetings held by Sammy Bell in the Admin. Block, which took the stewards off the sections for hours on end—sometimes to report back tales of big meals and free drink—were viewed with great cynicism. Andrew:

'Well, if he goes off as a shop steward with some of the big-wigs and they live it up and things like that. To me, it's all wrong. It's the blokes' money that's being put in. I think if you're going to have unions, you want people running them who's running them because they believe in 'em, but not for what they're going to get out of 'em. I know it's a hard job. You can't expect some bloke to run a union and not get something out of it really, but to me, it's the only way it will really run, you know, fair and. . . . Well, half the time I wonder if they're really interested in the workers and things like that. I don't think they are.'

It's not an easy business being a shop steward at the best of times and at Riverside some very inexperienced shop stewards were up against a very sophisticated management. So we talked with Andrew's shop steward—Donald—about the possibility that ChemCo were trying to buy him off.

'Last Christmas Sammy Bell was up at a meeting and he said, "You've got your overalls on" and I said, "I've just come from work." "Go and get changed, then come back", he said. And we all went out for a meal.

Last Christmas it was. Now I don't think that there is any ulterior motive behind him passing the cigars about and everything, I just think that he is a genuine bloke. In actual fact he knows that I do a bit with the car and he's offered to lend me his spraying equipment many a time. I never sort of took him up on it, but I know that if I went round to see him he would let me have it, so I don't know whether they are playing games or not, I can't tell.

I have never regarded it as a pay off, and I have never regarded myself as a "Yes Sir, no Sir, three bags full Sir" type of bloke. If I have got something to say—obviously I don't blurt it out you know, just for the sake of saying it and showing off in front of everybody, I take it as it comes—but if I feel that I have got to say something then I have got to say it. If I don't want to say it then I don't feel that way inclined. Don't feel bought off at all.'

Sammy Bell is—in many ways—a very likeable and personable bloke. But he is also the most polished of the professional managers at Riverside. At one level it is quite understandable that the stewards should see him as 'a genuine bloke' but it is equally understandable that other workers— not enmeshed in the 'personal' relationships of the consultation meetings —should think otherwise. Any steward who hoped to represent and still more to lead his members, would have to be very mindful of this. Which brings us nearer to the heart of the situation because it wasn't so much the cigars and the beer in the Admin. Block—although one or two men did couch their criticisms entirely in these terms—but rather the whole thing taken together which made the men lukewarm toward their stewards. It looked like a fix. And it did so because of a fundamental disagreement over what trade unionism *should* be about.

Nothing brought this out more clearly than the situation where stewards covered for supervisors. Donald was one. On the days when his foreman was off the plant he would be responsible for the section, for giving orders and making sure that they were carried out. He did this while he was the blokes' union representative. When we talked to him of the problem of being on two sides at once he agreed that it could be a 'bit tricky' and that if you weren't careful 'it can put you right in queer street'. But he didn't think the situation either impossible or wrong. He saw no *fundamental* conflict between managers and men; in his view the shop steward and the foreman share a similar concern for sorting out problems and ensuring that the section runs smoothly. Many of his members—who believe 'a steward has to get the best possible conditions for the men—he shouldn't be a firm's man'—disagreed. Indeed one of them who had thought a good deal about what 'a good steward' should be, went even further than this:

'A good shop steward should be for his men. And just for his men, not regarding his own feelings. If his men said, "Strike", I think he should strike, and if his men said, "We'll stay in", stay in, you know. But you know, I think that a shop steward really should be the voice of his men in a way. I think really that he should be a guiding light.'

A guiding light. Riverside workers received little such light from their stewards.

In trying to make sense of all this it is possible to argue that Riverside is an exceptional case. Several things might point to this. The fact that the site employed a 'green' labour force with only a limited experience of large-scale factory production; the separation of the workforce from the national union, which negotiates wages on its behalf; the introduction of the check-off arrangement; the blocking of the development of the shop steward committee; the *extent* to which the workers were exposed to management's way of looking at things. All these things taken together create immense handicaps for any sustained opposition to management's strategies within the factory. But perhaps they aren't as exceptional as they might seem. ChemCo chose its Riverside site with some care and it has chosen others like it. So have other multinationals. The NWA deal was no coincidence either; it was formulated carefully over a period of several years. Riverside is neither an exception nor a coincidence because giant corporations like ChemCo are in the business of creating the very conditions that exist on that site. In particular the way in which the Company systematically restructured its 'labour relations' points to a *general tendency* within big business. This tendency involves a clear attempt to deal with and incorporate trade unionism—to encourage trade union membership amongst the workforce; to grant special facilities to trade union representatives and officials; and all this to the end of *subjecting the labour force to a degree of order, regulation and control.*

The experience at Riverside can tell us a lot about this strategy; about the day-to-day practices of managers which take place within its ambit. It also points to some of the contradictions involved. The value of trade unionism to management lies in its (apparent) independence from capital. An independence which comes from the fact that trade unions 'represent the workers'. In as far as this independence is real it can create real problems for management. At Riverside the Friday meetings were an example of this. On the other hand where the union becomes seen to be simply another tool of management it can lose all claims to represent, speak for, and commit the people who are central to the whole thing—the workers on the factory floor. The antagonism which management's sponsorship of shop stewards created is again indicative of this.

So 'incorporation' is no simple process and the function of management in large corporations like ChemCo is to *manage* the contradictions; at all costs 'to prevent the system from running out of *control*'. In this task it had a lot going for it, because it is clear that the factory is wrapped in the hegemony of a capitalist ideology. An ideology which finds its expression not just (or even most importantly) in managers mouthing the Company line but in the whole fabric of day-to-day activity in the plant. The task of the working class is to break free of this. Our task now is to point to some of the ways in which workers struggled against their situation at Riverside.

Notes

1 Harry Braverman, *Labor and Monopoly Capital*, New York and London, Monthly Review Press, 1974.
2 See *ibid.* and also James Hinton, *The First Shop Stewards Movement*, Allen & Unwin, 1973.
3 An additional potential source of division within the workforce is that of skin colour. During our visits to the Riverside site we heard enough 'private talk' to convince us that a deal of racial prejudice existed there. But while we heard many stories of serious fights between blacks and whites during the early days of the site, we were aware of no such overt racial conflict between 1970 and 1973. In the Zap and Zap X packing areas black and white men performed the same jobs and worked alongside each other. Their shared, common situation dominated any prejudice or cultural difference that might serve as a serious source of division. At Riverside prejudice was a much less severe obstacle to united action than the plant and shift system.
4 C. Sofer, *Men in Mid-Career: A Study of British Managers and Technical Specialists*, Cambridge University Press, 1970, pp. 164–7.
5 It was for this very reason that Riverside became a 'show site', workers from elsewhere in the ChemCo empire being ferried down to see how the deal really would work to everybody's benefit. One of the northern convenors who came down chuckles when he remembers: 'Those lads down there. We told them it'd come to an end sooner than they thought. But then they've not got the experience with ChemCo that we've got.'
6 A deal of ink has recently been spent on the question of the class position of managers and the notion of the 'collective labourer' has played a prominent part in this. It is

pertinent to add here therefore that we are not hostile to the proposition that managers like those at ChemCo perform work which relates to the *co-operative* nature of the labour process, nor would we wish to deny that such managers are 'wage labour'. We would argue though that, devoid of qualification, the 'One Big Collective Labourer' idea is theoretically specious, and ideological (after all, if 'managers' and 'men' are all 'employees'—and if that's the main thing—everything suggests that they should 'all pull together', just as those who deny the relevance of class analysis have always said). What has to be emphasised is that managers, as Marx put it, are 'a *special kind* of wage labour'—'special' because in performing work which appears to be necessitated only by the co-operative nature of the labour process, they *also* perform the work of *control* which is necessitated by the capitalist character of that process and its inherent antagonisms. It is true that collective labour, in any society, requires 'organisation' but in the capitalist system this 'organisation' is no neutral process, as we hope to have made clear by our distinction between the social and technical aspects of the division of labour in Chapter 5.

7 We tackled Jimmy on this apparent conflict of views—asking him why it was that he could support an Act which intended to curb the use of union power while, in his own work situation, he advocated the greater use of that power. He then made it clear that he didn't think *all* strikes were a bad thing 'because some do have a good foundation, you know the workers have got reason to strike—but some I believe are Communist inspired and so if the Act can stop that sort of strike then I'm all in favour of it.' It becomes clear that it is not working-class action that is being rejected but working-class action as it is projected by the mass media. Not *militancy* but 'mindless militancy'. Jimmy and his mates are *told* that strikes are bad, that workers are led by Communists and they believe it. To an extent, that is. Certainly they believe it to the point of arguing it in a pub or of answering a public opinion pollster. But when it comes to daily activity at work they *know* that strikes can be justified. Maybe they won't go on strike but they won't decide *not* to strike because 'strikes are bad for the country' or because 'strikes are the result of agitators'. Their decision to strike, or not, will be geared to their own particular situation. It is this tension between generally propagated abstract ideas and practical necessity which explains why—even at a time when wider and wider sections of the workforce were involved in strike action—public opinion polls continued to find so many workers who considered strikes 'a bad thing'.

8 It is not without significance that when a worker wants to put in for regrading, it is often his manager who 'rehearses' him in what to say, who helps prepare him to argue his case to a panel—a management panel. There is, on purely practical grounds, no sense in raising false hopes, and the best way to avoid that is to explain the rules of the game. To explain how things have been fixed. For the rules *are* fixed; a Grade 5 job *is* a Grade 5 job; there's no room in this bureaucratic rationality for claiming that Grade 4 is too low a rate ('salary') for the job that you do. You could try to impress on national union officials that Grade 4—all Grade 4 jobs—should get, say £5 more, but the way things are fixed at ChemCo now this is a national, not a local matter. If you object that physical rating *should* count for more . . . well, this is why managers have to explain to workers that it can't, that this bureaucratic justice is not to be questioned. (For further details on grading and assessment, and for a systematic consideration of the control situation at Riverside generally, see

Theo Nichols and Peter Armstrong, *Workers Divided*, Fontana, 1976, Part I and especially Part II.)

8
The Workers' Struggle

IN A PIECE-RATE factory the workers are disciplined by the rate. In a time-rate factory, where men are paid by the hour or week at the same rate, no matter how much is produced, work discipline has to be established through organisation. A lot of the hard work eulogised by the northern foremen was done by miners who were paid by the piece; by the number of tubs of good coal that came from their part of the coal face. Employers have since found it in their interest to do away with piece-rate schemes (workers having used the rate to their advantage in the boom years), but this has left them with the problem of ensuring that the workers 'work productively' or, as the men themselves put it, 'sweat our cogs off'. One of the consequences of this has been the flood of 'consultants' into factories and the corresponding movement of managers and supervisors into residential and other courses on 'human relations' and 'man management'.

Under the NWA agreement at ChemCo the long established bonus schemes were replaced by a nationally agreed basic rate and shift allowance. The rate was a guaranteed one (i.e. it didn't rise and fall with the output of the plants) but it was also non-negotiable at the point of production. No longer could the men who packed bags bargain with the foremen over their bonus rates. The rate was fixed and it was linked to specific job grades. Yet if the rate was fixed, production was not. The period which followed the introduction of the Agreement saw an increasing pressure for production being placed upon fewer and fewer men (in the chemical industry generally productivity increased by 31 per cent between 1970 and 1974). At Riverside the manager of the Zap plant began setting the workers' output targets. The notice board in the workers' mess room was covered with figures indicating the 'records' achieved by particular shifts, and comparisons with the Company's other Zap plants elsewhere. Workers are taken off periodically to be given talks and be shown films in the Admin. Block about production costs, the problem of wastage, the needs of capital and so on. However the real pressure for production is applied on the plants themselves. There, day in night out, the organisation of work around costly machinery ensures that the men work.

The Zap plant pours out Zap at a fixed rate into a hopper which holds just sixty tons. On high rates the hopper is filled in an hour. Thus the system of production—in reality designed and programmed by management—appears to *automatically* put pressure on workers:

> 'Well actually you don't need a man to keep you working here because when you go out there to take over the work, you have *got* to work. If you didn't work then the foreman would be in there and the whole lot would be in there. But really a man works because he knows in his own heart that he has *got* to work, it is a case of *having* to do it. You have to work or else the packing shed would fall down around your ears, it is bound to. You have to work.'

You can work that bit faster to get a blow now and then but the foreman is still around, just in case, so he can be 'in there' if there is a hold-up in 'the system'. 'Sometimes', said one of the loaders, 'sometimes I think that they want blood. It's always another bloody record.' Someone else agreed:

> 'You never see our one. When things are going along all right he's inside drinking tea. But as soon as those bags stop falling on the lorry, he's out here shouting. Bawling, *"Do this. Do that."* '

We asked if some foremen pushed harder than others; if, for example, the blokes from the north were keener on the idea of hard work.

> 'As far as I'm concerned, no. They might be different in race but as far as I'm concerned they are all after the same thing—producing more tonnage than the other. They're all the same I think. They're all firm's men.'

To be a firm's man means to push the blokes for more production. For notwithstanding the participatory philosophy of the NWA and the technology, men do have to be pushed to hump bags. The truth of this is revealed in the fact that (despite the introduction of 'single line supervision') the packing areas have retained assistant foremen in the guise of 'co-ordinators': men not 'on the staff' but responsible for ensuring that their fellow workers go where they are supposed to go and work when they get there. To quote one of them,

'Ever since the early days we've had a problem of discipline on this plant. You see the average bloke just doesn't like being told what to do. And on this plant they work shifts and do heavy monotonous work as well.'

An important element in the NWA was the stress upon the devolution of decision-making, allied to notions of 'job enrichment' and a 'participatory' style of management. An implicit acceptance of the fact that 'the average bloke doesn't like being told what to do' and an attempt to let him 'direct himself'. In its practice the deal indicates the limits that the 'external' market and the internal structure of the Company place upon such an ideology. The workers in the Zap and Zap X plants, for example, had practised job rotation long before the deal was introduced—'eight hours loading and you'd be dead'. During the period that we were at Riverside these men attempted to modify the organisation of work even further. A few of the teams used the principle of rotation to work out a system which allows each man a long period of rest in the mess room.

'I mean this system that we have got down here now, I mean it is a system that we have only worked out ourselves. I mean management knows about it but they sort of turn a blind eye to it. I mean they don't "know" that we do three-quarters of an hour packing and three-quarters of an hour loading and then have three-quarters of an hour off. I mean it's just something that we have arranged ourselves. You know, perhaps we are meant to have three or four men out driving when we go into the other end of the shed but we cut that down to two men. We said, "two men there" and the other two men are in having a cup of tea. Well that is how it started see.'

So the men rotate the jobs to cut out work. Activities which in their view are unnecessary are left undone.

'When the NWA was about to come in—every day you come in you hear them talking about NWA. What NWA's going to be like; how hard you're going to work when NWA comes in and what job you're going to do. It gets you worried. Because they say you're going to be on NWA and there won't be any breaks—you're going to be allowed just one twenty minute tea break on a shift. It gets you worried and you think—"When NWA comes in, Christ I don't think I'm going to stick it." Then NWA comes in and it's nothing like what they said. It should be but, the rules that they laid down, they think it should be working that way—but we think different. We think their way is too hard. If we can work it our way we'll work it our way and let them think we're doing it their way. But our way's the way we're working it now, we make it easier for ourselves.'

They do it their way, which isn't the proper way. Jacko, for example, describes a situation:

'Where you've got spoiled product and clean product spilled on the floor. To do the job properly you should sweep it into piles and put it into the bins. I know that . . . but for some cussedness I won't do it. I sweep it all together.'

Jacko spoiling clean product, his mates practising their version of 'job rotation', regulating the size of their work teams and maximising the time they spend in the rest room—what these and other activities have in common is that they are entirely *covert*. They take place outside of established union–management relationships. The significance of this is that while in certain circumstances management is prepared to turn a blind eye to them, it may also—quite arbitrarily and with a monopoly of right—choose not to do so. If, for instance, blokes are caught 'sitting about' when there is spillage on the floor they face a bollocking. The co-ordinators find themselves in the middle of this.

'As I was saying, the average bloke doesn't like to be told what to do and I've had a couple of bollockings off Jack Steele because of this. On one occasion I thought all the lads were out working but they had in fact sneaked in around the back into the mess room. Jack Steele saw them in there and came straight to me. Mad he was.'

Shop floor activity at Riverside is rarely planned, in anything but a minimal sense. The blokes' 'counterplanning'[1] is often essentially negative; it is an 'anti-work' activity by way of which they kick back at the jobs they have to do, and those who boss them. Systematic skiving is intermingled with the occasional act of sabotage and the odd flare up with the foreman. Jacko again:

'I used to be a bit rebellious in the past. I just didn't like taking orders. Now I still don't like it but I get by most days. It suits me to do as I'm told. It saves me thinking. You get an off day when you're working hard and sweating—I just shout, "Fuck off!" He [the foreman] comes into the mess room and asks to me to go on a job and I tell him to fuck off.'

They do soft things like hoping on every day of their foreman's holiday that it will rain torrents. Crafty things like booking one day's holiday, months and months in advance, and taking it without reminding the foreman—all to turn the tables on him when he threatens to discipline them for not phoning in. At the root of their resistance, then, is a face-to-face, and personalised, conflict with the foreman. Only occasionally is this established within *collective* undertakings and arrangements that protect all the workers on the plant. But there is an exception to this on the Zap plant.

Under NWA each job at Riverside was graded and a man who was competent to perform that job did it, and received the appropriate rate. This system ran into difficulties with job rotation, which *in principle* is entirely at odds with the division of labour assumed in a graded structure. On the Zap and Zap X plants there are several distinct jobs, but for the most part the Zap packers are only involved in four of them—packing, sealing, loading and stacking. The grading panel decided therefore that competence in four jobs qualified a Zap packer for grade 4 and competence in yet more jobs (additional ones being driving, checkweighing and relief operator) earned the grade 5. The site management resolved the issue further in favour of the division, rather than rotation of labour by deciding that three 'grade 5s' per shift were sufficient for efficient working. On Zap X this directive was rigorously enforced but on the Zap plant the workers, by way of surreptitious haggling, pressure and black-mail, were able to make foremen push the numbers up. The shop steward was not involved in any of this. On one shift every worker made grade 5 before the plant manager discovered what was happening and issued (and received) a directive and a bollocking. Again, though, this was done entirely outside the ambit of union–management negotiations as oper-ated on the site and was limited to one of the plants. (The steward on the Zap X plant, for example, where identical work arrangements exist, didn't know about the 'agreement' which the Zap packers had established for themselves.) At Riverside, extra-union action, usually of a covert kind, is the rule. At the band-end and in the control rooms too.

The control room operators are in a situation that is, in many ways, different from the packers'. The organisation of work, the burden of responsibility for so much capital equipment and the impersonal control exercised by the very processes they monitor, combine as severe obstacles to the sort of 'anti-work' activity practised in the packing sheds. For example, in the packing sheds men miss shifts when they're 'fit for work'. 'It's an awful temptation on those two nights before the weekend. If you have those two off you're away from this place for five days. . . . Lovely.' The control room operators have similar temptations but they know that if they succumb their mates (whom they relieve) will end up doing their work for them—by working a doubler or, at best, being late getting home. Also while at work they know that if they leave the control room in a mess, or the plant a bit off line then the man who follows them will have to tidy up or spend an uncomfortable hour of hard work at the beginning of his shift. The relief system makes the control room operatives dependent upon each other and in doing so it shifts part of the 'problem' of labour discipline away from management and onto the backs of the workers themselves.

So the situations *are* different, but it's a matter of degree only. The 'technical imperatives' cannot prevent the operators having their games with the foreman. Anonymous notes are written in the log books, the foreman's boots are filled with water—'just to cool him down'—and any additional work is resisted.

'He's come over sometimes. He says: "Oh, we're having a scrap up. Operators will do the scrap," he says, sticking up a notice. I took it down and threw it away. He played hell about it, he come up and put another one up. Then I took that second one down and I took it down

his office and put it in front of his desk. I said: "You know what to do
with this." He said: "Look", he said, "I put that on your board" and
he said, "You're not to touch it." I says: "Colin", I says, "we're not
doing that." I said: "We're not qualified to do that." I said, "If you
want it done", I said, "put it up on *your* board and *you* do it." '

The monitoring, the 'responsibility'—all the pressures toward 'integration' and 'self-discipline'—cannot prevent control room operators
coming into conflict with management; and their conflicts contain all the
elements of antagonism that the packers experience:

'We had one manager here, like a real fairy he was I'm telling you.
"Twiggy" we called him. Laughed my head off I did. He would always
be down here [in the control room] altering the bloody running of the
plants. The flow of the compression—if it dropped he was altering the
bloody flow. Well anyway, Mike turned round to him this once and
said, "you bloody alter that again and I'll wrap it around your bloody
neck." Well he was right wasn't he? Mike was running the job. If he
wanted it changing he should have told him. Not fiddled about down
here.'

And sometimes angry words are not enough:

'Well, as I've told you, it's largely a matter of touch in this job and I
don't care what anyone says, if you've been on a plant for a few years
you get to know what's happening to it in a way that you can't get from
reading on the dials. Well anyway, we had a lot of trouble with this
plant [the Grinder] as you know, and this one occasion it had just
settled down and we had this new manager. A real slide-rule fella he
was. Well, he came in one morning and said, "*Do* this. *Do* that." And
I *knew* that if I did it, then that would be it. Well, we were all a bit fed
up with this particular manager so I said to myself: "If that's what you
want, that's what you'll have." And over she went—a couple of
hundred ton of shit on the floor.'

The sheer magnitude of Bill's cock-up—accomplished in a matter of
seconds—contrasts graphically with the amount of spillage a disgruntled

packer could manage in the same time. So does the possible magnitude of management's come-back, if he'd been found out.

There's a strange symmetry here however. The sabotage enacted by workers is in a sense equivalent to the 'psychology tricks' that managers play on them. For in this most modern of corporations, where a determined attempt is made to *process* everything, both management and workers find themselves covertly negotiating the reality of corporate production. Conflicts and antagonisms are contained beneath the surface by way of tacit understandings and unmentioned limits. ChemCo managers are careful to maintain this 'balance' and the wiser of them know that without it they could have a very hard time indeed. Edward Blunsen's experience is testament to this.

Blunsen had no respect for the men who ran the plants or for the 'rule of thumb' knowledge that they had gained as a result. He laughed about this in the Admin. Block, and relished Colin Brown's talk of social scientific proof that workers are like children. But Colin Brown was damn careful not to let 'his' workers hear him talk in this way; Blunsen, by contrast, went out of his way to. He told one man:

> 'If I was doing your job, even with your education—even if I hadn't been to university or a good school—I could see this [problem]. I don't know what's the matter with you. A child could do it.'

As you might expect, news of this got round in no time, to add to other reports that he'd called men 'thick'. By 1973, Blunsen's standard greeting to us had been: 'Do you know what the stupid idiots have done now?' But the 'idiots' acted their part. If he wanted to up-rate a plant another few tons, up they put it—and down. Plants got mysteriously 'gunged up'. Storage pits ran dry. Wasteful emissions occurred. Valves leaked expensively throughout the night and, come the morrow the log book told strange tales. Everybody had a job description, the log book was the Bible, but somehow 'the system' didn't work. Blunsen understood what was going on, but it did him no good. He was moved off the plant and when he went 'the idiots' knew that they were the ones who had got rid of him.

Resistance at Riverside is set in the context of an elaborate managerial strategy aimed at rationalising the system of production. It is a day-to-day affair which only rarely becomes organised on a collective basis, and it is rarer still for it to be captured by the trade union structure on the site.

Usually the struggle takes place *outside* the union; and most often it is based upon *individual* responses: a battle of wits in which management often turns a blind eye so long as the 'job gets out'. And in this there is no doubt that management was *forced* to turn a blind eye. They didn't like the way these workers practised the age old British art of 'getting by', and a strong ideological component of NWA was directed precisely against this activity. In an important way then this covert anti-work activity represents the *strength* of the workers; a strength which comes from the fact that it is they who are on the plants doing the work and running the jobs, and, up to a point, it serves them well—the Zap packers got their higher grades and the acid operators got rid of Blunsen. But equally when expressed in this form it can be seen as only a *muffled* challenge to capital. It sets limits to what a manager can do but it doesn't penetrate too deeply into the structure of corporate power. In fact, in terms of the 'formal system', it doesn't exist, and this often suits local management quite well. At Riverside, for example, the management exercised strong control over who applied for which jobs, and who got them in the end; who worked on which shift, when holidays could be taken, what was recorded on the personnel records in the Admin. Block. All of these things were important for the men who worked on the plants but they are only the details of a situation which is dominated by the systematic exploitation of all these men. 'Getting by' makes it easier but it doesn't solve it. And it doesn't even make it easier for everyone. For example, when Jacko tells the foreman to 'fuck off' someone else is told to do the work. It is for this reason that many of the blokes we talked to—even the most 'indisciplined'—felt the need for greater discipline in the factory. As it was, the only source of such discipline appeared to be the Company and its supervisory agents. And so men—like Jacko—talked endlessly about the need for foremen to be firmer and fairer.

This is the heart of the contradiction. Resistance established through the 'indiscipline' of anti-work activities is of limited effectiveness. To go further—and also to correct its own iniquities—it has to be organised and disciplined. Only in this way can the individual acts of resistance be co-ordinated and organised at the collective level. Without such organisation there is a real danger that men can turn (or be turned) against themselves and each other. If capital and capitalism is to be really challenged it has to face an *organised* working class.

By 1972, the workers were taking stock of a situation where they faced on the factory floor the strategies of the highly organised agents of capital. The NWA deal made clear the need for an organised response by the workers, for if one thing was clear it was that the deal was to have a lasting effect upon the structure of relationships in the factory. One of the men put it like this:

> 'The thing about this NWA is that it makes you forget a lot of things. It makes you forget your rights.'

Another man, Brian, who worked as a packer elaborated:

> 'When blokes leave they aren't replaced. I can see a day when there will only be ten men on a shift [instead of fifteen]. A lot of heads are going to roll down here eventually—in the near future too I wouldn't be surprised. Once the rates go down and ChemCo is fighting for orders.'

Up till 1973 the changes had not been particularly dramatic, but NWA had set the stage for the future. John, who worked in the sulphuric acid control room had seen his plant's capacity increased, he also knew that he had to be a bit careful.

> 'Under the NWA we've got a job description of the work, see. And if every bloke carried out his job description as he should do, he wouldn't have much spare time like. I mean I'm supposed to walk down the sulphur lines of the plant every hour or every two hours. Well we don't of course but if Rod [the foreman] wanted to get a bit funny about it like. . . . Or, you know, I might be gonna start bloody playing up about too much bloody work and that. He could quite easily find me a lot more to bloody do. Say: "Well that's your job and you've got to do it." And I wouldn't have a leg to stand on.'

NWA *had* affected the balance and in its introduction, and support, of the union on the site it also posed a real obstacle to any attempt that workers might make to upset it again. If a shop floor organisation of workers was to be formed at Riverside it would have to be created within the context of established union–management relations on the site. The policy of management on the site was to incorporate the shop stewards within the web of the office. So effective had it been in this that most of the workers had come to write off 'the union' as a source of organised strength within the factory. Generally they preferred to go their own way. But they learnt that there were contradictions within this managerial strategy itself. These could be exposed and used to advantage. One of the packers explained to us:

'These foremen, believe it or not, they don't like the union being boss, see. It looks bad for them if it gets higher up. So if I find them nasty— they can be quite nasty some of them—I just threaten them with the union. It pays to go to the union.'

Workers in the Zap plant have had similar experiences. In a dispute over manning levels, for instance, they walked off the job to find the shop steward. The foreman saw them:

'He wanted to know where we were going so I told him. But when I told him he hit the ceiling. He called me in the office. In the end he agreed to increase manning. After a lot of shouting, but that was that. He didn't want "the union" involved see.'

They learned that they could *use the union* as a threat against the foremen. The operators too were to find that there were circumstances in which they could use the bureaucratic apparatus as an adjunct to their activities on the plants.

After the introduction of NWA, management introduced, 'without consultation', a new job of 'Mobile Operator' at the top of the grade structure. None of the operators had really expected to be consulted by management over this new job, but what they had expected was that they should have some control over how the new operators were to be selected.

'They said they were going to introduce this Mobile Operator's job to relieve all plants, relieve the supervisors and do any other tasks he's given. It was to get the top grade—as usual like, he's paid more for doing less—but we didn't object to that: so long as everyone's got a chance to go through the job.'

But NWA, for all its talk of 'participation', marked a break with any idea of 'progression' through the jobs. The grade system—except in very rare circumstances—was not intended as a *promotional* system. And the Mobile Operator issue made this very clear. *Management* decided that no one on the plants was capable of filling the job and *management* decided to advertise in the local newspaper and demand that applicants had O-level qualifications. All this was a *management decision.* But when the new qualified recruits arrived on the plant the operators found that *they* were the ones who were expected to acquaint these 'superworkers' with the plant—in effect to train them to be their superiors. The operators deeply resented this: and they decided to systematically use the job descriptions *against* ChemCo.

> 'Well some of us were already doing the mobile job. I mean, they come up to me and say: "Right, we're short over sulphuric. Will you go over there?" Or on raw materials, "Will you go over there?" But since they've had these Mobile Operators, see, now I mean if they ask me to go over sulphuric, I say, "No, I'm not a Mobile Operator." Well that's what it says. It's true, isn't it?'

And they turned to the union. For once they pressed their stewards who met and put the issue 'in procedure'. After eight months, and two stages of this procedure, the Mobile Operator's job was reviewed.

> 'ChemCo's senior management came down with our national official *and they were on our side. They* said what *we* said was fair. . . .'

They'd 'called the union in' and they'd used it against management. They'd been able to exercise some control over management but the procedure couldn't get rid of the Mobile Operator's job altogether; nor could it compel management to recruit from the men already on the plants. 'The union' had narrowed it down to 'ChemCo employees' which was seen as a help but didn't really rescue them from the nagging feeling that in the long term the imported Mobile Operators would be running (and supervising) the plants. Their 'success' revealed the limitations of their action, but it served to make many of them think in a much more positive way about their situation and what they could hope to achieve.

There were other straws in the wind as well. One of the men who was 'brought in from outside' for the Mobile Operator's job, and the promise of a rosy future at ChemCo, found the experience 'an eye opener'. Rob has six O-levels and he'd spent a year in the sixth form before leaving to take up a job as a lab. assistant in a firm in Provincial. He hadn't liked that much—while he was there he decided to study for his ONC at the local Tech. He was at a bit of a loose end when he read the ChemCo advertisement and he thought it would make a change. He was started on Edward Blunsen's plant. On his first day Rob recalls how Alan, the new shift manager, met him.

' "I feel sorry for you", he said. "I feel sorry for you going over there. I don't know how you are going to get on with that lot." I had already had Blunsen telling him that the steward was the man to watch so I thought it was going to be interesting. I came on the plant and everybody told me that Blunsen was a bastard. "Well", I thought, "it's unanimous anyway. You can say that for them. But I will wait and make up my own mind." '

He worked on the section and decided that the blokes were right. He decided not to be an informer and not to think of getting ahead at ChemCo. He became deputy-steward. Alan was amazed—'There's a man who is going out of his way to make trouble for himself.'

Before these incidents the workers at Riverside had usually replied to our questions about 'organisation' with the dismissive 'you can't do anything'. But the months 'in procedure' led them to talk about and examine their strengths. One of them spoke for them all when he said: 'We've always got the last card because we're *running* the jobs.' But they had also come to know that this strength could slip away unless it was built on. NWA, the cuts in manning, the introduction of new jobs like the Mobile Operator, all this made the men who worked the plants think about the way things were going. It changed some of them. It led them to assess trade unionism and its potentials in a way that was quite at odds with the established practices at Riverside.

'The union men are fighting for their rights, for the right thing, I suppose. But they're always fighting when it's too late. You know they should look into a case before it goes too far. When they find it out its too much and they know they can't do anything. Well I think the union should try and get *everything* under control. You know, control it.'

In making such assessments it was clear that they had to deal not only with management but also—and perhaps most importantly—with the sort of trade unionism that had developed on the ChemCo site. During 1973 conflicts *within the union* were a central feature of life on the plants and, in the arguments that took place over what trade unionism *should* be about, much more was involved than the Company's strategy of incorporation. In an important way the arguments that took place on the site between these undisciplined 'cowboys' and the 'union men' reflected the presence of quite different traditions within the British working class. They made clear the crucial *ideological* obstacles that stand between the spontaneous 'anti-work' activities that we have described as being a central part of the struggle on the plants, and the organised strength of 'official' trade unionism.

Note

1 For a discussion of this form of extra-union activity in an auto plant in the USA see Bill Watson, 'Counterplanning on the Factory Floor', *Radical America*, vol. 5, no. 3, May/June 1971.

9
The Politics of Representation

ONE OF THE main forces that the working class has created for itself over the last hundred years or so has been its organisation on the factory floor; around the job, at the productive centre of capitalism. Struggles within factories have provided one of the central dynamics of trade union organisation and an important bolster to some of the crucial elements of working-class consciousness. This has not, however, been a simple, straightforward process. While it is true that one of the strengths of the British working class lies in the depths of its trade union or factory consciousness, this consciousness has many sides to it and has, historically, been channelled into various, different, political forms. Social democracy—as expressed through the Labour Party and the trade union organisations —has been the dominant form. The continuance of this dominance, though, is ultimately dependent upon its ability to relate meaningfully to the significant experiences of working-class men and women. Ideologies which become little more than abstract formulations are lost in the grind of history. Those that endure do so because their roots go deep into everyday life; because they become a part of people's lives. In the past syndicalism and revolutionary communism have challenged social democracy and remnants of these traditions are still alive within parts of the working class.

At Riverside—a place where there were 'no militants'—workers had some very clear ideas about what trade unionism needed to be like if it was to be 'theirs' in anything other than a nominal sense. For them the trade union organisation which dominated the Riverside site was of limited use and we have seen that in their criticism of it they were particularly scathing of shop stewards who were 'out for themselves'. Yet there were two shop stewards who were seen to be a bit different from this. Both of them were elected prior to the NWA deal; both had been active unionists before coming to Riverside and both were committed to the idea of building a strong union organisation on the site. They strongly disapprove of the stewards who 'deputise' for foremen—'you have to be on one side or the other'—and they are both critical of the more obvious ways in which ChemCo managers use the 'glad hand approach' as a method of control. Both these men (we have called them Alfie Grey and Greg Andrews) believe that ChemCo has to be opposed by the organisation of the workers, they both talk about the need for a strong and independent trade union movement and they both call themselves socialists. But these men disagree quite strongly on what all this means; they disagree about the union and the source of its strength and they have quite different understandings of their fellow workers and their class. While Alf is 54 and Greg 30 their differences aren't simply to do with their age. For both in the way they think and in the way that they conduct themselves as shop stewards in the factory these men can be seen to personify quite different interpretations of working-class experience. To an extent these can be related to different political traditions within the working class. And for this reason we think it's worth looking closely at these men.

Alfie Grey is the control room operator on the Zap plant, and as shop steward he is elected to represent all the men who work on all four shifts on the plant; around sixty of them, mostly loaders. Alfie has been elected unopposed as shop steward on each occasion he has stood, but the men who elect him were far from happy with the way he represented them 'in the office'. The loaders were particularly dissatisfied. They pointed to the fact that as a control room operator he had no direct knowledge of the problems they experienced around the bagging lines. They claimed too that he wasn't concerned to find out about these problems; that he was very reluctant to take up the issues they felt strongly about and that when he did he was unlikely to press them very hard. To put it bluntly, they didn't think that he represented their interests very well.

'If something's gone wrong in the packing shed, when we complain about it nothing ain't done about it. And he will say: "Oh, right, I will sort it out." And days pass, weeks pass, you don't hear nothing and when you see him: "Oh, I'm still working on it." And he don't. He just, you know, he just seem to think that we only go and face the manager with a big thing. 'Cos if we happened to say we want a meeting with the plant manager to discuss certain things, and we want him there to represent us, he says, "Yeah, yeah, yeah, yeah, yeah, that's right, that's right." Then afterwards you don't hear nothing more. And that's it. And that's why I blame him.'

The most cynical brand him with the rest: a man out for himself—for the white coat. But most of them wouldn't agree with this. They know Alfie is different. Even those men who blame him severely will tell you that they like him; that he's a good bloke; that they enjoy talking to him when they get the chance. As Steve puts it:

'If he could put into practice what he thinks about he'd be a great bloke. All the things he says are dead right but he's too friendly with management. There's nothing wrong with being friendly but Alf just can't put it to them, he can't lay it on the line.

You get old Alf by himself, you'd think he was a really strong unionist. Well, I think he is a strong unionist in that way but he just won't put it across to management, he won't stand up to them. We were pushing for extra payments for top rates some time ago [pre NWA] and he just wouldn't take it up. He said, "I can't do it. Look at the records. Look at the time keeping records of everybody down here." You know, he shouldn't say that. If we want it he should go up and try and get it but he won't.'

He can't 'put it to them' because he's too nice, too decent, too polite, too vulnerable, too old. But there is more to it even than this. He did 'put it to them' on one occasion in 1972. Steve was accused of not performing his job and in evidence the foreman used the secret checks that he had carried out with another operator. Alf was furious. He told the foreman:

'We're not having that. We're not having one member spying on another member. If you take this further I will have that man disciplined by the branch. All right so you think the lad isn't doing the job. Well that's for you to sort out. You've no right to drag one of my members into it.'

The foreman dropped the disciplinary action he had planned and apologised to Alf.

But this case was a rarity. Normally Alf doesn't take up strongly the issues that the blokes bring to him. Dave, for example, was disciplined for driving a fork lift truck away from the authorised roadways. 'It's common practice. Everyone does it. The fucking foreman *tells* you to do it and then they have the cheek to discipline you because the manager is on the plant.' Alf, however, was adamant: 'You shouldn't be doing it. The union doesn't condone it and if you get caught you've only yourself to blame.' Dave insisted that he wanted to contest the case. Alf agreed to accompany him into the office but once there he refused to argue for him. Dave's never forgotten it: ' "Thank you very much, Mr Steele", he said, "you have been very lenient." I could have smacked him around the earhole. That's what *my shop steward* said.'

Alf was born in 1919. He was brought up in a large docker's family through the depression. He tells you how he won a school scholarship and had a certificate from the London Chamber of Commerce but how he couldn't stay on at school. With a half-smile on his face, adjusting the dials in his control room he says, 'I'm older than you and I've known poverty. I've been hungry and ate crusts of bread. I've seen slump and I've seen boom. I just had to go to work. First thing I knew I was on a banana boat.'

Alf is a committed trade unionist. He believes in the TGWU and he gives it his *loyal* support. When we heard that some of the stewards on the northern plants were thinking of forming a national shop stewards' combine committee he told us, 'I don't believe in "unofficial organisations". It's got to be done through the union. The lead has to come from the national office in something like this I think.' He is vice-chairman of the Branch, one of the very few regular attenders and the man most likely to move motions in solidarity with other workers ('I was glad to see that our branch could donate £10 to the Fine Tubes strike fund. The Ford organisation could only manage a guinea I believe'). He is proud to call himself a socialist and a supporter of the Labour Party. He tells you how at a large conference which ChemCo called for 'all grades' he listened to one of the Directors speaking about the size of ChemCo and of its total autonomy.

> 'I walked right up to the front of the hall—there were several hundred people there—and I said that while he was partly right in what he said there was something that could affect ChemCo. That the Labour Government could take it over and nationalise it. He had to agree.'

After years as a seaman right through the war Alfie had returned to Provincial to work on the dock. 'You had to be a union activist there.' He was very active during the big strike that took place on the dock in the late 1950s. 'We lasted out for over a month. It was the most amazing solidarity I've ever seen. We stayed out against everybody.' Yet this solidarity, linked with the poverty of his youth, serves, in Alf's case, as the basis for a withering moral criticism which he directs at the lads on the Zap plant at Riverside. It is his *moral* antagonism, more than anything else, which prevents Alfie from acting as the militant spokesman for the packers.

'That's the trouble down here, the blokes just don't seem to care. Well I've seen hard times, I've been involved in the Labour movement, my father was in the Labour movement, my father carried a banner for the T & G. But the younger element just haven't got this tradition. They just don't care. They just grab. *Grab. Grab. Grab.* They're all going in for colour tellies now. Can you understand them? Colour tellies and then they'll want overtime to pay the instalments. It's beyond me. I think it will take another slump to make them care. The only people on here who have experienced that sort of times are some of the foremen. Now a lad like Alan, now Alan is a good socialist.'

In an important sense, then, Alf cannot strongly represent the lads on the packing lines. He has little contact with them, he cannot understand what they're after and he is critical of their attitudes. In a real sense he has washed his hands of them. His commitment is to the union and not to them. Like the northern foremen he is, to an important extent, locked into the past the time of *real* poverty, *real* hunger, *real* slump. A past which 'the mighty T & G' represents in the present. This came out clearly on the issue of overtime. Alf is opposed to overtime working. He thinks that his members don't really need the extra money, and that for some workers to be demanding extra hours at a time when many others are unemployed is indefensible. So he refused to argue for overtime, and he was appalled when his members demanded that strikers from a Provincial factory who were working for contractors be banned from the site.

'All they are concerned about is this bloody overtime. They don't think about anyone else. About where these blokes are going to get their Christmas dinners for their families from. It's just greed.'

Whatever the rights and wrongs of this particular issue it makes clear the basis and depth of Alfie's *moral* condemnation of his members. And it contrasts sharply with Greg's approach.

Greg was married with three small children when he'd come, like everybody else did then, to chase the overtime and bonus money at Riverside. He had previously worked on the buses where he had become active in the union.

'When I came here first I asked one of the blokes who to see to join the union. No one knew so I walked around a bit until I found somebody in the Zap plant. A chap called Davidson was the branch secretary then, but he was doing the foreman's job "unofficially" at the same time. The trade union was really in name only. It's getting a bit better now I think.'

Greg's father had been active in the Labour party and Greg joined at 16, trying to form a group of Young Socialists in his ward.

'A couple of Councillors helped us start it but then after about a year when we had started to get something going they wanted the right of veto. That was the start of a lot of conflict and I left the Labour Party a couple of years later. I'm not a member now. In fact if I was going to belong to a party I would join the Communist Party. It's the only one that speaks for my class of person.'

Greg was the one thorn in the flesh of the management on the fertiliser section. As an operator on the acid plants he represented the control room operators and the men who worked in the raw material store. He had been the man, above all others, who had contested the issue of the Mobile Operator; who had argued and argued over the grading of the sulphuric operator's job. To management he was 'our Communist', and they made no secret of the fact that they'd be glad to be rid of him.

They had tried—unsuccessfully—to get him voted off as shop steward. A foreman who had been moved on to Greg's section told us that he'd been given firm instructions to build up a dossier on Greg—'something that we can really throw at him when the time comes'. In 1970—in the middle of the NWA negotiations—a motion of no confidence, typed on the office typewriter and signed by the section's arch anti-Communist, was passed around the plants. No one else signed it. Then a new recruit to the section suddenly stood for shop steward. He got one vote.

All this is further evidence of the extraordinary lengths to which ChemCo management went in order to bring 'the union' under their effective control. But in this case it didn't work. And it didn't work because the men on the plants recognised Greg for what he was:

'Well I think he's pretty good myself. I think that he's a good chap. He gets things done as far as I'm concerned. I can simply accept him by what he does. I'm not nearly as left-wing as he is but I can see that he's doing the right things in here.'

All but one agreed: 'I just think he sticks up for the rights that he's fought for, and that's it.' This is it.

Greg isn't even an active trade unionist. He rarely attends branch meetings, and he doesn't give a lot of time to thinking about how to develop a strategy to embrace all workers on the Riverside site. Occasionally he reads the *Morning Star* or the *Soviet Weekly* but he doesn't go to political meetings and he has never joined the Communist Party or, since his youth, any other Left political group. All that he has done is to stick out *openly* for the workers on his section. It was for doing this that he became branded an 'agitator' and a 'Communist', so revealing the shallowness of management's ideology of 'participation'. His members stick with him and give him more support than any other steward on the site receives —because he is *their* steward, and because he represents *their* interests. The difference between Greg and Alfie is to be clearly seen on the question of overtime. Both of them disagree with it 'in principle' but Greg is much more inclined to be 'realistic'.

'I suppose as a trade unionist you should say when there's unemployment there should be no overtime. But you've got to look at it realistically. The average bloke down here, he's got, not a bad wage—let's be fair—but it's not a *good wage*. But if a married man with three or four children is taking home—let's say £30 a week [this was in 1971]—you can live on it, but it's not the kind of wage you're really going to enjoy yourself on. So you get used to working a certain amount of overtime.'

With a fixed rate, overtime (i.e. working longer hours) is the only way that blokes can affect the level of their wages. And Greg knows that the Company use it to suit themselves.

'The firm say overtime is worked "when it is justified". But on the other hand it's *always* justified through five months of the summer time. . . . Those who don't want it then are pressured all the time to work. But in the winter time. . . .'

Although he's basically opposed to overtime working he recognises the reality; that for his members overtime is an issue—'this is one of the few things they get active about because it affects them *personally*'. And he argues that the shop stewards should work out a site policy on overtime:

'See, they want us to work in the summer. That's the very time of year that we don't want to work. That's when we want to be out with the wife and kids. We'd put up with that but then they come back and say we can't work in the winter which is when *we* want to work. . . . We'll get them in June, July or August. They'll be crying out for us to work lieu days then—and we'll say "No".'

Such a tactic—were it to be adopted—clearly offers a bridge between the day-to-day interests of the men who work on the various plants and the longer term need of uniting those interests against the Company. The importance of the tactic comes from its recognition of both the strengths and the weaknesses of the day-to-day activity on the site. Any strengths that the workers revealed at Riverside took the form of activity which lay, in important respects, outside the established union–management relationship. Alfie Grey, for reasons which weren't to do with self-interest but rather with his strong commitment to an idea of a working-class morality, found it much easier to sympathise with this established relationship than with the covert activities of his members. In fact Alfie found himself well and truly caught. Morally preoccupied he was also politically ineffective, the 'big' things, about which he cared, having already been fixed nationally between the Company and the union. What is at least as important though—for as Greg saw, overtime *was* a big issue to his workers—is that corporate capitalism with its emphasis upon fairness and reason, upon the need for rules and consultation rather than confrontation, has colonised the rhetoric of a particularly British brand of socialism. To men like Alfie it can appear extremely persuasive. And it can lead them to lose faith in their fellow workers.

Alfie's moral condemnation of the 'greed' of his work-mates is so strong that he cannot make that step toward them that is necessary for him to understand them and then perhaps help to change them and their situation. When he looks around the site what he is overwhelmed by is waste and extravagance. We talked to him once about nationalisation, and the possibility that ChemCo might become a public corporation. We asked him what he felt the problems were likely to be.

'The problem—and make no mistake about it—will be with the labour. If we were to run this as a nationalised organisation the first thing we'd need to look at would be the waste that goes on every day on the factory floor. Men get a pair of gloves; they get dirty and they *throw them away.* They don't think about washing them; they just discard them. That's a little example but it describes what's true generally here. No one really cares.'

Now in an important respect he is correct here. In spite of NWA and the psychology tricks and the ideological sessions no one does care very much at Riverside. And this lack of concern about work and what goes on there—this antagonism toward the work process and the product— seems to be a feature of a growing section of the British working class. So much so that firms like ChemCo devise elaborate schemes to 'motivate' their workers, and the Labour Government has set up a 'Work Study Unit' to enquire into possible solutions. The problem which Alfie Grey faces on his section; the dilemmas that he finds himself in; these are shared—in differing degrees—by the captains of modern industry and by those in positions of leadership in the British Labour movement. The 'problem' is to do with the working class that has been produced since the last war.

The post-war period with the long years of expansion, comparatively low rates of unemployment and the establishment of a Welfare State stands out as a distinctive (perhaps unique) phase in the development of capitalism. Thirty years and much else divided the 1960s from the 1930s; and the 1970s were to be different again. Workers born just after the war, turned (despite ten years of schooling) on to the 'unskilled' labour market, found that they could earn 'good money' working in the mass manu- facturing sector of British industry. During the 1960s employment in this sector became increasingly concentrated around a hundred or so gigantic corporations. Almost all of these corporations had learned to recognise trade unionism, learned too that 'high wages' (passed on in high prices) could mean good business and that the workers needed to be looked upon as 'an investment'. A good deal you might think; certainly it looked a much better one than had been handed out before the war when the deal was the means test. But workers, like these at Riverside, stayed off work, moved from job to job, did bad work. In a situation of full employment where 'good money' was offered in exchange for hours of dull, repetitive slog, in a society dominated by 'consumerism', it made increasingly less sense to talk of a work ethic. The slogan 'If a job's worth doing it's worth doing well' came out of a *particular* class experience. It has little meaning on the band end at Riverside to men who live in a world where selling (yourself or anything else) is the ultimate value.

A central feature of the ideology that has come to dominate 'official trade unionism' during this century has been the notion of obtaining a fair deal over work. The union agreement is one which sets wage rates, arrives at recognised disputes procedures and modifies the unilateral use of power by the bosses. But above all in the period of *established* trade unionism (and of an established Labour Party) fairness means winning or defending a percentage on the given wage, that the union should be 'listened to' to a greater extent, that 'the worst employers should be brought up to the standard of the best'. Even seemingly radical demands, like calls for worker representatives on company boards, are put forward within the ambit of class exploitation and capital's division of labour. To be a shop steward— to be sandwiched between 'the union' and the established order within which it works, and the men, and their experience of that established order—is often to be caught between potentially different conceptions of what is 'fair'.

The steward is elected to handle the grievances of the workers on a particular section, to be involved in negotiations often conducted in offices far away from the factory floor in face-to-face contact with the manager. This move into the office is not one that should be taken lightly. The war of words can be a tricky one which needs preparing for, and if any threats are to be made you have to be sure of your support. The office is 'another world' and all too often shop stewards find themselves caught in the nether world between the direct experiences of their members and the terms which dominate the discussions in the office. Some—as we have seen at Riverside—use, and are used by, the position. Those who take the job seriously find it a very difficult one to cope with. And the biggest problem often relates to representing the day-to-day problems and grievances of the workers. No steward in his right mind will take up every issue and complaint that is brought to him. He will need to check it out, know the people involved, anticipate management's arguments and so on. Then he will have to decide on the basis of his experience how hard to push. This process therefore involves issues of tactics and of ideology: questions to do with whether the case can be won, the level of support on the section, the implication for other cases etc.; further questions about whether or not it is a real 'trade union issue', whether it is *right* to make such demands. Tactics and ideology are bound closely together and for this reason there can be no such thing as 'pure and simple trade unionism' or pure and simple *economic* demands. All forms of trade union activity involve ideological elements—particular ways of understanding social and political action.

For Alf trade unionism involves the demand for a decent wage and the obligation of a fair day's work in return. It involves a union hierarchy which you respect because the officials represent *you*: because it is they who personify your strength, an organised strength that links the past with the present, the strength of 'the mighty T & G'. Alf is a trade union loyalist and faced by members who shared no such loyalty and who expected 'the union' to commit itself to each and every one of their grievances Alf washed his hands of them. For him they are 'bad trade unionists' and he can never see them changing.

Greg contrasts with Alfie most clearly here. He is no T & G loyalist and he is very sceptical of the integrity of the union officials that he has met. He talks a lot about 'the rank and file'; about the need for them to be *really* involved in the union because they really should be what the union is about. For Greg (and for the others who hold this 'rank and filist' view) trade unionism is seen to be much less rigid and formalised. The need for leadership is accepted—'someone has to be a bit out in front, putting the arguments'—but trade unionism is linked much more deeply with the day-to-day activities of the workers in the factories and what is stressed is not so much the strength gained from the bureaucratic use of 'constitutional action' but rather the autonomous collective action of the members themselves. It is this action which is seen as the basic means of building a shop floor organisation and developing a collective awareness amongst the rank and file. The workers are not seen as a 'membership' who may be good or bad unionists but rather as people who can change and be changed by their own collective agency.

Greg—although without any real experience of industrial struggles or support from activists at Riverside and Provincial generally—attempted to operate in such a fashion on his section. Bothered by the overtime issue, he also saw it as something that had to be tackled and built on. But in this he came up against one of the major problems of rank and filism. The immediate demands that come out of working on a particular job on a particular section are often demands that are peculiar to that job or section. Important as it is, organisation built around these demands is limited by its exclusiveness. There are many sides to this issue but at Riverside the issue of overtime (in effect control over pay) made it clear that a problem faced on one section could not be tackled adequately by organisation on that section alone. The problem with Greg's strategy of using the overtime issue against the Company was that (given the inter-relationship of production) the strategy had to be a site-wide one. To refuse overtime (cut production) on one plant would cut overtime (and even lay off workers) on another plant. Without co-ordination, antagonism and not unity would be the likely consequence.

It was for these reasons that Greg and Alf argued about the union and what was involved in building a strong organisation on the site. And in these arguments Alf frequently talked of the 'apathy of the members'; he would point to the fact that the union constitution made ample and adequate provision for the democratic involvement of the membership through the branch and the other elected lay committees, but that the workers just weren't interested in such involvement.

'They just aren't interested in the union. I just can't understand it. They seem to want everything on a plate. They moan but they don't seem to want to influence what's happening in a constructive way. They're just apathetic. That's about it, I think. They don't care about the union and they don't care about anything else.'

Activists have raised similar criticisms with the same sense of frustration throughout this century.[1] And there is no doubt that this view of the working class as an 'apathetic mass' is still prevalent today. This however needs to be recognised as a strongly ideological view[2] which should neither be taken at face value nor totally ignored. The workers at Riverside, for example, gave a very strong impression of being a docile 'apathetic mass'. But when we tackled the blokes on Alfie's section with this charge—asking them why they didn't try to alter things if they disliked them so much and why they didn't oppose Alfie as shop steward—our conversations, though a bit difficult to unravel, revealed something a deal more complex than this stereotype of 'the apathetic worker'.

For the members, the rank and file on the Zap plant, Alf was 'the union man'; a man who they had respect for because he so clearly stood for something, but who was of little use to them, for the things they wanted sorting out. Commonly their reaction was to 'let him get on with it' and dig ever more deeply into the subterranean world of getting by. Occasionally though, they'd decide to give Alf's unionism a try. On one such occasion some of them decided that they would go to the next branch meeting, to find out what was going on and to try and get some of the issues that bothered them sorted out. They weren't impressed. They came back on the plant with a report of a badly organised meeting where there was 'all mouth but no one saying anything. It was all talk.' (Greg, incidentally, never attended the branch meetings. . . .) They have thought, too, about deposing Alf. They go through lists of names working out who could do the job. When we talked to them they had concluded that no one could do it properly:

'We've talked about it. We talked about it a lot at one time. You know, about who we could get to do the job. But nobody wants to know it. There are one or two who could maybe do it all right but they've all got lots of kids, families you know. And to do that job properly takes a hell of a lot of time. The one or two who do want to do it, we don't want. Because they're either crazy like Steve or, you know, we think they'd be more trouble than anything else.'

Steve agrees. In some ways he'd really like to have a go but he's afraid to —'I'd just be too temperamental.' And other blokes dwell on their limitations as well.

'I've often pictured myself in a union job. I just know I'd end up being led by the management. I couldn't be hard . . . and if you're not hard you end up being led by the management.'

Either way management is seen as a big problem.

'If we did get someone to take over Alfie's job and he tries to sort the job out right—to do it right like it should be done—then the manager will say, "Well we'll have to move him on; put him on another section, or else make him up [to foreman]." '

What these men saw very clearly was that the job of being a shop steward was a very tricky one. Few of them could see themselves laying down the line when they were over in the Admin. Block by themselves and up against all the spoof and the word games. They knew that most of the stewards on the site had succumbed without much of a struggle. What they wanted was a shop steward who was hard, who would put their case straight to management, who would state their views clearly at the branch and protect their interests at meetings in the factory. They would support such a man. But men with this experience and dedication are pretty thin on the ground—particularly in the Provincial area, and certainly no one easily fits the bill on the Zap plant. To many workers the odds against getting a good steward—one who will fight and stay—seems so great that it doesn't even seem worth a try. For these men's 'apathy' is rooted in their experience just as much as Alf's loyalty is rooted in his. And what they say is this:

'If you had the right representative it would be really fine. But I have never seen a right good representative. I never did.'

Notes

1 In 1920 Carter Goodrich found that 'the average British workman' is often said to be 'interested in "mere wages"'. He cares nothing about control; he doesn't want to run things.' Goodrich is quick to point out that this is not 'merely an employer's view of working class psychology. I heard it from an impatient leader of shop stewards who said that working men were "not interested beyond wages and hours" and that therefore he had no intention of waiting for the majority.' Thirty years later in the USA, Sidney Peck, after discussions with many shop stewards, concluded that 'although he speaks as the leader of the workers, the steward is appalled by the unappreciative, unconcerned and disinterested response of the rank and file to his leadership tasks. . . . The most widespread explanation of worker apathy is linked to the image of complacent, self-satisfied, rank and filers.' (See C. L. Goodrich, *The Frontier of Control*, Bell, 1920, pp. 21–2; reprinted by Pluto Press, 1975. Sidney Peck, *The Rank and File Leader*, New Haven, College and University Press, 1962.)
2 As Raymond Williams has said: 'there are in fact no masses, but only ways of seeing people as masses'. See his 'Culture is Ordinary' in N. Mackenzie (ed.), *Conviction*, McGibbon & Kee, 1958.

10
Trade Unionism, Corporate Capitalism and the Working Class

IN TRYING TO draw together some of the things in the past three chapters it is well to begin by remembering two important facts. 'ChemCo' is not a small-time, one-off, firm: it is a giant multinational chemical producer and one of the largest companies producing in Britain. Its strategies are the strategies of large-scale, progressive, corporate capital. The other fact has to do with the location of the Riverside site. It is situated miles away from the nearest urban centre and has recruited a green labour force widely dispersed across an area in which there is no militant trade union tradition. It is hard to think that these factors weren't important ones in determining ChemCo to purchase its 1,000-acre Riverside site; harder still when you consider that Riverside is but one of several new chemical complexes that have been located in such situations. Riverside was—and is—a part of ChemCo's international strategy and with the advent of NWA it became very evident indeed that trade unionism was a part of that strategy also.

At Riverside the men we talked to were quite glad to join the union and they were not opposed to NWA. The union, they felt, gave them some sort of protection. They knew that when they were sick they'd get sickness benefits; that if they had an accident the union would help them with its legal department; they knew too that firms—even 'good firms' like ChemCo—need pushing over wages and that the union's national negotiators would push for increased pay. They got all their benefits and they were thankful for them. The NWA deal and subsequent negotiations gave them 'a pretty good basic rate' and it gave them a degree of security. All these things are very important for men who—like Michael Kennedy—have never had 'a permanent job', and they become increasingly important as the chances of getting such a job elsewhere become less and less likely. So they would say that they were 'lucky at ChemCo'. But often they would wonder whether they'd been 'good lucky' or 'bad lucky', and 'the union' became a central focus of this ambivalence. Crucially these men experienced the union as a *service organisation*: a deductor of taxes and a provider of facilities. Something important. Something to fall back on. But not *their* union. In no sense did they feel that their membership of the TGWU made them a part of something—in no way did they see themselves being involved in a union *movement*. And this absence, this sense that unionism ought to be something more than it was, was fundamental to their frustration with 'the union'.

These feelings of frustration extend beyond the union; they are felt about politics and about most of the established ways of doing things in our society. And this isn't surprising. The corporate strategy practised by ChemCo fits into the increasingly corporate practice of the State. Since the war innumerable areas of life once brought under the (limited) control of an elected committee are now the domain of the highly paid official. The field of 'industrial relations' is but one example of a general trend; but the State has been particularly active in this area. In 1964 one of the first decisions of a marginally elected Labour Government was to set up a Royal Commission to investigate the activities of trade unions. Its final report made it clear that of all the things that needed changing one thing stood out above all else and that was the relative autonomy exercised within 'the formal system' by shop floor elected workers' committees. In its consideration of unofficial strikes and the pattern of union–management agreements it concluded firmly that '*the root of the evil* (our emphasis) is our present method of collective bargaining and especially our method of workshop bargaining'.[1] This bargaining—organised between shop steward committees and plant managers—had to be integrated into an established national system. To this end the Commission considered the check-off a 'useful arrangement' and advised that 'trade unions who do not collect subscriptions in this way might usefully consider doing so; and that employers should sympathetically consider requests . . . for the facility'.[2] The solution lay in extending the area of collective bargaining and establishing it within a system of formally established rules and regulations. This idea of 'facilitating' trade unionism at every level, combined with the establishment of strong *centralised* bargaining structures was to become the dominant tendency. In the Left's celebration of the defeat of *In Place of Strife* and the Tory Government's *Industrial Relations Act* this fact has often been overlooked. What came out of the 1960s was not a 'system' based upon coercive, legal sanctions, but rather a deeper, more complex web of controls which were exercised at the level of the factory, the corporation and the State.

ChemCo is a company that the Labour Government would consider to be a 'good employer'. It's a progressive company and its views and practices find favour in the offices of the many government departments that now deal with industry. Companies like ChemCo produced deals like the NWA in the context of discussions in and reports from the various committees of the NEDC. Its plans to revolutionise its industrial relations fit well into the perspective presented by Donovan and into the subsequent recommendations made by the (now abandoned) Commission on Industrial Relations.[3] Its ideas about work, about 'enriching' jobs and the like, find sympathy with those being propagandised by the Department of Employment's Work Study Unit.[4] The NWA agreement was established within the context of an increasing trend toward the centralisation of union–management negotiations, accompanied usually by company-wide agreements and the establishment of fixed rates of pay. Add to this the increasing number of Tribunals, the new arbitration and conciliation facility established through ACAS and the trend becomes clear. The trend in our society is a *corporatist* trend and Riverside in the early 1970s is just one example of this.

But it *is* only a tendency, and it has its contradictions. The crucial feature of this form of corporation (or, as it has been termed, Labourism) is that it seeks to enmesh, rather than confront, independent trade union organisation. Its aim is to bring this independence under the canopy of the corporation and the state, to then use it as a method of regulating the working class. But often management will be unwilling, or in other cases unable, to make the necessary concessions to this independence. At Riverside, remember, the Friday meetings were quickly terminated and management fought shy of the idea of recognising a full-time convenor— lest he be a trouble-maker. For management the independence of the trade union movement (the fact that it somehow contradicts the logic of hierarchy and 'the system') is at the root of an ideological and political conflict. It is something that they are forced to recognise, but in their hearts they wish that they didn't. In cases where they don't have to face up to it—as in the demand for supervisory unionism at ChemCo—they will back-track if they can. And this—in a different way—is true for union officials too. There is no denying the fact that many officers have slipped easily into the corporate mesh. But not all of them have. One of the national officers who deal with ChemCo had been a shop steward and convenor in the 1950s when such people weren't smiled upon by the union hierarchies. He still sees the real importance of shop floor organisation and he is very wary of the ideology of participation and involvement:

'We're trying to use it all back against them at the moment. If they want participation we say "all right let's have equal participation—open the books". But it's a tricky game because they can come back at you and say "look . . . the cupboard's bare". And we've lost the right to say "That's your problem".'

It is a tricky game but that's the game that's being played. The name of the game is corporatism and the rules of that game are the ones that the working class are increasingly having to deal with.

The tendencies which produced NWA were tendencies which asserted bureaucratic procedures and categories over the ChemCo labour force. At Riverside the establishment of the union was a part of this tendency toward rationalisation, a tendency which also involved the lowering of manning levels (through 'natural wastage', 'early retirement' and—in some plants—redundancy) and a systematic grading and restructuring of the manual and managerial labour force. Along with this came a new 'grievance procedure'—the means whereby 'fair treatment' would be guaranteed. The managers at Riverside lay great stress upon the fact that they treat each worker *as an individual*. They claim that each case is treated on its merits and that their kind of system is used simply to ensure 'fairness'. But the difficulties the old foremen face with the new style of supervision are experienced, much more severely, by the people they supervise.

On building sites, on the farm or the dock 'the gaffer is the gaffer'. If you've got a problem you tell him, if he does nothing about it you tell him again, you refuse to work or you leave. If you cross him you know the score. Not so at ChemCo. There everything (and everyone) is *processed*. And although the constraints that bureaucratic processes can put upon the arbitrary use of power by individuals should not be underestimated, it must be said that at ChemCo these processes have a strong *mystifying* quality. At many points they give the appearance of fairness and reason but taken together they do not add up to a fair and reasonable whole. The 'reason' and 'fairness' of ChemCo's bureaucracy is rooted in inequality. This inequality can only ever be overcome by the use of the power that lies in workers as a collectivity. But at ChemCo, as in other bureaucratised corporations, it is this very collectivity that is denied by the new rationality with its stress upon *individual* cases, discussed on the basis of the 'evidence' in offices away from the plant, the point of production.

At one important level the managers at Riverside recognised this. They knew that talk about 'participation', 'pushing responsibility downward', 'involvement' and so on, was often just so much talk. They knew that for the corporate ideal to become reality would require a special 'race' of workers; and that such a 'race' had yet to be bred. They knew the dangers and it was for this reason that they took such great care in their dealing with the shop stewards. That was why they told men like Billy King that he could 'go places', that he was more reasonable than his fellow workers, that he should think about becoming a steward.

Apologists will argue that, however distasteful management's manipulation may be, it is in fact a necessary (if regrettable) part of modern corporate society. That if Britain is to survive then firms like ChemCo must make a large profit. And so on. This argument denies totally the possibility of alternative forms of society but it has the virtue that it makes clear that it is not the power of the individual manager or even of the particular capitalist firm which ensures the exploitation of workers but the existence of capitalism as a system. Only the *political* transformation of society can alter this and in Britain the dominant political ideology on the Left has been social democracy; a reformist politics which links the day-to-day practice of trade unionism with the piecemeal, centralised, tinkering with the capitalist apparatus.

Historically, workers have developed controls over the decisions made by the boss which have provided a degree of that autonomy necessary if the rule of the boss (his power and the ideas that justify that power) is to be challenged at all. These controls provided the important base for the formulation of an alternative politics. For while factory politics is, without doubt, politics in a stunted form, it can—in the context of different ideologies—be one source of fundamental strength. At Riverside though, the Company's restructuring of labour, the system of grading, and many of the other things we have considered have raised severe impediments to even this (in the broader view, limited) rank and file activity. So too, especially with respect to its national level negotiations, has the national union. Assuredly the union was the workers' main strength; unfortunately it didn't make *them* strong.

Many of the managers and foremen would occasionally thank their luck that there wasn't a militant on the site. One foreman put it like this: 'I dread to think of what some of the lodge officials would make of this place. The issues they'd have to go on.' This is quite right. Just one good militant *would* make a hell of a difference—but he would have a hell of a lot to contend with. The extent to which ChemCo's rationality separates the individual from the group and one group of workers from another has a pernicious effect upon any attempt to establish the primacy of the collective. To assert such primacy at Riverside *is* to be 'unreasonable'; to act as its representative involves you in hard-headed *unreasonableness* in the office. That is why men can say that they 'never have seen a right good representative'. Alfie Grey's situation constitutes just one particular statement of this. He is a decent, unselfish man who believes in reason, in discussion, in seeing the other person's point of view. Without such qualities a socialist society wouldn't be worth much. But the political tragedy is that we live in a society where 'reason' is the property of the controllers, where 'fair' dealing reproduces inequalities of power.

All this raises the final point: the issue of the nature of the working class in the post-war era, and the position of chemical workers within it. At Riverside it was clear to us that the forces of institutional integration had succeeded in only a limited way in encasing the detailed activities of the workers. The institutional changes were important but they didn't put an end to struggle; what they did do was to force the struggle outside of them. There it was mostly uncoordinated and rarely expressed in a form which threatened the overall control of management but it represented, nevertheless, an important ideological 'distancing' from the hegemonic embrace of capital. At Riverside the men we talked to on the plants were working for ChemCo in name only. They didn't believe in the Company in any real sense and most of them would consider the notion of being a 'firm's man' to be an insult. At work they resisted. They did what they had to do but no more. They were industrial spoilers. And in this respect we found there to be no substantial differences between the men on the band end and those in the control rooms. The actual content of the work obviously made *some* difference. It affects what you have to do and how you can get by. The operators did feel that they had the better jobs (some of them felt their jobs to be more important) but they didn't consider themselves a class apart, and the practice of their work gave them no ideological commitment to a reorganisation of the chemical industry based around their 'skills'. That they didn't talk much about their 'skill' is not surprising. Mostly they were glad to be away from the band end but in the practice of their—easier—jobs in the control room they 'monitored', rather than expressed any skill, and in this monitoring they were subjected to the increasingly sophisticated vigilance of capital.

None of this adds much substance to the view of a new working-class vanguard of scientific workers.[5] The scientific work that was practised at Riverside—and, we think, throughout ChemCo and the chemical industry generally—is established within the parameters of bureaucratic power.

The application of science to industry has (under the general auspices of capital) produced a managerial technocratic class, not a powerful class of technicians or process operators. These 'technocrats' experience their own contradictions but none of these, we feel, are likely to push them into leading the working class into a radical or revolutionary politics. The working class is the object (rather than the practitioner) of industrial science. In considering the extent to which this class is 'new', and considering the nature of its political and social consciousness we will need to extend our view beyond the factory and look at modern capitalist society. For it is there in the context of a growing State corporatism, that changes have been most significant.

Notes

1 *Royal Commission on Trade Unions and Employers' Associations 1965–68*, Cmnd 3623, HMSO, 1968, p. 128.
2 *Ibid.*, p. 193.
3 See, for example, the Commission's report *Shop Stewards*, Cmnd 4668, HMSO, 1971) which recommends, among other things, a 'joint review' of the steward's role, the written formalisation of credentials, areas of responsibility, etc., and the provision of facilities—offices, filing, typing, time—to enable the steward to carry out these responsibilities.
4 See, for example, Work Research Unit Report no. 1, 'Improving Satisfaction at Work by Job Redesign', Department of Employment, May 1974.
5 For a statement of this vanguard view, set in the context of French industry, see Serge Mallet, *The New Working Class*, Spokesman Books, 1975. Aronovitz's discussion of this 'new class' within the context of the chemical industry in the USA is by contrast more consistent with our experience of the situation in Britain. See, for example, Stanley Aronovitz, 'Does the United States have a New Working Class' in George Fischer (ed.), *The Revival of American Socialism*, New York, Oxford University Press, 1971.

Part IV

Living with Capitalism

THROUGHOUT THE 1960s there was a great deal said about 'affluence'. There was the idea that with increased growth rates the economic and political problems that had afflicted western society during the twentieth century could be solved. And politicians, social scientists, mediamen were all pointing to the 'affluence' of the working class as a source of stability. Given the vision of an ever flowing cornucopia, 'affluence' was seen to have exorcised Marx's spectre of capitalism producing—in the working class—its own gravediggers. In this view a new 'life style' had developed within the working classes of Western Europe and North America; a life style which was based on the motor cars, the television sets and 'consumer durables' that growth itself had made possible, and which had detached this 'new working class' from the class conscious traditions of yesteryear. These workers, so it seemed, did far less unpleasant work than their parents had done. A deal of talk was to be heard about 'the problems of leisure'. There was even speculation in some circles whether they were really 'workers' at all and in the case of the chemical industry the 'personality' of these new workers was seen to 'tend . . . toward the new middle class, the white collar employee in bureaucratic industry'.[1]

Yet the reality is that 'affluence' and pleasant work have become nothing like as widespread as was supposed.[2] And whereas some people have become comparatively well-off this has sometimes cost them in other ways. Chemical workers, for example, are paid some of the highest wages for manual workers in Britain (for management staff, too, chemicals along with banking and finance is one of the two industries which pay the highest salaries to a large group of middle and senior management). But the 'affluence' of ChemCo workers doesn't alter the work they have to do or the hours they have to work; nor the fact that while at work they have to conform to a system that is ChemCo's system. The 'affluent worker' lives in a society that is structured by the same inequalities as the one his parents lived and worked in. In many respects it is the *same* society.

There are, of course, ways in which things have changed a great deal.

None of the workers we talked to at Riverside had experienced a long period of unemployment, they had not had to fight in wars or be conscripted into the armed forces; those who were brought up in Britain had received compulsory full time education until they were 15; they all owned television sets and two-thirds of them had cars and mortgaged houses as well. In this final part of the book we try to make some assessment of how people—not just any people but 'affluent' people—have come to understand this amalgam of change and constancy. And in doing this we raise further questions about class and class consciousness.

The few sociologists who have been concerned to look at class as process and not to 'stop the time machine', have only rarely appreciated the complexity of the processes involved. The one major investigation into the effect of 'affluence' upon the British working class, for example, begins with the assumption that the sort of understanding which workers have of their situation can be analysed in terms of its overarching *consistency*.[3] Given this assumption 'models of consciousness' can be arrived at in which one set of ideas are seen to relate in a formal logical manner to others. The problem with this view of things is that it fails to root 'consciousness' in the structure of the real world where experience is more characterised by *contradiction* than consistency. At work, for example, ChemCo workers face the power of management, the inequality of work and of reward. But they also experience—through the technical division of labour and the continuous barrage of managerial ideology—a sense of the job having to be done; of there being no other way, given the fact that 'someone has to do it'.

Outside the factory they know that they are expected to be politically involved, and that 'apathy' is frowned upon; but they know too that the 'politics' that is offered to them is one in which choice is severely limited. Television provides them with a 'window on the world', but it is a flawed window on a flawed world. One day, for instance, we were shown tomatoes being dumped to rot in the Channel Islands. We were told that the hot weather had produced a glut and that most of the crop 'couldn't be sold'. Earlier we had seen scenes of starvation in Ethiopia. We had also been left to ponder the situation of the million-odd unemployed . . . and the rampant inflation. But the tomatoes 'had' to be destroyed because they 'couldn't' be sold. On top of this there are the commercials—packages of fantasy and hope. Their images bear little resemblance to the lives which millions of men and women lead; regimented in factories and on estates. Really it would be surprising if people *didn't* carry within themselves conflicting feelings and understandings.

An appreciation of this, of the essential complexity of people's thoughts and experience—and, by extension, of class consciousness—should be of great political importance. To look at things in this way shifts us away from dogmatism and stereotyping—from the use of simple slogans and labels which allow people to be dismissed and written off the historical map—toward an appreciation of the many-sided potential of the sort of understanding which comes from being an 'affluent worker' in this society.

In this Part therefore we attempt to look at Riverside in the context of the broader society. ChemCo managers, for example, are plagued by 'the problem of motivation' but this—which is indicative of a contradiction at the societal level—is not a simple product of work or power relations at Riverside. It's a 'problem' which troubles many managers and for a solution quite a lot of them also look to the creation of 'trust' between 'management' and 'men'. It is with a brief examination of the limitations of this particular managerialist notion that we begin.

Notes

1 R. Blauner, *Alienation and Freedom: The Factory Worker and His Industry*, University of Chicago Press, 1964, p. 181.

2 On the basis of his research into the work experiences of people in the USA in the 1970s, Studs Terkel arrived at the conclusion that 'in a terrible way Charles Dickens' London is not as far away as long ago'. Scrooge has simply been replaced by the conglomerates and Dickens' people by Beckett's. (See S. Terkel, *Working*, Vintage Edition, New York, 1975.) In Britain in the late 1960s a study set up to examine 'the affluent worker' in the context of a pleasant Southern town (Luton) with new owner-occupier estates and new factories, was unable to find a sizeable group of workers earning high wages and involved in satisfying work. Most of the workers in the sample earned their affluence by working shifts and on assembly lines. (See J. Goldthorpe *et al.*, *The Affluent Worker: Industrial Attitudes and Behaviour*, Cambridge University Press, 1968; and J. Goldthorpe *et al.*, *The Affluent Worker in the Class Structure*, Cambridge University Press, 1969.)

3 *Ibid.*

11

The Politics of 'Trust', and the Lack of Trust in 'Politics'

AT RIVERSIDE NO capitalist is to be seen to finance and direct, to hire, exploit and fire. The plain fact is that ChemCo's investment needs are so massive that they far outstrip the resources of any one capitalist. Like other big corporations the firm is owned by an impersonal aggregation of tens of thousands of shareholders, the largest of which (insurance companies and pension funds) themselves constitute further aggregations of depersonalised private wealth. In a real sense, then, the existence of 'private' firms like ChemCo depends on the socialisation of private ownership. Today indeed—at a time when a poor outlook for profits has led to a 'strike' by investors—it is becoming increasingly clear that for capitalism to survive investment must be socialised yet further. And, as State assistance and part State ownership become a commonplace, private enterprise is becoming less and less private; the 'private' company itself develops into an impersonal mass of capital.

However the depersonalisation of property has interfered not one whit with profit as the *raison d'être* of capitalist enterprise. Nor has the so-called 'separation of ownership and control'. Within the big corporations thousands of managers now exist to perform specialist tasks, to be held to account by a top stratum of management accountants. Rational men, the management accountants define rationality in terms of profit and loss. Paid high five-figure salaries, they preside over a differentiated structure of Sales, Research, Technical, Personnel, Legal, Public Relations and other departments: all these ultimately to increase and to realise more smoothly the surplus created at the point of production.

No wonder, then, that Riverside managers talk in terms of 'the system' and think 'systems-think'. The system is a system of control, of power, and it regulates their lives at work. Accountancy and accountability are structured into the very organisation of the big corporation: what power managers have is delimited by rules and regulations, by job descriptions, and by their immediate bosses' scrutiny of the measures designed to monitor and improve their performance. As for the manager accountants themselves, they too are subject to the very accountancy of profit and loss they use to control those beneath them. A system of private appropriation, capitalism, once set in motion, is driven by *capital*'s need to accumulate.

When, in the middle to late 1960s, ChemCo profit margins came under threat the manager accountants turned into yet more accountant-like managers. The pressure to 'economise' was on. The management structure was streamlined. The fat was cut out. Managers were invited to 'ask their price'. Those who remained were left in no doubt what was expected of them, or that their performance was to be watched still more closely. Accountancy meant costing and costing meant cutting overtime, cutting absenteeism, reducing manning. All this represented in charts on office walls, where the activities of people became no more than 'labour costs'; a commodity like any other. As sulphur had to be bought at the right prices, fed through the chemical system to produce sulphuric acid, so too had labour. Labour, like the technology, had to be programmed; to be rendered predictable.

Now the corporate planners could achieve much by 'rationalisation' (redundancy and 'natural wastage') and by securing more control through the new accountancy. But for them it was not enough to harness more effectively whatever human energy was currently being expended or to simply have fewer workers (and fewer foremen and fewer managers) do more work. 'Economising' was not enough because labour power is a unique commodity; labour power is *people*. And what capital buys is people's ability to produce. This ability can be withheld and for capital this raises the problem of 'trust', of 'teamwork', and what Riverside managers call 'the problem of motivation'.[1] Rather than having to force out more work, they hoped, in the long term—and this was the 'new philosophy' aspect of the NWA—to be 'trusted'; to reach a situation where men spontaneously and voluntarily co-operated with them and each other. They wanted men to put their ability to produce unreservedly at their disposal.

Of course when managers regard the people who make up their work-forces as just so many people—and this is what they do at Riverside when they tell you 'the organisation *is* the people in it'—it really does seem very little to ask of them—these other people—that they should give managers their trust and co-operation. But 'trust' is not the easy answer that it at first appears. Sure enough if Riverside is regarded purely and simply as a couple of hundred men who have come together to work, some by hand

and some by brain, to make bags of fertiliser, then it does at one level seem unreasonable that they don't all work as a team, don't trust one another and don't produce more. But the reality is different. Trust rarely arises out of compulsion, and it is only in a peculiar sense that these workers might be said to have 'chosen' to work (rather than not to), and to have 'chosen' to go to Riverside. As they see it, ChemCo is somewhere they have 'ended up'. If the bargain they have entered into with ChemCo is a 'voluntary' one, many would not describe it like this.

Obviously, some managers are trusted more than others. Blunsen's attitudes weren't the most likely ones to achieve either the respect or support of 'his' men. Other managers were less officious, more likely to be called 'good blokes'. But this doesn't alter the fact that 'personally' is not institutionally, socially is not structurally and that, whatever workers or managers would like, managers inhabit an institutional structure in which workers sell their labour power and thereby relate to capital as impersonal commodities. Politically articulate or not, Riverside workers know this: know that whatever social pleasantries managers may exchange, whatever relationships they may have with them 'as people', they represent a system, the logic of which is to serve capital not labour.

Given their own relationship to capital, managers sometimes feel trapped themselves. Like the foremen, who feel this even more acutely, managers are trapped because there is only a poor chance they could get out of ChemCo now—and also trapped because they don't want to give up what they've got. Their wives, though, suspect their husbands don't really want to leave ChemCo. For while a crisis on the plant can disrupt home life, they don't always accept at face value their husband's complaints about being called out at all hours. Talk about 'getting out of ChemCo' is apt to be greeted with wry humour. So are the sort of rural reveries in which it seems an increasing proportion of the salaried middle classes now indulge: 'Every year he starts this thing about a croft in Scotland. Not that he'll ever do anything about it.' It is in the actual process of their work, however, that managers are entrapped most closely of all. There they have little room for manoeuvre, for though their new found 'responsibilities' please them, they also serve to make them still more accountable to capital.

As just one link in a chain of organisational positions and decisions, they cannot always be 'reasonable'. Not when 'dealing with people as people' interferes with extracting a surplus from them; not when being 'reasonable' might erode the system of control. Talk about 'participation' aside, they learn early on that to fail to defend management's 'right to manage' is to ask for trouble. The international management consultants who specialise in 'people' are also well aware of this.[2] The truth is that it just isn't rational—for capital—to let workers participate in decisions to alter their conditions of work if this interferes with profits; which means that 'Mickey Mouse' jobs won't be abolished if men can be bought more cheaply than machines. No more—again from the standpoint of capital—is it at all 'rational' to leave workers to determine their rate of production, or to determine what happens to the product of their labour.

The manager accountants can only safely enlarge the sphere of 'participation' to the extent they do not forfeit control. Their predicament is that in order to serve the ends of private appropriation they want to socialise production: to have it recognised, by workers, that production is collective, social, labour. But this development is itself held back by the end of private appropriation. This is the contradiction.

As for the plant managers, though sellers of labour power themselves, they stand in relation to other workers as the subalterns of the manager accountants; as agents of capital, of 'the system'. And 'the system' constrains them. 'Failure', as the manager accountants define it, can mean more management redundancies. So: 'ChemCo exists to make profit, not chemicals.' And: 'You can be a bastard or a bad bastard.'

None of this makes for 'trust'.

Although Riverside plant managers appreciate that investment has to some extent been socialised already, a socialist solution is not for them. As they see it, Government grants and allowances are one thing; nationalisation and policies which 'interfere' with management are quite another: 'Management must manage'. All the same—and despite their firm conviction that the business of business is profit—they do want to work with 'their men', and to have their men work with—not just for—them. Perhaps they deceive themselves about how close they really were to the men in 'the old days', before the new accountancy and the 'economising' pushed them away from the shop floor into the office. But they do value production and productive labour. They have no relish for 'paperwork', and they do feel at times that becoming what they have become, and having to do what they have to do, costs them something. (Or if not them personally, then other managers.) Maybe one reason they value productive labour so much is that they are partly paid for their technical ability, for the exercise of their own mental labour. Anyway, sitting in their centrally heated office block they do regret the existence of 'Mickey Mouse' jobs; do regret that they can't stop themselves 'counting numbers'.

For their part, Riverside workers have no illusions about the business of business. Ask them about why the job is like it is, where the money goes to, or why they are the ones 'on the outside looking in'—'that's the capitalist system' they tell you. That's the way things are. Things like these are what living with capitalism is all about. It has come down to them from father to son that it's not for them to say what the business of business should be. No illusions then. But not much hope either.

These workers expect little from work—and in return for their wages they give management as little as possible: hence 'the problem of motivation'. There is another side to these workers' lack of enthusiasm however. They are not just unenthusiastic workers in the service of capital: they are unenthusiastic about politics too—about Conservative and Labour and about what in their experience has passed for socialism. In the past the struggle against the boss has, at moments, opened up the possibility of a new social order. For the workers we talked to at Riverside this vision has become blurred.

The idea of 'workers' control of industry' has been an important one in the British working class, and at no point was this of greater significance than in the decade that followed the Russian revolution when demands were made for 'workers' soviets' and the 'nationalisation of the means of production'. That these demands weren't realised is part of our history; the wounds of defeat and of a decade of severe unemployment have only recently healed. But this healing has taken place in a post-war world of Labour Party nationalisation and Stalinism in Russia, both of which (in fact, and as propagandised in the capitalist press) have dealt a severe blow to the development of socialist thinking.

In 1945 Bob Edwards of the Chemical Workers Union could preface his attack upon the owners of the British chemical industry with the clear statement that he looked 'at the industry through socialist eyes . . . biased in favour of public ownership'. Few chemical workers today find any solace in the idea of nationalisation; it no longer exists as a strategy in the same way as 'the mines for the miners' existed for the miners between the wars. The 1971 miners' strike made this very clear. Riverside workers, for example, supported the miners. Not actively perhaps—although one of the shop stewards did turn the heating in his control room on to 'full' 'in solidarity'—but the sympathy they felt for the blokes who worked down the pits confirmed them in their view that the miners hadn't benefited from nationalisation; that the State is just about as bad a boss as a capitalist. In this, of course, they were substantially correct: nationalisation as conceived and implemented in Britain was not designed to achieve socialism.

By a similar reasoning, but with much less available evidence, the Soviet Union is seen by these men to be little different from the West. Sure enough Greg reads the *Soviet Weekly*, but he is in a minority of one —as is the site's Monday Club supporter. The vast majority reason that the worker's lot, here and there, is pretty much the same.

Reg:

> 'They haven't solved it either, have they? I don't know too much about it like, but I'm pretty sure that over there there's the people with the big money, the people with the power and the people who do the work. Just the same as here. Except for the salt mines, and the Secret Police.'

Martin:

> 'I think there should be a way around it but I don't know what way to be honest—short of making it a Communist state, and I don't think that would be the answer. But I can't see any other way. They haven't solved the problem in Russia so I'm sure they won't solve it over here. . . . I suppose it's everybody's problem really—but I can't solve it, I can't see any answers at all. It's just the system we live in. Probably not on the same scale but the same things are happening in Russia, which is supposedly equal shares for everybody. I expect you've got blokes over there earning, say, £200 a week and the average worker's down to £16–20.'

The cold war period, the scaremongering, the propaganda are all at work here. But important too is the reality of the Soviet Union and the day-to-day operation of 'power bloc' politics which has effectively discredited it as an agent of world socialism. For most workers (the overwhelming majority at Riverside) the Soviet Union offers neither the elements of a utopia (a possible new order) nor a reminder of an international socialist movement.

'Politics' make many of them angry.

Jimmy:

> 'Look. No matter who we vote for it's still the working man that gets it all the time. Let's be fair. I don't think it matters who you vote for.'

His two mates agree. Roderick:

'The smaller you are, you know like the workman, the poor people, well they don't have no say in no country. None of these people is boss. Nobody hear his voice. The big man, like the big merchant and such like, when they speak they got to hear his voice or they can't run the country. They run the country but the working-class man don't own anything.'

Vic:

'Yes that's right. I think it is the Big Bosses that have the say. I don't believe that people like us have any say. But it doesn't worry me, see. It doesn't worry me at all. Because I can't see any change in it. It might change but I can't see it. It's only the Big Boys who have the say. It's not fair I know but as I say: What can you do? If you could have a system where everybody could have a say . . . everybody would be glad like. But they say, "I have the money, I am the one who has the money. I am the one who employed you. So I am the big boss and what I say goes like." '

Given the existence of the Big Boys, any politics which fails to come to terms with them appears remote.

'Well, I've always been Labour to be quite honest. I mean, I make no bones about it down here or anywhere else. But they've got really as many faults as what the Conservatives have. I don't think there's a hell of a lot to choose between them to be quite honest. . . . The only thing is that Labour do have to be a bit more artful you know. To make it look as if they care a bit like. I don't think there's much difference otherwise. I mean it's obvious they've got to be a little bit artful to make it *look* as if they're concerned but they're not really. . . . They're all out for themselves, I think, to be honest.'

Austin agrees:

'Well, I don't see no changes. I don't see no changes. They think things will be all right after this party comes in [Tory Government in 1971]. But things start to go up more and more and more. Mr Wilson's party was putting up prices, now Mr Heath's party is putting up prices. Well now everybody comment that they want to put him out and put Mr Wilson in again. Well, I don't care. And if they do put Mr Wilson in things won't change—because it is just the world.'

When they talked about the bosses, the Big Boys, the people who run things, most of the workers we talked to echoed Grandpa Bonnemore in Zola's *Germinal*: 'the bosses are often swine but there will always be bosses won't there? What's the good of racking your brains to try to make sense out of it?' They put it down to luck:

'Yes, in a way it's wrong, you know. To pay them the sort of money they're getting—to a man [shareholder] who doesn't work. But if he can get away with it let him get away with it. If he can get away with it good luck to him. As for me if I could get away with it, I should be glad. It's hard to say. It's just one of those things. They're just the lucky ones to have those sort of jobs.'

Luck it is then—perhaps it will come our way too. 'Win the pools. That's what we all want isn't it? Eight draws.' Because,

'The job I'm doing here, I don't believe it will make me rich. As an ordinary labourer I don't believe you could ever work for riches. You know, it's impossible. But still you can be happy if you are really satisfied with what you are, but if you try to be rich when you can't earn it, you will find yourself unhappy.'

Situated in a world not right in the head some despair, and give up all hope of understanding it. Some vote Tory. A few look for the emergence of another Churchill or a dictator.[3] Most try to make sense of their lives. They try to live from day to day, to construct reasonably coherent pasts and futures, to maintain respect for themselves. As to work—they have no respect for 'firm's men'; and they are far from giving management their 'trust'. As to 'politics'—the politics of the politicians—this engages them hardly at all. The enemy not being so much a readily identifiable capitalist as *capital*, and a class politics being ill-developed, they are thrown back upon themselves. In this, as we shall see, the idea of sacrifice is central.

Notes

1 For a more detailed consideration see Theo Nichols, 'The "Socialism" of Manage-

ment: Some comments on the New "Human Relations" ', *Sociological Review*, May 1975.

2 As Herzberg puts it: 'there is a danger you can participate beyond your level of competence.' See David Jenkins, *Job Power: Blue and White Collar Democracy*, Heinemann, 1974, p. 169.

3 For an account of one ChemCo worker who does at some level look to 'a dictator' for a solution to his problems see 'Roger' in Theo Nichols and Peter Armstrong, *Workers Divided*, Fontana, 1976, Part III.

12
'Success' and 'Failure'

IN THE WORDS of one of his mates, 'Jacko just likes going the opposite way to what everyone else is going. He's just one of them type of people.' Of all the workers at Riverside, Jacko was clearly the most 'bloody-minded'. 'If he thinks something then he will say it, whether it's to Bell or bloody Brown or whoever it is. He won't be pushed about.' In the opinion of most of the foremen he's 'a cowboy'. But he's no fool. His foreman says 'he could go places if he put his mind to it'. But he doesn't. He doesn't want to go to those places.

Before he came to ChemCo he'd had hundreds of jobs: 'how many jobs have I had? . . . You want me to tell you *all* of them? You'd fill a few books with them if I did, I can tell you.' Apart from numerous factory jobs he'd been in the Army, a lorry driver, an attendant at the local swimming baths, a coal man and a milkman. Usually he'd just got fed up and moved on, or he was sacked. He'd been at ChemCo for four years in 1970—'I've never stayed in a job that long before'—and he was thinking of moving on. He had come to ChemCo with the expectation of working for a super-efficient, technical, rational, space-age corporation. Like others who thought this—'it's an idea you get like'—he was soon disillusioned. They listened to management talk about the importance of competition and the vulnerability of operating within an extremely cost-sensitive industry: then they found themselves packing Zap into the bags of their chief competitors. While they were given lectures on the plant about the need for cleanliness and 'good housekeeping' ChemCo acted as a major pollutant. Then there were Sammy Bell's 'surprise visits' which, as they soon discovered, took place the same time every month and were always prepared for with the same frantic sweeping and polishing. All to keep them on their toes. As Jacko saw it, ChemCo was 'a madhouse'.

Jacko blames the management for this state of affairs. He blames his mates too:

'It doesn't have to be like that mind. . . . There could be other ways of doing things. It's just that the working-class man is a bloody fool. He's so uneducated he can't take it in any other way. Mind you they [the management] feed them enough guff. It's all guff here. We're forever arguing about it in the mess room and I'm always being called a bloody fool. They feed the blokes so much and no more. And it's always *their* interpretation.'

Most deeply of all, though, he blames himself:

'Now what you should look for is a man who is content in his job. But who's looking for contentment? They're few and far between here. It's education again see. Most of the blokes here aren't content in their lives. The only way they can enjoy themselves is by spending money. They don't realise that there are other things in life apart from boozing and lasses. Now my wife and my father-in-law read all the time. You could put my wife in a chair with a book and she'd stay there for hours —if it was interesting that is. She wouldn't move. Now me: I can't read. I should: I'd like to. I should wear glasses too but I don't. That's me see.'

He wants to read but he can't settle to it. He wants to 'get somewhere' but he can't help telling the foreman to piss off when he's being stupid. He wants to work—'people are happier when they're working'—but he can't bear packing bags. In all this he ends up blaming himself: 'It's me though, see. It's my manner. It seems to offend people.' Himself and the working class: 'They're so uneducated: they're fools to themselves.'

This mixture of self-doubt and recrimination is not exceptional. Jacko's anguish is all too common in our society. The educational system is to blame for a lot of this. It is truly ironic that Jacko and men like him end up blaming themselves and their class for failings which are directly attributable to what passes for an 'education' in Britain. But the effects of education are not just to be seen in the self-doubts of workers, nor in the limited opportunities it has left them with, nor even in the felt vulnerability of the foremen, at least of those who fear the rise of 'educated' workers, 'them with O-levels'. The effects of education are also to be seen amongst managers—'education' here meaning a system which hives off the technical from the social and which has marked out a career path all the way from O-level Science to A-level Science to BSc to PhD to the research lab. Edward Blunsen's arrogance—'a child could do it'—is in part a function of this. John Baird's puzzled reaction to workers' reactions to him is another. Baird is a product of an education system which insulated the 'educated' from the realities of a class society.

Science and engineering students rarely seem to have been to the fore in student revolts. Maybe of course there's a chance that one day yet more of them will end up like Riverside's most 'successful' manager, Dr Jones: end up frustrated because they cannot make full use of their almost exclusively technical education. But, generally speaking, politico-intellectual trauma is not for them. Their education is only political education to the extent it doesn't raise questions, treats the world as unproblematic and confirms them in the conventional wisdom. For working-class children, by contrast, 'education' means school. Quite often—and perhaps increasingly—it cannot be seen to impinge on their lives in any meaningful way. School, like the factory, is time lost.

True, in the factory things are clearer but they are not simple. The workers are together there, they are organised and, to an important extent, *with* each other in a common shared situation. But there is still the managerial guff; the ideological offensive that always gives '*their* interpretation'. And there is still the idea of 'success' and 'achievement', for though children now leave school at 16 its effects don't end there. The education system *systematically* produces failure. These men left school at 15 as 'failures'; they worked where they could, moved when it got too much for them or when they could get more money elsewhere and were branded as 'cowboys'. However, the dominant ideology of bureaucratic capitalism has not seduced them entirely.

Strongly utopian notions of *work* and its significance for mankind persist within the working class. A few of the workers we talked to at Riverside had previously worked in the sort of jobs that have helped to promote such ideas in the past: skilled jobs where they'd been trained by old men who loved their craft, open air jobs in fields without supervision where the dreams of being at one with nature came easily. Take Steve; he'd left school at 15 and followed his father onto the railways:

'Before I was here I worked for British Rail, I used to be mad keen on steam engines. When they brought the diesels in the interest went, I just didn't want to stay with the diesels, you know with the old steam engine it was great. You'd hammer along about 90 getting shot to hell. Daft it was but it was great, I used to love it. Not one engine was the same you know, not one day was the same either. You'd get a derailment or you'd be snow bound, there was always something happening. But as I say, when they brought the diesels in it just wasn't the same.'

The interest went, he got fed up and his neighbour told him that ChemCo was 'pretty good'. As Steve saw it, he had 'no qualifications, so for me this is a fair job, it's a pretty fair firm. Of course I've got no love for management but as firms go this isn't a bad firm to work for.' Steve started as a packer, a job which he hated, and when we met him he had taken the job as second operator on the Zap plant: totally isolated, stuck in a filthy, sweaty control room for eight hours a day. It didn't compare to the railway but he was away from the foreman and it was better than packing bags:

'No one wanted to take it but I jumped at it. I read. I'm not supervised. What could be better? Down there packing bags you go fucking mad.'

As a driver of a steam locomotive Steve had found a sort of happiness; the contentment that Jacko talks of. Diesel power destroyed that for him. But the memory of his relationships with steam locomotives stayed with him as he packed and humped bags of Zap for ChemCo, and provided him with the basis of a critique of life at Riverside. At one and the same time he feels both cheated and superior.

Few workers have ever obtained this sort of satisfaction from their work. Steve is part of a declining majority that is becoming increasingly remote from the mainstream of industrial life. Like Brian—who had worked the land, who 'loved farming' and would 'rather do the extra hour's work and be back out in the fresh air'—he knows that those days are gone. So too do the men who travelled to Britain from the West Indies in the 1960s. Hamilton left Barbados in 1961. He worked for a while in London and moved to Provincial in 1962. Like many others he found difficulty in getting a job at first. He was unemployed for three weeks before he was taken on as a packer at Riverside. He thinks the job at ChemCo isn't bad. The money is OK and you don't get the sack. But:

'It's different here y'know, man. Before I came here I never done shift work. I go to work at 7 and I finish at 4. And that's it—finished until the next day. You get a lot of rest in between and you enjoy yourself. You really enjoy yourself. There's not the same amount of enjoyment here as over there. You all work more; you does more work. It's more The Man. You work more for The Man. But I don't get out a lot here, not with this shift work. I don't get out much 'cos I figure that when you get home you so tired you just feel like having a bath and, you know, bed. I don't think there's a lot of harm in having a good time.'

He misses the 'good time', and he and his friends talk about going back. They talk, they 'have it in mind' but when asked seriously, they are realistic. They just 'can't see it happening'.

'At home there's not enough jobs to go around see. This is the trouble in the West Indies. I mean people say, "Why did you come over here? All that beautiful sunshine, blue sea and beaches." Well you try to explain to them but some don't understand. Coming over here it's the job, you know. You can't live off sunshine and all, and sea and things like that. You must have some money. You must have clothes and things like that. You can't live off the beach. It's all right if you got the money: a millionaire over there is made.'

Metropolitan capitalism through companies like ChemCo provides the jobs; the money to buy clothes and shoes for the children. That's one way of looking at it. But it's not the only way. While ChemCo 'provides the jobs' it provides them by extracting raw materials from the under-developed countries, forcing workers to travel half way around the world to earn a living and, at the same time, ensuring that the underdeveloped world stays that way. A playground for the millionaires.

Most of the men who worked on the plants at Riverside have never experienced the sort of satisfaction from work that Steve misses, or the enjoyment that Hamilton talks about.

When Ted joined the Army and was asked whether he was interested in a career or money, he had replied 'money'. But, looking back he is quite clear that 'it's not what I'd say now though'. He had previously had the chance to take on a greengrocer's shop with his wife but had turned the offer down, he hadn't fancied it. But of this too, he says, 'If I'd known what I know now I would have jumped at it like a shot.' Recrimination and regret dominate Ted's talk of his life and these emotions were by far the most common ones at Riverside. These emotions are healthy ones, at least in that they indicate that men retain some idea of life having potentiality; of struggle and alternatives. Far more shattering, and shattered, are the few who, having been particularly ill-served by society, feel no sense of loss. Beaten down they just feel lucky that they have a secure job, with good money. Lucky and grateful.

Graham came to ChemCo when he was 21. Before that he had been indentured for *three* different apprenticeships. Each time his employer went bust and Graham's apprenticeship was terminated:

'Everytime I get something I'm really interested in something goes wrong with it. . . . I would really have liked to be a carpenter.'

He speaks the words without anger. He blames no one. Not the bosses who went bust; and certainly not capitalism. He is emptied.

'Fair enough', as Graham would say, greengrocery shops fail and Army careers can turn out to be falsehoods; and even as a carpenter he might have ended up unemployed. British society is structured in a way that makes the 'failure' of men like him extremely likely (even necessary). But the dominant interpretation of such failure offered by this society, and generally accepted by workers at ChemCo, is the common-sensical one that men are their own masters. If they fail they must blame themselves, or the fates. And the price of failure is a job at ChemCo; quite a good job 'for people like us'. Stuck there they dream of better things. They hope for luck, they fill in football coupons and they work out new possibilities. Fantasy and strategy jumbled into notions of possible futures. And running through many of these is the idea of being 'your own boss': to get a shop or a smallholding. Notions of independence that belong more to an era of cottage industry than the epoch of international capitalism and giant multinational production. David, in whom entrepreneurial calculation runs deeper than most, had worked out his plans most clearly.

'You see I live in Burbridge [a seaside town] and don't intend stopping here for the rest of my life. I don't intend catching bags for the rest of my life either. When we've got together enough money we're going to set up a business and when that comes I'll just jack in. A lot of blokes down here don't seem to worry but there aren't many light jobs down here, I wouldn't like to be stuck down here when I got older.

Well I've got a wife and a little girl and we've been married two years now and we live in a flat in my brother-in-law's house. My wife has been in the hotel and catering business all her life and what we think is that we've got to get together a decent deposit to have a large detached house, that would be good. I think being my own boss for a start would be good, I don't like being told to do things. I don't like having to work to a standard routine and I don't like shifts at all. No, I think we would be comfortably off.'

When we first talked to David he was working as many double shifts as he could. Travelling thirty miles to work and staying there for sixteen hours. But it began to tell and increasingly he was having to turn down the chances of overtime. Nobody asked him about the hotel any more. Others had had similar, if less precise, plans:

> 'I'd like to have a business of my own, I'd hate to think of catching bags when I'm 45. I'd like a shop. It's the sort of dream that goes through your head. I'm trying to get some money together. I do window cleaning rather than overtime because there's more satisfaction in it.'

All but the most single-minded find it 'difficult to put aside more than a hundred quid a year: and most of that goes at Christmas'. But in spite of this, the idea of a shop, a place of your own is something which goes through many of their minds as they pack and load the green bags. A dream for a future. And one that is becoming increasingly impossible as more and more small businesses go bankrupt. But people need their dreams.

Men like Graham are drained by the experience of being a worker in this society. It has left them without hope. Not so Jacko and Steve. Both of them in their different ways (Steve by driving a steam engine, and through his father, Jacko by arguing with his father-in-law—an old member of the Communist Party) have access to a tradition of working-class thought. What appeals to them are the utopian aspects of this tradition. This has not provided them with any clear idea of how to change society. In a number of respects both of them hold quite reactionary political views. But it has left them with an understanding of themselves as active agents. It is no coincidence that Steve and Jacko were pointed out as the leading 'cowboys', or that they provided their foremen with the greatest headaches. Nor was it surprising that eventually they got away from ChemCo and the bagging line, Jacko to a smallholding; Steve to a job on the dock.

It is not too difficult to see how workers (particularly those living in areas which are isolated from the mainstream of working-class militancy) end up placing the blame for the ailments of society upon themselves and those near to them. Despite this they don't lose all their edge; for they still *experience* the reality of a class society. They still pack the bags and the boss still comes to inspect, to check up on things. And as long as they can remember they have known what John Baird had to find out, about factory production. George put it like this:

'There is the bosses and there is us, man. I know that. There's him who tells us when to jump and we who jump.'

And NWA hadn't changed this. Bill:

'I thought NWA would make life down here a bit more interesting—you know—more responsibility and all that. But as far as I can see that was just sugar on the pill. You know? They still jump on you all the time and I'm just as fed up with it all.'

That is how things are, so:

'The blokes are down here to earn as much as they can in as short a period as possible. A bloke isn't going to come to work and sweat his cogs off for nothing. And a manager is going to want to get the most out of him as possible—for himself and the firm.'

One of the central principles of the ideology which justifies the existence of a capitalist society (the ideology that holds men responsible for their own fate) is that people who have to sell their labour on a free market are, in some sense, free. Their freedom is expressed in their choice, which in turn makes their bargain with the employer a fair one. 'If you don't like it you can go somewhere else.'

Many of the people we talked to at Riverside accepted the judgment of themselves as failures, and some of them felt that the particular bargain they had made with ChemCo was (relatively) fair, but all save a few of them sense the unfairness of a situation that commits them to pack bags and the like, while others sit in offices and get well paid for it. Michael:

'I mean you take the people up there. Dr Jones—I suppose he gets about fifteen or twenty thousand quid a year. And that's terrible isn't it? After all, the likes of the working man, the working man boy, he has got to come in here whether it is raining or snowing and work pretty hard. And his own wife is saying when it is snowing or fog: "How will you come home?" worrying like hell. All for a few pounds, isn't it? . . . At Christmas time when you're working here and when that bloody hooter goes, right out you go at about six o'clock in the morning. You are dead tired, loading trucks all night, up till Christmas night, and then you come Christmas morning and put a candle up in the window. Up in one window you see, to show the light to Christ walking around. Well, I think about this. All those "Big Books" as I call them, getting about twenty or thirty thousand pound a year. And them out drinking whisky on it. It makes a man think doesn't it? And yet you can't do nothing about it, can you? What! What!!! What can you do about it? They have the upper hand all the time. They are the firm and you can't do anything about it. But it's terrible really.'

The chairman of ChemCo is paid around £50,000 a year; £1,000 a week. This fact came as a surprise to all but a few of the men who made ChemCo fertiliser at Riverside. A lot of them couldn't believe it, and they all felt that it was 'a lot of money'. Freddie thought that it was 'a hell of a lot of money! And I suppose he don't do a lot, do he?' He certainly doesn't pack bags.

'Well fifty, forty, sixty thousand when you think of it. I mean you must get angry when you think you're humping bags and there's a bloke, he just walk around from plant to plant and he give orders and because he's giving orders he's getting that amount.'

You get angry but what can you do? The boss is the boss; bosses give orders and get paid a lot more than you. To boss you around while you do the awful jobs. It's wrong, rotten, terribly wrong but what can you *do*?

'I mean, well, you might say why couldn't he be getting say twenty thousand and you getting a bit more. Say five or six thousand. You know break it down a bit. Well you wouldn't expect to get as much as him, but to bring it a bit closer like you know. He get twenty, thirty thousand; take off ten thousand or so off him and give us another thousand. I think you'd be a bit more satisfied with that.'

Freddie has not given too much thought to the chairman of ChemCo; to how The Man spends his time. Much less to possible ways of restructuring society on a more equal basis. For him, as for most of the people we talked to and argued with at Riverside, these things are part of the established landscape of a world which is not of their making but which they have to live in nevertheless. Yet whereas the landscape is established, immovable, solid, its contours are not clear. Capital today is personified by the manager accountants but for most workers such men are just 'them'. Typically, outside their own firm or industry they don't know their names. And the managers whose names they do know, the ones they deal with, are clearly not 'capitalists'.

The chairman of ChemCo has enormous political and economic influence which can bear directly on the lives of those who work for Chem-Co, and indirectly on the rest of us. The enormity of the sums paid as top salaries (£1,000 a week to men who earn a fraction of this) is almost too much to cope with. Especially when it is the £1,000 a week men, and those who rub shoulders with them, who insistently instruct workers that they are the ones who must tighten their belts and exercise wage restraint 'in the national interest'. People do try to make sense of all this. 'He *must* deserve it', they say of their own five figure a week man. 'Well, he must have a lot of qualifications. And there's the responsibility.' And there's the tax: 'he won't take so much home after tax I suppose.' But as they say it, it all sounds a bit off-centre, as if the arguments are being voiced to push back the possibility that there *is* no sense to it; that it is *really* wrong and that they really are being screwed. This sense of the unreal is less pronounced, but still operates, when you talk about the economics of Zap production.

Zap is packed on top rate at 60 tons an hour and at one time it sold at £40 a ton—£2,400 an hour, £10,200 a shift. All made by fifteen men who were paid a total of £100 a shift.

> 'That can't be right. It must be the maths. That *can't* be right. Let's see. . . . Yes it *is* right. Christ! But you know, they don't make all that profit I suppose. We had a talk from Sammy Bell the other week and he told us about, you know, the investment on the site as a whole; depreciation on this plant and that. I think this plant is keeping this site, from what he said. But it *is* a hell of a lot isn't it?'

Yes it is a hell of a lot. So much so that it has to be justified by all the guff that Jacko talked about earlier. Not that it is *all* guff because, as managers would hastily point out, it isn't quite true that Zap is made by just fifteen men. Chemicals flow into the Zap plant, produced by yet other men who are aided, to concede this too, by the technical inventiveness of managers. But if you add all these wages and salaries together there is still a surplus. Moreover, workers have no say in what is done with the product of their labour. No say as individuals. No say collectively. And not as a class. 'Production is for profit.' And 'management must manage': manage for capital. They make fertiliser and pack it into bags in quantities which they cannot question. It is sold at a price which they cannot influence. They have no say in the way the profits are invested, in the amounts which are distributed to shareholders or in the salaries that are paid to the directors.

So they carry on, look for a bit of overtime for the family, dream of opportunity, of 'luck' and 'success'. Were they to do anything else, for example to try and exercise direct control over the things which so deeply affect their lives, they would quickly come up against the disapproval of those in this society who control access to, and define, this self-same 'success'.

13
The Ideology of Sacrifice

PEOPLE MAY BE used as machines but they are not the mechanical products of the forces that have fashioned them. In spite of the inequality, the exploitation, the media, workers do not exist as totally conditioned social beings. They make something out of what they've got. The true strength of the ideology of workers' control, of militant syndicalism, was that it allowed workers to come to terms with both themselves and their exploitation *through their work*. The worker's skills gave him a dignity. At the same time they made clear that the bosses were unnecessary exploiters. At the end of the day the boss took the surplus, but his dependence upon the worker's skills was clear.

At ChemCo the men we talked to had no such relationship with their work. They knew that they, as individuals, weren't really needed by ChemCo—that others could come in 'off the street' and do their job. They are told this day after day. With the exception of a few of the process workers, these men understood their time at ChemCo as a sacrifice rather than a dignified exercise of their physical skills. The only dignity they felt they had was the dignity to be found in holding themselves back from the work.

They work for ChemCo. They give up their evenings and their rest days to work shifts. They endure the pain of the hundredweight bags on their shoulders. They suffer the mental stress of alert loneliness. They see green bags in their sleep. They suffer in order to get the money: to buy things. They talk of getting a nice house of their own, for the kids, and many of them have achieved this. Of taking the wife and kids away for trips in the car. Of providing a good life for their families. A good life that is based upon their sacrifice. When you're packing bags, self-sacrifice and a determination to see things through become central to your world; just as they do for wives and *their* sacrifice in the home. She sacrifices herself for her husband and her children just as he sacrifices himself for them. And if you still can't get by the wife works too. It's a terrifying totality. His exploitation in the factory justifies her oppression in the home; and notions of masculinity and motherhood reinforce their mutual dependence. It is only through *sacrifice* that a wasted life has value.

The foremen, who are 'successful' (or once thought they were) and who are also older than the workers they now supervise, know this well enough; but they also know that the thanks of the children whose future happiness justifies the sacrifice cannot be guaranteed. And, because of what their children do—what they dare to do—they have their doubts. Told by a daughter 'I'm not going to give my life to ChemCo as well. I'm going to get a bit out of life' it's sometimes difficult as we've seen to entirely hold back the thought, 'Perhaps she's right.'

Tom's son had joined the Army:

'He was out in the States. There for about a month I think, training with the tanks. Out in Cyprus. Then he got fed up with it and he wanted to give it up so we bought him out. Two hundred quid. But I don't know whether it did him any good or not. He come out, he had a couple of jobs, he's out of work now. He says why should he work? He's quite happy. He's got himself a flat in Oakfield [the student quarter in Provincial]. . . . Well, the lad that he's living with, he had a good job. They were making brake linings and so on. He was on over twenty quid and he packed that in. He's on the dole now. I mean I can't make these young lads out these days. They'd rather go on the dole and do a bit of fiddling I suppose. I can't make them out. I mean I'd rather work for me living. Maybe I'm old fashioned, I don't know. Am I? Eh? I mean I can't see why they'd rather loaf around though. I wouldn't, I'd rather have a definite job where I know I got a pay cheque coming in.'

But Tom himself isn't totally convinced about the virtue of work.

'What we want is the pools up, isn't it? Or the premium bonds would do. I wouldn't mind that, you know. But you know, it makes you wonder what went wrong or how we went wrong. You know, something must have gone wrong somewhere, I don't know. I was going to try and get him a job down here but George Smith said there was somebody down on the Day Gang had applied for it. So of course there was no job here for him. I don't think he'd have stuck the shift work anyway. . . . Well, it's no work for a single lad, shift work, is it? I don't think so.'

Now fathers have always fallen out with their sons, and it is easy to talk of a 'generation gap' as if it were a new phenomenon. It seems likely though that the length of the post-war 'boom', and the immense rate of technological change that accompanied it, led to a more pronounced change of emphasis between generations of workers. And the foremen were in the middle of this.

Most Riverside workers have children who are still at school. They have no love of shiftwork. They stick it out because they have to, just like Tom and the other foremen did a decade or so earlier. There are times though when they talk about what it must be like not to have to work. To live the 'good life'. Born around the last war, these men have lived their lives on the fringes of the colour supplement world. (A world which, ironically, the chemical and plastics industries have made possible.) The world of television and advertising; a Bounty Bar world of sea, sunshine, sex, indolence and happiness. An impossible world with no real substance but which just could be a possibility if they struck it lucky and won the pools. A few of the blokes we talked to felt that an approximation to the fantasy world might be there for the taking at the local university; the girls in short skirts, late night parties and long mornings in bed. Time and again though, they'd think of football: 'That would be great that, being a professional.' There's another side to this, however. These men have sacrificed their lives working for the boss so that their children can lead a decent life. They resent pop stars—and footballers—who behave like 'spoilt children'. Above all other superstars they resent George Best. It wasn't his fame, it wasn't his money, it wasn't the dolly birds. It was that he could have easily been one of them, that they couldn't have been him—and he quit—

> 'He's got it made, that lad. Getting paid that money for kicking a football around. He's got it made. He's a fool to himself: and he'll regret it.'

To escape the world of ambition and hard graft, then throw up the good life, that was Best's offence. Work just isn't life: to *live* at work—to be able to excel at it—and then throw it up—that was incomprehensible.

But those who throw up the *hard* life—who actually throw up *work*—or who are often depicted as doing so, are also resented.

None of the men we talked to had experienced a period of unemployment that lasted longer than one month. Those who had been unemployed for a short period hadn't liked it, and many of them, as we have seen,

feared the dole queue. Yet in offering an explanation of unemployment
they most frequently referred to the 'laziness' of the men on the dole.

> 'If you happen to go down the Labour some time and you see men that
> is stronger than you, you know, taking that free money you know,
> and some of them can get work but they just don't want to work—
> they're just, you know, lazy.'

If you pack bags at 60 tons an hour, catch them on your shoulders until
they ache permanently, it perhaps isn't surprising that you object to
laziness. Barney was born in South Wales and is recognised to be the
hardest worker on the site. He works all the overtime he can get (at times
as many as six double shifts in a week) and he is utterly determined that
his children will have a better life than he had. He thinks that malingering
on the dole is 'this country's biggest problem':

> 'There was a bloke who used to live in our street back home and he
> never worked. Well he worked down the pit once but all the time I
> knew him he never worked. But you know, he always had a roll of
> fivers in his pocket. I couldn't do that. In fact it drives me wild.
> Those buggers with a lazy bone lying around when they're fit to work.'

But it isn't just a matter of 'laziness'. These men work hard; they know
it doesn't do them any good but few if any of them would praise the
virtues of hard work. And whereas they don't pour scorn on the idea of
shareholders doing nothing to receive a dividend from ChemCo—'Good
luck to them' they say—this bonhomie isn't extended to the men on the
dole. The fact is that such men, or more correctly the idea of such men,
constitutes an immense *threat* to the ideology of sacrifice. In fact it makes
a mockery of it. The archetypal 'doley' is working class, has a wife and
several children, lives in a nice house paid for by the corporation, takes
home 'over £20 a week' from the social security (perhaps over £40 now,
in 1976)—and spends a lot of it on ale. Such men may exist; what is
certain is that there are not many of them. The men who work at ChemCo,
however, often speak as if a large proportion of the unemployed is made
up of such men. Ambrose thinks so:

> 'I don't know why there is so much unemployment you see. I am not a
> politics man myself because I don't know much about politics but
> what everybody seems to be saying is that it is the Government like,

you know. Because you find a lot of people out of work and they will tell you, "I am married with three children and I am going down to the Labour Exchange and I am going to get £20 a week. I can get a job for £25. I have to get up every morning to go to work, after deductions I will be coming home with £21. What is the point of going to work?" You can't blame someone for thinking like that, well this is the Government's fault, isn't it, this is it. Because if I was on the dole and taking that money from the dole, I would never go to work myself. I don't believe that nobody would, why should you?'

And Phil agrees with him:

'I blame the Government, you see. The Government should say to the majority of the people who are unemployed: "Right, we will extend to you a certain amount of money for a certain number of weeks." And if they don't pay that off and get a job the Government should say: "Right, no money." Then people will try to get a job for themselves and start trying to get the money. That's what I blame the Government for. Things would be fairer then and there wouldn't be so many unemployed. Because you tell me something: would you work if you could get £22 a week for *not* working?'

One of the foremen from the plant saw it like this:

'The Conservative Government is deliberately using a policy of unemployment at the moment. It goes wrong though because people are paid too much when they're unemployed. Now if it's right that a man can earn as much on the dole as I can at work I'll show my arse in Lewis' window. It's the same with a bloke on strike. His family shouldn't be supported. If a man's prepared to go on strike, if he's prepared to suffer for something, he should *suffer*.'

Derek would go further, he'd stop *all* dole payments.

'A chap who doesn't work! I would sort him out. I would literally see him *starve*. I would step over him starving in the gutter. . . . But as I say, I would take all that money for not working away from them and see them starve or work for the money. Whereas perhaps years ago I would have said: "Oh well, give it to them." But now it's got to the point where there are so many of them and they go round openly boasting that they do no work. And here's me, I do a full time job, then when I get home with my money the wife goes down the supermarket and she can't afford to buy perhaps three packets of chocolate biscuits. We have to make do with one a week, and the people on the social security who have done no work for the last ten years, his wife comes in, you know, takes about four cakes. My missues has to *make* them ... well, not 'has to' but we prefer them. But it's also for the cheapness as well. You know, I mean we just couldn't afford to go on the way they do.

There's a firm near us, advertised a job for a driver, £33 a week. They had *one* application I think for the job. It speaks for itself. Well to my mind, they're doing so well out of the State that they haven't got to work. I mean if it wasn't for my guilty conscience I'd rather go on the State myself, you know. But I shouldn't be that lucky, I should be disqualified for some reason because I own my own house or because of something. You know, I mean perhaps I'm prejudiced because I can't do it, but I'd be one of the unlucky ones. Just for some reason I wouldn't get it. You know, I'd end up on £10 a week selling everything to keep body and soul together.'

It is not difficult to see where ideas like these get their support. The popular press make regular 'exposés' of welfare malingerers. (In fact the story about the £33 a week driver job came straight out of the local paper.) But workers don't simply believe everything they read in the papers; and propaganda has to have something to feed upon, for which there is nothing better than fear. The virulence of the 'doley' myth can only be explained in terms of the damage that the possibility of the 'doley' life can do to men who have, if nothing else, *sacrificed*. When Phil asks 'would you work if you could get £22 a week for not working?', the dilemma is clear. Phil is working. Perhaps he's been a fool to work so hard, perhaps his life has been a farce, perhaps nothing of it has been worth while. But Phil *is* working.

14
Production, Consumption, Waste

WORKERS GO TO Riverside to 'get a bit more'. But for practical reasons working there means a car, and a car means petrol, tax, insurance, repairs for the MOT. Of course it's handy to have a car for holidays, for a trip to the sea; cheaper as well. Capitalism has brought benefits then, except that what with the cost of petrol, the 20p to park the car when you get there, ice cream for the kids—what with all this you're forced back to looking for that 'bit extra' again. And working the Continental there aren't many sunny weekends you can spend with the wife and kids. So, yes, Riverside workers 'consume': consume petrol, consume ice cream and the rest of it. They borrow as well: HP for the car, a mortgage for the house—a mortgage they couldn't take out on less money but which, once taken out, harnesses them more firmly to production. It's capital's money trap. Hamilton's had to learn all about this:

'But you find it hard to save it. When you come into this country you earn more than what you are earning in Jamaica but it is easier to save the money in Jamaica than in this country, because every money that you earn in this country you have to spend it every day.... You understand. You have to *spend* that money.'

His foreman knows about the money trap too. Part of his job is to set it:

'When I look for a bloke to take on I look for a married bloke with a mortgage and a couple of kids. I do it deliberately. When a bloke is working here I try to encourage them. If I can, I get them to buy a house.'

Politicians, Government officials and businessmen frequently pontificate to workers about how 'what you don't earn you can't spend'. They understand well enough that consumption depends on production. What they don't understand—or certainly don't shout about—is at what human cost the money is earned. Yet to explain what a DEP Report[1] saw as a 'paradoxical situation'—that 'absence rates keep rising in spite of the improved conditions of work and rising living standards'—it is necessary to concretely relate consumption ('rising living standards') to production ('conditions of work'). 'Production' is no mere *abstraction*: it is the collective application of human labour power. 'Production' is jobs. And most jobs at Riverside have very little meaning. One worker—the only one at Riverside who refused to talk to us—summed up his job like this: 'It's fucking awful. Just do it. That's all. *Do it.*' We didn't do it. If we had, we'd have folded in five minutes flat, but we have tried to convey what it's like.

Working at Riverside generally requires less ability than driving the car to work. What it means is getting physically worn out and mentally shattered. Take this into account, and the administrator's paradox appears less paradoxical. Take into account as well that in this society pretty well everything has a price and the further apparent contradiction—that it is sometimes the same men who miss shifts and go 'sick' who also work doublers and do overtime—also disappears. Outside Ford's Rouge River plant in Detroit workers have painted in large letters the words: 'WE COME HERE FOR EIGHT HOURS—DO WE HAVE TO WORK AS WELL?' Such attitudes are less strongly in evidence at Riverside. But as we have seen, they have developed enough to perplex the northern foremen. Moreover, they seem to be present in a growing section of the working class. Even at Riverside, however, the only dignity most workers find in work is in *not* co-operating voluntarily and spontaneously, in *not* acting out their potential, and their dissatisfaction with a society which forces them to waste their lives finds its expression in different individual forms, especially in absenteeism.

Yet work is not simply about 'meaning', about jobs: work at ChemCo has a purpose, profit. And being labour for capital, being subject to capital's seemingly impersonal imperative to accumulate, can induce a sense of lack of purpose. One of ChemCo's workers, Brian, who had worked on a farm, had a clearer than usual impression of the purposelessness to which working for the 'Big Bosses' can lead. Recollecting what it was like when he first went to the factory he remembers that he was 'quite surprised':

'I was coming from the outside world into a factory y'know. Just wondering what it would be like. And to me none of them seem—

well I can't make 'em out meself, even after five years to be quite
honest. Well half of 'em, they don't seem to have no purpose in life,
to what they're working for, or anything else.'

Ambrose, who came from the West Indies, saw the same problem.
Describing boys and men walking around the streets of the 'ghetto' area
of Provincial he said 'They won't work, they steal and beat people up.
This is because they have nothing to work for and because work is not a
delight.'

There's precious little 'delight' to be had at Riverside—and regrettably,
the lack of purpose which 'surprised' Brian *shouldn't* be cause for surprise.
Not if you consider the lives these men have led; the schools they have
attended; the jobs they have done; the jobs that are open to them. They
have been *produced* for a purposeless existence. The choice extended to
them has been the 'choice' of working at Riverside, or at somewhere else
like it, and whereas at Riverside they get 'a bit more' things are structured
in such a way that they have no say in the major decisions about purpose.
These are the very decisions which management and politicians will not
let, and cannot let, them have. Really, then, 'purposelessness' is no surprise. Not if you think about these things for a moment, and multiply by
generations.

Riverside, in so far as it is technically advanced, is a tribute to the power
of human imagination. It is also, for workers, a treadmill upon which
they wear themselves out. But Riverside does more than trap workers in
a technico-bureaucratic apparatus, make them dream of green bags, hump
their backs into pain at 40 and form an unholy symbiosis between
production and consumption. For though it is above all the working class
which capital sucks dry, in this society of 'success' and 'failure' even those
who are supposed to enjoy 'success' can come to win little of human
value. Managers and foremen also work for capital; in their different
ways they too can pay cost. The malaise which afflicts this society is a
general one which is structurally rooted.

In this context it is worth going back to Edward Blunsen, the manager,
and to Jacko, who worked for ChemCo in a physically much more onerous
way. It is, as we see it, rather silly to say they are both 'alienated', or to
pretend that they share the same life-fate. But both of these people have
come to live lives which bring the general malaise to light in a particularly acute way. Edward Blunsen for instance comes far closer to the
stereotype of the 'ruthlessly ambitious manager' than anyone else at

Riverside, and Jacko comes far closer to the stereotype of the 'bloody-minded worker'. When Jacko was at work—he held the site 'record' for absenteeism with a third of his time off in one year—he took 'nothing lying down' and was driven by one desire only, 'to get out that fucking gate'.

Now to exist and persist stereotypes have to have something to feed upon, but stereotypes also deceive: they fail to capture the totality, and Edward and Jacko have to be seen *in relation to one another*. It has to be seen that they were born into a society the social organisation and economic foundation of which must necessarily produce agents to be controlled and exploited, and yet other agents to perform the work of control. It is because at some level they both know this that there can be little 'trust' between them, and there is no respect either. But there is more to Edward and Jacko than this; it is no more the case with them than with anyone else that they are the *mechanical* resultant of class forces. Edward, the 'technical man' who wanted 'success' and who put his technical ability in the service of capital to get it, also wanted to *share* his technical joy. And Jacko, the man who did the 'donkey work', wanted to *share* it. At least he had *once*:

> 'I've been here for four years now and the place has lost all the interest that it had. I look up [from packing bags] and it's got no interest for me whatsoever. Look at those pipes over there. All different chemicals. It should be interesting. But I don't know. . . . I used to want to do the Control Room but I don't think I ever will now. There is a lot of interest there really. But I'm just not interested.'

As we have seen, Jacko blamed himself for his lack of interest. Himself, his class, and his lack of 'education'. But packing bags afforded him no joy at all, nor had a long list of other unskilled jobs. His interest—which is another way of saying his human potential—had been bludgeoned out of him. Locked into a mode of production which is not of their own making, managers like Edward Blunsen come to think of workers like Jacko as 'stupid', even though they have 'the education' and sometimes want to share it. But there's another side to this too: because workers like Jacko despise managers for their 'psychology tricks', for their attempts to treat them as people-objects.

The problem, to be clear about it, isn't that some managers and some workers don't 'get on', though obviously this can be the case. It isn't just, as we are so often told when the issue of almost any reform of work relations is raised, that workers 'lack the education'. Nor even is the problem the impersonality that increasingly characterises the modern corporation, and which we have come across so often in this book in relation to ChemCo as a company, its ownership, and indeed the union. The real, underlying, problem is the existence of a mode of production which continually reproduces people without 'the education', which has structured into it very good reasons for managers and workers not to be 'reasonable' with each other, and in which impersonality serves as a means to a sectional end.

Cynical about 'politics'—and knowing very well what Blunsen meant when he said 'I'd be all for socialism if I could be one of the bosses'— Jacko turned his back against any collective solution. He got out of Riverside to start his own smallholding. But as other workers noted, when in under six months Jacko was driven back to a factory job again, such solutions do not and cannot work, except for a tiny minority.

Edward of course 'left' Riverside too, but the real problems of work in this society aren't caused by a few people like him. For the greater the capital at stake the greater the need for 'clever' people to keep yet other people, who are apt to do 'stupid' things, in line; to stop 'the system running out of control'. The fact is that the system's demands are increasingly contradictory demands: it wants to engage people as a commodity, as labour power, to be managed, directed, *controlled*; it also wants them to become engaged, to be 'involved'—but not to *control*, not to manage for themselves. Indeed this is just what other managers learned from Edward getting the 'style' wrong: that in the big corporation today managers do have to be that bit more 'clever'.

In general terms we can say that, objectively, capital socialises production to a quite unprecedented degree; Riverside for example draws its raw materials from the labour of workers in Morocco, Senegal, South America and elsewhere and supplies other UK plants with some of its products. But so far as any truly purposeful, collective, work effort is concerned, the socialisation of labour—its subjective socialisation—is limited. To an important extent the collective potential which is labour power, remains a potential only. Because of this—as the systems theorists might say—the system's optimum, socially and economically, is low. But to talk of 'systems' in the abstract as the systems theorists do, or of 'labour costs' like the economists, or of 'job enrichment' like the theorists of psycho-sociology, is to mask and distort reality.

This is why throughout this book we have attempted to see the effects of the general on the particular, to see the way class relations bear on the individual and to locate individuals always within class relations. In this way it becomes evident for example that to categorise Jacko's leaving Riverside as just another case of 'natural wastage' is a travesty: a travesty because so much of Jacko's life has been *unnatural* wastage. For the facts of the matter are that despite all the talk about making work a meaningful experience, most people do not do meaningful jobs. That despite all the high-sounding formulations about 'technical systems' and 'social systems' and the rest, the ChemCo system—and the wider capitalist system of which it is a part—is not a neutral one. That in this system, whatever the management 'style', and whether particular managers are good blokes 'personally' or not, relations between people who are workers and managers are class relations. Grasp these central facts and a lot of things begin to fall into place—why men waste the product, why their lives are wasted; why managers play childish games, why they think 'their' workers 'childish'; why though they sometimes say they want 'participation', they do not really want it; why some 'progressive' companies favour a policy of union incorporation, why, even for management, this is not enough; why it is that at Riverside's particular 'modern factory' there are so many respects in which everything remains essentially the same. And this despite ChemCo's 'change programme without parallel in British industry'.

Note

1 *Absenteeism*, Department of Employment, Manpower Papers no. 4, HMSO, 1971, p. 4.